The International City Management Association is the professional and educational organization for chief appointed management executives in local government. The purposes of ICMA are to enhance the quality of local government and to nurture and assist professional local government administrators in the U.S. and other countries. In furtherance of its mission, ICMA develops and disseminates new approaches to management through training programs, information services, and publications.

Managers, carrying a wide range of titles, serve cities, towns, counties, councils of governments, and state/ provincial associations of local governments in all parts of the United States and Canada. These managers serve at the direction of elected councils and governing boards. ICMA serves these managers and local governments through many programs that aim at improving the manager's professional competence and strengthening the quality of all local governments.

The International City Management Association was founded in 1914, adopted its City Management Code of Ethics in 1924, and established its Institute for Training in Municipal Administration in 1934. The Institute, in turn, provided the basis for the Municipal Management Series, generally termed the "ICMA Green Books." ICMA's interests and activities include public management education; standards of ethics for members; *The Municipal Year Book* and other data services; local government research; and newsletters, *Public Management* magazine, and other publications. ICMA's efforts for the improvement of local government management—as represented by this book—are offered for all local governments and educational institutions.

Editorial board

Municipal Management Series

Managing Local Government: Cases in Decision Making

Published by the International City Management Association

Editor
James M. Banovetz
Northern Illinois University

Municipal Management Series

Managing Local Government: Cases in Decision Making

Effective Communication

The Effective Local Government Manager

Effective Supervisory Practices

Housing and Local Government

Local Government Police Management

Management of Local Planning

Management of Local Public Works

Management Policies in Local Government Finance

Managing Fire Services

Managing Human Services

Managing Municipal Leisure Services

The Practice of Local Government Planning

The Practice of State and Regional Planning

Small Cities and Counties: A Guide to Managing Services

Library of Congress Cataloging-in-Publication Data

Managing local government:cases in decision making/James M.
  Banovetz, editor.
        p.   cm.—(Municipal management series)
     ISBN 0–87326–060–0
     1. Local government–Decision-making—Case studies. I. Banovetz,
James M. II. International City Management Association.
III. Series.
JS78.M27 1990
352'.0004725—dc20

82-26829
CIP

Printed in the United States of America.

959493929190
54321

Foreword

Over the years, ICMA has maintained a strong link with the academic institutions that educate tomorrow's local government managers. The Municipal Management Series, or "Green Books," are developed with substantial input from those who teach in the various public administration specialties, and the editorial staff continuously monitors trends in the art and science of public administration education. A more formal institutional linkage between academia and practice is maintained through a Task Force on Local Government Management Education, composed of academic participants appointed by the National Association of Public Affairs and Administration (NASPAA) and city and county managers appointed by ICMA.

It was through these two routes that the idea for a casebook in local government management emerged. The Task Force proposed that ICMA publish a casebook. The concept was received enthusiastically by professors nationwide, for cases are compatible with the diversity of approaches that are employed in the teaching of public management courses.

As editor for the project, ICMA turned to James M. Banovetz, Professor of Political Science and Public Administration and Director of the Division of Public Administration at Northern Illinois University, and a member of the ICMA/NASPAA task force.

Together, ICMA and the editor selected an editorial board of respected professors, seasoned city

and county managers, and others with knowledge and experience in local government management. Simultaneously, ICMA issued a call for cases to its members and to the academic community. In response, over one hundred proposals and full-blown cases were submitted for consideration. These in turn were distributed to members of the editorial board for review. Based on the advice of the board, the cases were winnowed down to twenty that cover a broad range of local government problems.

Each case presented here is based on a real-life decision that faced a local government administrator. To improve their usefulness for teaching, cases have been altered to clarify issues and eliminate extraneous detail, and the editor has provided questions for discussion. ICMA and the editor do not intend for these cases to be regarded as factual portrayals of the circumstances on which they are based. In all cases, the names of jurisdictions, persons, organizations, and other identifying elements have been changed to maintain anonymity. In several cases, the authors asked that their cases be published anonymously to further protect the privacy of those involved.

ICMA is grateful to Dr. Banovetz for his diligent work in conceptualizing the project, overseeing the case review and selection process, and assembling the cases into a coherent volume.

Special thanks are also due to the editorial board, who among them reviewed the hundred-plus cases to select the ones that are presented here: Eric A. Anderson, City Manager, Eau Claire, Wisconsin; Wayne F. Anderson, Distinguished Professor of Public Administration, George Mason University, Fairfax, Virginia; David S. Arnold, Publications Consultant, Falls Church, Virginia; Stephen R. Collins, Assistant to the City Manager, Ferguson, Missouri; John E. Dever, Retired City Manager, Long Beach and Sunnyvale, California; John J. Gargan, Professor of Political Science, Kent State University, Kent, Ohio; James R. Griesemer, City Manager, Aurora, Colorado; J. Thomas Lundy, County Manager, Catawba County, North Carolina; Charldean Newell, Professor of Political Science and Associate Vice President for Academic Affairs, University of North Texas, Denton, Texas; Lodis Rhodes, Professor and Associate Dean, LBJ School of Public Affairs, Austin, Texas; Jewel D. Scott, Director of Research and Planning, Civic Council of Greater Kansas City, Kansas City, Missouri; Jeffrey D. Straussman, Professor of Public Administration and Senior Research Associate, Metropolitan Studies Program, The Maxwell School, Syracuse University, Syracuse, New York; and James H. Svara, Professor of Political Science and Public Administration, North Carolina State University, Raleigh, North Carolina.

The editor also wishes to thank the following persons for their contributions to the project: R. Ben Bifoss, City Manager, Manistee, Michigan; June M. Kubasiak, Roberta Horsman, and Audrey Banovetz.

The Municipal Management Series is under the general direction of Barbara H. Moore. Other staff members who worked directly on this book were Sandra Chizinsky Leas, who worked with the editor in the initial stages of the project; Susan M. Gubisch, who designed the cover and adapted the Municipal Management Series design to fit the special needs of this material; Dawn M. Leland, production director; and Mary W. Blair, publications secretary.

This casebook takes its place in a series of distinguished books in local public management published by ICMA. The pioneering book for the local administrator was *The Technique of Municipal Administration*, published in four editions between 1940 and 1957. Among the many persons who worked on successive editions of the book were Louis Brownlow, Herbert Emmerich, Lyman S. Moore, Orin F. Nolting, John M. Pfiffner, Don K. Price, Clarence E. Ridley, Charles S. Rhyne, Herbert A. Simon, and Donald C. Stone. The successor to that book was *Managing the Modern City*, edited by James M. Banovetz, published by ICMA in 1971. In 1983 ICMA published *The Effective Local Government Manager*, by Wayne F. Anderson, Chester A. Newland, and Richard J. Stillman II, with contributions by F. Gerald Brown, E. H. Denton, and Joe P. Pisciotte.

In 1964 ICMA published a casebook as well—*Case Problems in City Management*, compiled by Edwin O. Stene.

Like the other books in the Municipal Management Series, this book is dedicated to the improvement of local government management.

William H. Hansell, Jr.
Executive Director

International City
Management Association

Contents

Matrix of coverage

Matrix of coverage

A major advantage of the case approach to teaching is the flexibility it offers the instructor. Following is a matrix listing topics that are typically covered in urban management and other public administration courses, with an indication of the cases that relate to those topics. As the matrix shows, these cases can be used with virtually any course outline and in conjunction with a wide selection of other materials.

Subject	1	2	3	4	5	6	7	8	9	10	11	12	13	14	15	16	17	18	19	20
1. Kind and level of government																				
County								8			11		13			16				
Small city	1													14			17			20
Large city				4		6				10		12						18		
Medium-sized city			3		5		7		9						15				19	
Special district		2																		
2. The context of local government																				
Governing structure	1				5		7										17			
Politics	1		3	4	5	6	7				11				15	16			19	
Public/private interface		2						8		10					15			18		
Intergovernmental relations		2					7	8	9		11							18		
Race relations				4																
3. Professional administration																				
Bureaucracy						6		8	9				13		15	16				
Policy making		2	3							10							17	18		
Administrative leadership	1		3	4		6						12		14	15	16				20
Administration in a political setting	1		3	4				8			11	12			15	16			19	
Administrators and policy making			3		5		7				11									
Relations: elected and appointed officials	1		3					8			11					16			19	
Relations: appointed official & community				4	5	6		8						14						
Ethics	1						7				11			14					19	20
4. Management theory																				
Organization theory									9			12	13		15					
Administrative organization		2			5				9				13		15					
Decision making			3				7		9	10						16		18		
Program analysis and evaluation								8	9	10	11					16				
Finance		2				6			9	10	11				15	16	17	18		
Budgeting								8								16	17			
Personnel	1			4								12	13	14	15				19	20
Labor-management relations													13		15					
Affirmative action				4								12								
Management of change			3		5				9	10							17	18		
5. Policy and service functions																				
Planning							7				11						17	18		
Economic development							7										17	18		
Housing			3					8												
Human services								8			11									
Public works		2								10		12					17			
Environment		2																		
Land use							7				11							18		
Parks and recreation						6														
Police	1			4										14						
Corrections							7									16				
Fire															15					20
Sanitation		2								10										

Part one:
Introduction

The case approach

John J. Gargan

This volume presents twenty cases focusing on management problems that were actually faced by county or city administrators. Covering a significant range of local government concerns and problems, these cases were designed and written to serve as educational and training materials for individuals with varying backgrounds. Graduate students will find an in-depth exposure to the kinds of problems found on the daily agendas of professional government managers. Undergraduates can read the cases to familiarize themselves with the basics of local government management and politics. Advanced graduate students have here a body of data for hypothesis testing and theory building. Midcareer professionals will find reference points for discussing common experiences and for formulating insights about public administration.

The use of cases has been adopted in several academic fields and has proven to be an effective tool for learning, teaching, and even research. The idea of a single case as the unit of analysis is the foundation of legal and medical education. Intensive analytical discussion, centering on the specifics of a case and the impact of internal and external variables on organizational decisions, has also been widely used in business administration education. In public administration education, case studies have long been used to expose students to the scope of public administration, to specific public management problems, and to issues in a given field of administration.

By offering a set of cases to students for analysis and discussion, this book adapts the case approach to the study of public management at the local level. As their titles suggest, the cases here deal with substantive, process, and structural issues in the practice of public administration and management in city and county governments.

The case study in the classroom

The case approach involves a unique style of learning and teaching. Golembiewski and White comment:

> The heart of the case method is its basic orientation to the humbling, even numbing, analytical challenges offered by even apparently simple cases. If the case approach . . . has one dominant goal, it is the induction of a reflective and searching posture by the learner. . . . Perhaps the primary skill is the disciplined ability to suspend judgment while data are being gathered, the mental toughness to "dangle" while the mind's complex processes are at work isolating, assimilating, and integrating the multiple cues triggered by the typical case study.[1]

As students will readily discover when they examine and discuss the material presented, the editors have chosen cases that illustrate the "humbling, even numbing, analytical challenges" presented by real-life situations in city and county government.

There are no inherent limitations on the use of cases in teaching; cases can be used as the core material in a class or to complement other materials.[2] Indeed, while cases are, in effect, stories, " . . . one measure of a good case is its generalizability to some larger class of managerial or analytical problems."[3]

Nonetheless, cases have proven to be more effective for achieving some educational objectives than others. If a distinction is made between education for technical knowledge and skills on the one hand, and for reasoning and judgment abilities on the other, the case approach is more relevant to the latter.

Fundamentally, case studies allow instructors to familiarize students with the stages, processes, and circumstances of management decision making. Case assessment is a mechanism through which instructors can demonstrate to students the importance of clarifying value positions and recognizing fundamental relationships between political conflicts and value conflicts.[4] From a pedagogical perspective, cases and the case approach lend themselves to " . . . the orienting of students, the cultivation of analytic judgment for use in problem-solving, and the building and enriching of administrative value systems."[5] The extended discussion that is the key to case analysis is most appropriate for "development of understanding, judgment, and even intuition."[6]

Cases are, by definition, artificial, and case analyses and discussions are, at best, only approximations of decision-making reality. At the same time, well-written and properly analyzed cases do help students to "see" the multiple dimensions of problems and the interrelationships of individual and organizational objectives in policy development. Case analysis and discussion give them practice in "scientific or systematic thinking by learning to look at problems and situations objectively, by examining the facts available, and by considering a variety of solutions or proposed courses of action for a particular difficulty."[7]

Active participation in class discussion requires students to articulate and defend interpretations and positions to their peers and to participate in the dynamics of group decision making—a decision-making mode that will prevail for the duration of their professional administrative careers. Students should be able, after group discussion, to formulate generalizations and theoretical insights from the specifics of each case. They thus begin to develop an "administrative point of view" in an environment that is more forgiving than the operating administrative world. They can gain an appreciation of the context and complexity of real-life decision making without the responsibilities and risks.

To facilitate consideration of the cases and to assure some continuity in the way in which a class approaches its work, each case is structured around the same themes:

1. *Background*. An introductory section provides general information on the context of a problem or issue—situational factors, city or county social and economic trends, governmental arrangements, political developments.
2. *The case*. The next section describes the case under consideration.
3. *The decision problem*. The decision problem section covers the management or administrative issues that need to be resolved in the case.
4. *Discussion questions*. The first set of questions allows the class to consider how the case and the associated decision problem might be resolved.
5. *The aftermath*. After discussing the case, students learn the outcome of the actual case—how the decision problem was addressed and some of the consequences of the decision.
6. *Final discussion questions*. A second set of questions helps students relate the specifics of the case and the decision to more general issues and themes in public administration and management.

The decision to begin using the case study approach is a major one for students and their instructors. For the transformation of a class from lecture to case format to be successful, real care needs to be exercised in redefining class roles and in arranging the class setting. Matters that might appear to be of little significance in lecture classes can have a significant impact on the quality of case consideration.

The effectiveness of case discussion is shaped by the capabilities, preparation, and mindsets that students bring to the class. When one of the pedagogical objectives of the case approach is learning by discussion, students have to be willing to express themselves and be prepared to defend or modify their positions in the face of opposing points of view. If mastery of the details of a case is fundamental to understanding an issue or decision, students need to allocate sufficient time to studying cases prior to class meetings. For some students, this may necessitate a virtual reintroduction to the principles of studying and learning. According to Charan:

Skill in case analysis is developed through regular preparation and defense of one's views, rather than occasional massive doses of overwork that examination-based lecture method courses frequently encourage.[8]

Since there is rarely a single correct interpretation of any case, students need to understand and tolerate ambiguity both in their own case assessments and in their instructors' responses to questions. For students who are most comfortable as passive learners and accustomed to deferring to an instructor's intellectual authority, the transition from lectures to cases may be initially traumatic. To minimize trauma, instructors must help students alter their approach to learning and remain sensitive to, and supportive of, student efforts.

Instructors, too, must alter the way they approach their work. If they are to be effective, instructors must be prepared to play two roles. The first is that of substantive expert; the instructor must be able to relate the materials in a specific case to a body of knowledge (e.g., budgeting, planning, organizational development). In this role the instructor should guide class discussion to "a high enough level of abstraction to address principles of management or analysis."[9]

The instructor's second role is that of process leader, a role that is often unfamiliar to those who have relied exclusively on lectures in their teaching. As process leader, the instructor has the primary responsibility for guiding class discussion by drawing on details in the cases to make general points, by illustrating those points with relevant data, and by raising the right questions at the appropriate times. An effective process leader needs to have mastered the case under consideration. He or she also must have mastered the art of guiding a class from one major point to another, of moving from the specific to the general and back, all the while maintaining a high-quality discussion. To fill this role, the instructor must have some skills as a group facilitator and must be aware of innovations in facilitation practices.[10] The instructor must also be prepared to draw out the views of the reticent student and limit the commentaries of the exuberant. This means that the instructor has to know the backgrounds, talents, interests, and skills of the students so as to be able to activate their "intellectual and emotional involvement"[11] in the case discussion.

Whatever the backgrounds brought by students and faculty to the class, the success of the case approach ultimately depends on the quality of discussion. It is therefore important that class requirements and the class setting be conducive to a fruitful exchange of ideas. During initial class meetings and through the syllabus, the instructor should delineate course objectives, case scheduling, and individual and group responsibilities. Since many students lack background in the case approach, they may be apprehensive about performance criteria. Student anxiety is allayed when the course syllabus specifies the relative weights, for grading purposes, of participation in group projects, written assignments, and examinations.

Class quality is affected by other factors as well. Optimal class size is variable, but the best discussions occur in classes of no less than ten and no more than forty students. Regular class attendance assures that a group memory is brought to the discussion of new cases and a continuity is maintained in class organization.

Further, those who teach with case studies note the significance of the physical layout. Properly arranged classrooms and class seating facilitate interaction among students, encourage discussion, and downplay status and authority differences between students and instructors. Room acoustics, chalkboards or flip charts for recording ideas, wall space for hanging summaries of major discussion, all can improve the learning environment.

Relating cases to local government in the 1990s

The cases in this volume highlight a number of important realities regarding local government in the 1990s. Foremost among these is the fact that problems confronting public officials, public managers, and public employees are typically multifaceted; in the day-to-day work of local government, most situations involve two or more perspectives, and determining which, if any, is correct is no easy task. A public interest that is clearly discernible in the abstract to the philosopher or public economist is less evident to the city manager or city council member who is forced to choose, in the concrete, between spending more for recreation in poor neighborhoods and hiring new police officers. Calls for strategic planning to get the city or county moving toward a rationally chosen future usually go unanswered when they do not fit the political agendas of individual office holders. Ethics problems may (but rarely do) involve instances of honest public managers uncovering illegal behavior; more often, they arise from competing definitions of appropriate professional or political behavior.

On these and related topics, the cases affirm premises of public administration theory and lessons of public administration practice. Some of the premises and lessons are of long-standing, critical importance. Practitioners know, and students learn, that "much that happens in local management is 'firefighting' as well as seizing opportunities as they come along. In brief, purposeful calculation must be balanced with serendipitous action."[12]

The cases also show how fundamental changes have transformed local government over the past quarter of a century. City and county governments of the 1990s are qualitatively different from those of the 1960s. More so than in the past, elected officials, managers, and administrative staffs have to cope with changes of three major kinds:

1. Heightened complexity. An increasing number of problems facing local governments have many intertwined parts; solving them requires coordinated action on subsidiary problems. Frequently, policy choices are limited by a lack of technical knowledge about what should be done. In other instances, technically feasible solutions prove to be either unduly expensive or politically unpopular.
2. Heightened interdependency. City and county conditions result from forces and causes internal and external to particular communities. Over time, the relative importance of the external forces and causes has increased. Thus, for example, the health of the local economy now depends on developments in a global economy; local employment levels and pay scales respond to stock prices on foreign exchanges. Similarly, local government personnel and capital improvement plans are affected by administrative decisions made in Washington, D.C., and party policy decisions made in state legislative caucuses.
3. Heightened expectations. Growth in local government expenditures and the range of services provided with those expenditures has been substantial. The growth reflects public-sector reactions to public problems. It also reflects heightened expectations on the part of citizens (or at least the most vocal segments of the citizenry) as to what they can expect from government in terms of services and performance levels in service delivery. The task of balancing community interests

and formulating policy compromises has been complicated by two factors. First is a vigorous, intrusive media. Second is a reluctance on the part of the public to tax itself, a reluctance manifested in referenda to limit taxing or spending and in electoral support for candidates promising to lower tax rates while maintaining service levels.

This general theme of change in complexity, interdependency, and expectations is demonstrated in specific problems and decisions covered in the cases. The ability of city and county governments to deal with change is a test of the viability of their resource bases, governing capacity, and management professionalism.

In considering the cases and the discussion questions, students should remember the elemental certainty of resource constraints. At the local level, resources are limited, and reductions in federal aid, citizen resistance to new taxes, and pressures for increased spending have made them even more so. To some degree the seriousness of the constraints is related to government size; the larger the government, the greater the likelihood of slack resources that can be allocated to pressing needs.

Unfortunately, slack resources are rare or nonexistent in most places. Even though the United States is a metropolitan society, it is not, and never has been, a big-city society. The bulk of the population resides in, and is served by, local governments in communities that would be considered small or medium-sized by most standards. In these local governments a significant percentage of direct expenditures goes to a few functions (police and fire protection, highways, sewerage and sanitation); and the smaller the local government, the larger the percentage. Professional staff frequently concentrate on the direct provision of services, so management and planning activities may be limited and directed primarily to pressing immediate issues rather than longer-term goals.

Small size and resource constraints do not automatically lead to ineffective or inadequate governing capacity. City officials have made extensive use of management tools to build capacity citywide or in individual departments. Streib and Poister report that, since the mid-1970s, there has been a substantial and widespread diffusion not only of such familiar techniques as zero-based budgeting, management information systems, and program evaluation, but also of newer management tools, including financial trend monitoring, revenue and expense forecasting, and strategic planning.[13]

The tools and techniques surveyed by Streib and Poister constitute the management infrastructure of local government; they are a necessary condition for the efficient conduct of large-scale programs and routine activities. Other things being equal, city and county governments in which executives give high priority to management practices will perform more effectively than those in which such matters are not of high priority. Several of the cases offer testimony to the utility of management tools and techniques and, conversely, the unnecessary problems created when these tools and techniques are not used.

While the importance of management tools and techniques is demonstrated here, the cases do not convey detailed information on their underlying logic or furnish students any opportunities for hands-on experience. There are good reasons for this. The case approach does not lend itself readily to the transmission of technical knowledge. Moreover, the challenges to local officials—elected, managerial, staff—do not revolve around the question of whether or not to use one or another management technique. The issue of management tools and techniques is a settled one. Any city or county government dealing with heightened complexity, interdependency, and expectations is in a precarious situation if it fails to make use of demonstrably effective management practices. Those working in such governments are constantly in a reactive stance, responding to crises and recognizing too late (or not at all) that some disasters are avoidable if suitable plans are made.

The critical challenges to city and county officials in the coming years are strategic choices resulting from alterations in the practice of government and politics. Even more than in the past, boundaries between politics and administration are blurred; the domains of policy formulation, adoption, and implementation overlap more than ever. Executives find themselves managing local governments with extensive functional professionalism, greater structural decentralization, and service delivery based on citizen participation and coproduction. Appointed county and city managers—the classic neutrally competent public administrators—are expected to be politically sophisticated in their relations with city councils and federal agencies, serve as community change agents, and play a major part in policy initiation as well as overseeing ordinary operations. Commenting on the changing role of the city or county manager, Svara predicts that "managers' repertoire will increasingly require brokering, conflict resolution, and human relations skills."[14]

If they are to meet the changes and challenges of the coming years, city and county officials must engage in strategic management complemented by a commitment to excellence. Strategic management requires an action orientation, listening to citizens and employees, and constantly monitoring developments in the internal and external environments in which their governments operate. Local officials who practice strategic management bring to their jobs a set of process skills that help them focus simultaneously on the policy direction in which their organizations are moving and the capacity of their organizations to move. They recognize that "the strategies of public agencies and the way those strategies change over time result largely from the interaction of organizational intention and capacity with external environment."[15]

The knowledge relevant to strategic management and excellence in local government is of a special kind. It is based on an awareness of state-of-the-art developments in many technical fields, a recognition of the importance of linkages between urban management professions, and a sensitivity to the centrality of the public interest in deliberations. Such knowledge and talents are not easily or readily obtained. However, it is precisely that knowledge—and hopefully wisdom—that the authors of the cases and the editor of this volume have sought to convey to students and practitioners.

1   Robert T. Golembiewski and Michael White, eds., *Cases in Public Management*, 2d ed. (Chicago: Rand McNally, 1976): x.

2   Ram Charan, "Classroom Techniques in Teaching by the Case Method," *Academy of Management Review* 1 (July 1976): 116–23.

3   Dorothy Robyn, "What Makes a Good Case?" *Journal of Policy Analysis and Management* 6 (1987): 294.

4   This important point is emphasized by most who write about case studies in management education. See, for example, James R. Killingworth, "Narrated Knowledge: The Public Affairs Case Study Approach," in Ann-Marie Rizzo and Richard Heimovics, *Innovations in Teaching Public Affairs and Administration* (Kansas City and Miami, offset, 1981): 110–22; and Thomas J. Barth, "Case Studies in Public Administration: Linking Theory to Practice," in *Proceedings of the Twelfth National Conference of Teaching Public Administration* (Charlottesville, Va.: The Federal Executive Institute, 1989): 35–43.

5   Killingworth, "Narrated Knowledge," 121.

6   C. Roland Christensen, "Teaching with Cases at the Harvard Business School," in C. Roland Christensen, *Teaching and the Case Method: Text, Cases, and Readings* (Boston: Harvard Business School, 1987): 20.

7   C. Kenneth Meyer and Charles H. Brown, *Practicing Public Management: A Casebook*, 2d ed. (New York: St. Martin's Press, 1989): 7.

8   Charan, "Classroom Techniques," 119.

9   Robyn, "What Makes a Good Case?" 294.

10 For an overview of some of the developments in group facilitation in the public sector, see Carl Moore, *Group Techniques for Idea Building* (Beverly Hills: Sage Publications, 1987).

11 Christensen, *Teaching and the Case Method*," 30.

12 Wayne F. Anderson, Chester A. Newland, and Richard J. Stillman, II, *The Effective Local Government Manager* (Washington, D.C.: ICMA, 1983): 43.

13 Gregory Streib and Theodore H. Poister, "Established and Emerging Management Tools: A 12-Year Perspective," in *The Municipal Year Book 1989* (Washington, D.C.: ICMA, 1989): 46.

14 James H. Svara, "The Complementary Roles of Officials in Council-Manager Government," in *The Municipal Year Book 1988* (Washington, D.C.: ICMA, 1988): 31.

15 Barton Wechsler and Robert W. Backoff, "The Dynamics of Strategy in Public Organizations," *Journal of the American Planning Association* 53 (Winter 1987): 34.

The nature of local government

James M. Banovetz

Persons born at the turn of the twentieth century experienced what may have been history's most interesting time to be alive. It was a time of radical change. In the space of a single lifespan, society went from the horse-drawn carriage to the horseless carriage, to the automobile, to the airplane, to the spaceship. Labor went from the sweatshop to the assembly line to the robot. Calculation went from the adding machine to the mechanical calculator, to the electronic calculator, to the computer. Afro-Americans went from the farm to jobs in unskilled labor, to factories, to colleges, to positions of leadership in business, industry, and government.

By the turn of the century local government, too, had come a long way from the days when Tom Lincoln, Abe's dad, had his property taxes reduced if he used his horse and farm implements to maintain the county road that bordered the Lincoln farm in Kentucky. Local government had grown from a self-help, neighborly arrangement to a very large and very corrupt business, especially in urban areas. In fact, the condition of local government was such that James Bryce, in *The American Commonwealth*, wrote: "There is no denying that the government of cities is the one conspicuous failure of the United States."[1]

This condition, too, changed dramatically in the early twentieth century. Like every other institution, local government was affected by advances in transportation, changes in industrial methods and technology, and vast sociological transformations. At the same time, local governments moved to reject the characterization given them by Lincoln Steffens when he wrote *The Shame of the Cities*.[2] The operations of local government were significantly altered by the good government movement, with its Australian ballot, nonpartisan elections, use of the referendum and recall, elimination of corruption, and emphasis on merit and the Protestant ethic in public service; by structural reforms that produced at-large elections and the council-manager system; by the invention of the private automobile, federal housing programs, and the resulting emergence of suburban communities and governments; by *Baker* v. *Carr* (which established the one-person, one-vote principle), the reemergence of wards for legislative representation, and decennial reapportionment; and by the nineteenth amendment and the civil rights movement, which opened the door to participation in local politics and government for people who had been excluded.

Democracy and local government

Through all of these changes, however, the basic nature and function of local government remained the same. Local government has always been the government of the community; it is the social, economic, and political ordering of people's activities where they live and work. It is interaction among neighbors for the common good.

In the earliest American communities, local government was simply the social organization of the people who lived in the same frontier community—the people who helped each other with barn raising, birthing, and healing; the people who farmed, hunted, worshiped, and sometimes fought together for the common defense. As communities grew, the structure of social organization—of government—became more complex with the selection of leaders and the assignment of duties. Even then, however, government retained its essential linkage to the people: It still drew its leadership from the local citizenry and provided the social organization and the physical services needed to support people as they went about the tasks of daily life.

Local government also was the cornerstone of the governmental system. The New England township, the Atlantic coastal city, and the southern county offered the structure within which early citizens met, interacted, and debated the issues of the day, and from which they sent representatives to serve in colonial legislatures. It was in these local governments that American democracy first emerged. It was to these governments that Thomas Jefferson referred when he spoke of the "cradle of liberty" and "grass-roots democracy." It was from the local governments west of the Appalachian Mountains that Andrew Jackson brought his concept of "government by the common man" to the nation's political culture. It was from the small towns of the Midwest—the New Salems, Vandalias, and Springfields—that Abraham Lincoln brought his sense of government "of the people, by the people, for the people."

Local government today

Even today, local government is still the level of government that is closest to the people and that delivers the public services that are a part of people's everyday lives. Henry Churchill best captured the relationship between the people and their local government in the title of his book *The City Is the People*.[3]

National and state governments are housed in distant capitals. Their leaders are persons who make a business of government and politics, and who depart from their home communities to legislate, execute, and adjudicate the laws. National and state governments are responsible for crucial functions: national defense, maintenance of economic stability, protection of civil rights, economic regulation, environmental protection, public health, and interstate highways, for example. They are responsive to citizen action and opinion, but most citizen interaction with these governments is channeled through interest group activity.

Local governments, on the other hand, are close to home. Except in the largest communities, their leaders are friends and neighbors who hold elective office on a part-time, temporary basis, serving out of a sense of civic obligation rather than career ambition. These local governments provide another array of services: They build and maintain streets, parks, and schools; they supply clean water and treat sewage; they pick up and dispose of the garbage; they provide police services, ambulances, and fire protection; they offer aid to the impoverished and the handicapped; they support mental health services, senior citizens' programs, and youth activities; they are the first source of assistance in emergencies. In short, they provide the direct public services on which people depend every day. They, too, are responsive to citizen action and opinion, and most citizens deal directly and personally with their local officials without the intervention of lobbyists or interest groups. This means that pressures from constituents are more immediate and direct at the local level. As Churchill noted, local government "is the people."

Local government administration

These governments are served by local government administrators, and these administrators are responsible for the basic public services the governments provide. The way in which administrators perform this function ultimately affects not only the effectiveness of local government but the viability of grass-roots democracy as well. In this sense, local public administrators are custodians of democracy, discharging the "sacred trust" about which Woodrow Wilson wrote in the 1887 essay in which he laid the foundation for professional public administration.[4]

The evolution of professional local government administration was a major plank in the reform platform of the good government movement that emerged late in the nineteenth century. Professionalization evolved during one of those rare times in history when everything came together:

The American middle class . . . was growing as the nation's economy changed from artisanry to industry. Public service professions were forming, beginning with public schools and public health in the mid-19th century and expanding later as associations of public officials were formed in finance, planning, recreation, parks, personnel, and city management.

It was not enough to organize a campaign and elect a reform mayor and council. Local governments had to have accountants, engineers, planners, and park and playground superintendents. From there it was just a short step to the manager.[5]

A strong commitment to professional administrative leadership and the merit concept in employment continues to be a cornerstone of the Model City Charter promulgated and kept up-to-date by the National Civic League.[6] That commitment is reinforced and extended by the codes of ethics adopted by the American Society for Public Administration (ASPA) and the International City Management Association (ICMA).[7]

Despite its efficacy at producing good government in an era of politics and corruption, professional local government administration grew slowly and, initially, only in cities. It wasn't until after the second world war, at mid-century, that professional local government administration really took hold. Council-manager government became the most common form of government in the nation in medium-sized and large cities; strong mayor-council governments began to incorporate professional chief administrative officer positions; and county governments began adopting county administrator forms. Special districts, municipal leagues, councils of governments, and associations of local government officials also relied with increasing frequency on professional administrators to function as their CAOs.

With such administrators serving as role models and emphasizing professional competence as a standard for performance and promotion, the trend toward professionalism radiated outward and downward in local government organizations. Clerks and treasurers established programs of professional certification for those offices; administrative departments, especially in police, fire, public works, planning, finance, personnel, health, parks and recreation, and social services, were increasingly headed by persons with professional education and experience. Currently, the trend toward professionalization is reaching to middle-management supervisors—to police sergeants, fire lieutenants, and public works division heads—and to such specialists as management analysts, planning aides, health officers, accountants, data management technicians, and social workers.

The difference a professional makes

The presence of professionals in local government does not mean that government is raised above the level of the common citizen. Professionals supplement, rather than replace, the civic-minded community leaders whose assumption of local government office ensures that these governments are run for and by local people. Professionals perform a role quite different from that of the elected leadership. Specifically, they add four values to the operation of local government:

1. Technical competence based on training, experience, and access to information

2. An informed, long-range vision of contemporary trends and their intersection with community needs
3. Political neutrality
4. A principled commitment to serve the public interest.

Ideally, professional administrators should be selected on the basis of their training, experience, and demonstrated competence in both organizational leadership and technical skills. Administrators should know how to acquire the information they need to perform their jobs and to advise on policy matters, and they should be expert in methods of analyzing that information for policy makers. They must be skilled at working with constituents, elected officials, other administrative leaders, subordinates, and representatives of other agencies. They must, in short, be capable of solving a local government's problems, not by reflexively turning to "the way we handled this the last time," but by the creative application of new knowledge and experience.

Such problem-solving technologies should also encompass long-range vision. Democratic notions of responsiveness—calling for official accountability at intervals corresponding to the timing of elections—tend to emphasize short-range, immediate consequences in public-sector decision making. Increasingly, however, the public interest requires a longer-term perspective. Although city councils are elected for two- or four-year terms, they are most effective when working to improve the quality of life five to twelve years in the future.[8] To achieve that time perspective, they need the help that professionals, trained to study long-term trends, can give in terms of vision, insights, information, and empirical analysis of the likely consequences of alternative courses of immediate action. They need both encouragement and support from their professional staffs if their work is to venture far into the uncertainties of the future.

The tenets of professional public administration demand nonpartisan official behavior from the local government administrator. Such a position frees the administrator from dependence on electoral time frames as well as electoral politics, thus facilitating long-range planning and policy making. But the principle of nonpartisanship in administration means much more: It means that professional administrators are committed to "serving equally and impartially all members of the governing body of the [local government] they serve, regardless of party."[9] It means that they leave politics and legislative policy making to elected officials while they concentrate on the delivery of public services to the community.

These objectives of professional public administrators are reinforced and supplemented by the professional's principled commitment to serve the public interest. As articulated in their codes of ethics, professional local government administrators are expected to "demonstrate the highest standards of personal integrity," "serve the public with respect, concern, courtesy, and responsiveness,"[10] "recognize that the chief function of local government is to serve the best interests of all of the people," and "be dedicated to the highest ideals of honor and integrity in all public and personal relationships in order that the [administrator] may merit the respect and confidence of the elected officials, of other officials and employees, and of the public."[11]

All of these attributes are meaningless, however, if professional administrators are not responsive to the people they serve—the citizens of the local community. In a democracy, the ultimate test of efficacy is less efficiency than responsibility, less effectiveness than responsiveness. Professional administrative leaders are better than political appointees only if they are equally responsive. To promote such responsiveness, local government practice has been to appoint local chief administrative officers to serve "at the pleasure of the council" instead of for a fixed term. As county and city managers are wont to say, "My term of office lasts until the next council meeting." Since the council can remove them at any time, they trade job security for public responsiveness, thereby achieving this last, and ultimate, value for professional administration.

Professionals, elected officials, and the public

As powerful as it is, the imminent threat of dismissal is not by itself a sufficient base for defining the relationship between professional administrators and the political system they serve. That relationship also encompasses three other considerations: the role of elected officials, professional principles, and public accountability.

Role of elected officials

Of these, the most functional on a daily basis is the role of the elected officials. They are the central elements in the organizational structure of local government; they are the foundation of the representative system, assuring that local government remains the government of the common person run by local people. Local elected officials typically are long-time residents who are elected because of the breadth of their personal contacts in the community and the esteem in which they are held locally. Their contribution to local government is based not on their knowledge or experience in dealing with the technical issues of government administration but rather on their ability to reflect community values in policy discussions and to work with local residents in building support for needed public policy changes.

The rudiments of the relationship between elected officials and professional administrators is typically defined by law—by state statute or local ordinance spelling out the duties of the administrator. The Model City Charter articulates a standard format for this relationship: All powers are vested in the council except for those specified elsewhere, an exception that includes the delegation to the manager of specific responsibility to make appointments, direct administrative operations, enforce the laws, prepare and administer the budget, and advise the council on policy matters.[12]

Strict adherence to such a delineation of roles can prove to be more troublesome than helpful, however, and the prudent manager will work out an understanding with the council relative to their respective roles rather than standing inflexibly on statements of principle. In practice, the manager may become involved in some questions that could be construed as policy, and the manager may find it useful to include the council in a consulting role on key personnel appointments, even though these are technically the manager's responsibility. The local government administrative structure functions best when its participants—elected officials, chief administrative officer, administrative staff, department heads, and employees—work together as a coordinated team, performing mutually understood roles and supporting one another.

The responsibility for defining roles and relationships is best left to negotiation between the administrator and elected officials, not to the language of statutes, ordinances, and codes. Such negotiations should be repeated, at a minimum, whenever new persons assume elective office. Most important, the negotiations must always be based on a mutual recognition that it is the elected officials who most directly represent the citizens, who are the direct link with democratic theory and principles, and thus who must carry the burden of reporting to, and interacting with, the citizenry.

Professional principles

This recognition of the role of elected officials, however, does not reduce the administrator's responsibility. Indeed, the second consideration defining the administrator's relationship with the public in a democratic system—professional principles—demands no less. No fewer than seven of the twelve tenets in the ICMA Code of Ethics refer to the administrator's relationships to elected officials and responsibilities to the public. The code requires dedication to "the concepts of effective and democratic local government by responsible elected officials" and to "the highest ideals of honor and integrity in all public and personal relationships" and directs administrators to provide elected officials "with facts and advice on matters of policy" and to "keep the community informed on municipal affairs."[13]

Public accountability

Keeping the community informed is an important component of public accountability—the third consideration defining the professional administrator's relationship to the political system. Public accountability—the need to operate in the goldfish bowl of public information, public observation of official behavior, public oversight, and public reaction to administrative activity—is a constant in local government administration. The intensity of such accountability, of having to work within the narrow confines of open meeting laws, freedom of information acts, publication requirements, and neighborhood-level public hearings, serves both to limit the administrator's freedom of action and to assure direct and immediate responsiveness to the public. Perhaps more than any other administrator, in either private or public organizations, the local government administrator must work closely with, and under the direct supervision of, the individual members of the public being served.

What does it all mean?

Local government, and the professional administrator's role in it, is a big job. It is big not just because of the number of people or the volume of resources involved in it on a national scale, but because it is so important to people's everyday lives.

Local government serves the people directly, immediately, daily, and personally. It is the part of government that citizens can best understand and appreciate, to which they can most easily communicate their grievances, from which they are most able to achieve responsiveness, and against which they can most effectively retaliate when they are dissatisfied. It is the cornerstone of their democracy, the base from which their political principles have been derived and from which they will continue to evolve. It is the ultimate manifestation of "government by the people."

Because the professional administrator serves a central role in local government, whether as CAO, department head, or supporting staff member, the challenge of serving at this level is enormous. It is a challenge that manifests itself in the big issues, such as economic development, neighborhood design, and tax policy, and in the everyday matters of cost containment, humane and fair treatment of citizens and employees, and relationships with the public.

The administrator's response to this challenge contributes significantly to the success of local government and, consequently, to the quality of life in the nation's communities and the quality of democracy at its grass roots. In this sense, the responsibility of the task is awesome.

The administrator's success in fulfilling this responsibility is best measured by the aggregation of the decisions—small as well as large—that make up the pattern of daily activity. This book is designed to mirror that aggregation through the presentation of a representative sample of actual cases requiring administrative decisions. By so doing, the book provides a unique insight into the real-life challenge of local government and also offers a vehicle through which practicing and future administrators can develop, test, and evaluate their own decision-making capabilities.

The book is designed to promote a fuller understanding of local government administration. The cases are presented in an order commonly employed in local government courses, but the matrix of coverage that precedes this introduction provides a supplement to the table of contents by showing how the cases can be applied to other kinds of courses or educational formats. The matrix shows the range of administrative topics covered by each case, suggesting the various kinds of discussions that can be supported by its use. The essay by John J. Gargan explains how the case approach can be effectively employed in teaching and learning.

By making this collection of cases available, the book seeks to sustain and promote the ultimate goal of professional local government administration: local governments that are both effective and responsive in the service of the people they represent.

1 James Bryce, *The American Commonwealth*, vol. 2 (London: Macmillan and Co., 1988), quoted in William J. Murin, ed., *Classics of Urban Politics and Administration* (Oak Park, Ill.: Moore Publishing Co., 1982), 3.

2 Lincoln Steffens, *The Shame of the Cities* (New York: Hill and Wang, 1904).

3 Henry S. Churchill, *The City Is the People* (New York: Reynal & Hitchcock, 1945).

4 Woodrow Wilson, "The Study of Administration," *Political Science Quarterly*, II (June 1887).

5 David S. Arnold, "ICMA and the City Manager: The Plan, the Profession, the Association," exhibit at the ICMA Annual Conference, Des Moines, Iowa, 1989.

6 National Civic League, *Model City Charter*, 7th ed. (Denver: NCL, 1989). See especially Articles III and IV, pp. 33–43. The charter "stresses the basic principle of the council-manager form that the manager is a *qualified, professional administrator*" (page 37, emphasis added) and "should

strongly state the commitment to the merit principle" (page 42).

7 The ICMA Code of Ethics is reprinted as an appendix to this book. A convenient reference for the "ASPA Code of Ethics and Implementation Guidelines" is Elizabeth K. Kellar, ed., *Ethical Insight, Ethical Action: Perspectives for the Local Government Manager* (Washington, D.C.: International City Management Association, 1988), 161–66.

8 Laurence Rutter, *The Essential Community: Local Government in the Year 2000* (Washington, D.C.: International City Management Association, 1980), 17.

9 Guideline for tenet 7, ICMA Code of Ethics.

10 Excerpts taken from the ASPA Code of Ethics.

11 Excerpts taken from the ICMA Code of Ethics.

12 National Civic League, *Model City Charter*, Articles II and III.

13 "ICMA Code of Ethics," tenets 1, 3, 4, 5, 6, 7, and 9.

Part two:
The role of
professional
administration

Introduction to part two: The role of professional administration

Future political historians will remember the twentieth century as the one in which professional administration came to local government. Council-manager government was born in the century's first decade; the concept of professional administration quickly took root in school districts and special districts, but it had to prove its value and its compatibility with local politics and grass-roots democracy before becoming widely accepted as the preferred form of municipal administration in the second half of the century. Counties were slower to employ administrative professionals, owing to the closer linkages between their elected leadership and state-level politics, but as the century entered its last decade counties, too, were adopting forms that provided professional administrative leadership.

Part Two presents three cases that give different views of professional administration in local government. In the first, a manager is faced with political pressures as he seeks to apply professional values in the recruitment of a police chief. The case contrasts the manager's professional leadership in a reformed government with traditional nonreformed, or spoils, politics.

The second case describes a government's experience in employing private industry to provide a public service. The ensuing problems make it clear that, even when private industry is involved, professional public management—management that has a primary commitment to the public interest—is an essential interface between private industry and local elected officials. Ultimately, professional staff must provide leadership in helping elected officials "manage" the work of the private firm. In this instance, two levels of management were involved: The managers of the firm worked to protect the firm; the professional public manager worked to protect the public. From the clash of these competing interests evolved the decision problem on which this case is based.

The third case focuses on the critical relationship between the professional public manager and democratic values: popular control of government, managerial responsiveness to the people directly and through elected leaders, and local sovereignty. It describes a triangular relationship among local citizen groups, an elected council, and a professional manager, highlighting the kinds of considerations that affect the decisions of professional local government administrators on a daily basis.

Although these three cases all describe professional administrators at work in city government, the problems they pose, the challenges they describe, and the managerial roles they explore are fully representative of those facing professionals in other kinds of local governments as well.

Replacing the police chief

William R. Bridgeo and Paul M. Plaisted

Editor's introduction

Professional managers are expected to increase the efficiency and economy of local government operations. Even more important, however, they bring to their job a set of values that emphasizes the public interest over private and personal interests, that considers long- as well as short-term consequences, that demands competence and qualifications as well as compatibility from employees, and that places integrity over politics in decision making.

These values are usually endorsed by both the general public and the professional administrator, but that endorsement does not ensure their easy application. No matter how much a person or community espouses good government values in principle, the daily operations of government present frequent temptations to put such values aside in order to solve tough problems, achieve personal goals, or simply acquire more power and influence for the governing challenges that lie ahead. Such temptations are fairly common among elected officials and local influentials, who may seek to use government action to achieve private ends, but the temptations can also afflict professional managers, especially when the manager's job is on the line.

This case describes the dilemma of a manager whose attempt to administer in accordance with the tenets of professionalism runs into strong opposition from a politically influential family. The result is an all-too-common scenario: Politics intrudes on the manager's prerogative to appoint department heads, threatening a basic tenet of council-manager government. An important value of good government (i.e., the commitment to merit in personnel recruitment) is challenged; long-term community welfare is pitted against short-term political tranquillity; local politics and state legislative politics become intermingled; obvious options are all flawed; and the manager faces conflict between his personal well-being and his commitment to professionalism.

The case shows council-manager government in action, facing one of the most severe tests that can confront this form of government. Situations such as the one described here can quickly lead to a two-fold demand—not only to fire the manager, but also to change the form of government to one that will "respond to the wishes of the people" (or at least to those people who want more influence over local affairs). It also describes precisely how council-manager government works at its best, making it the most commonly employed form of government in all but the nation's smallest and very largest cities, and in a growing number of counties as well.

For those interested in comparisons, the case shows in stark contrast the difference between a purely political approach and a professional approach to leadership recruitment. Competing head-on in this case are the pre-reform and the reform (professional) approaches to local government. The politicians are determined to have their way even if this means circumventing the authority of the manager.

Unhappily, as long as community leaders and elected officials are tempted to expand their personal influence beyond that prescribed by law, the management decision described in this case will be all too common in cities and counties of all sizes.

Case 1
Replacing the police chief

Background

Will Spanning had been in Dover, in his first city manager's job, for five years. When he took the job he was as well prepared as most novice city managers, having served for three years in another city as an assistant to a seasoned and well-respected city manager. During those years he completed an M.P.A. degree by attending night classes. Shortly thereafter, he had been urged "out of the nest" by his boss and mentor, had applied for several city manager positions, and was hired in Dover.

A northern New England community of about 5,000 residents, Dover serves as the regional center of urban activity in a sparsely populated section of the state. Getting established in Dover had been a constant professional challenge for Spanning, but, after five years of hard work, he found himself happy and well adjusted. By then a board member of the state city managers' association and the state municipal league, he was respected by his professional peers.

During his time in Dover, Spanning had revamped the city's financial structure and taken the community from a serious budget deficit to a healthy surplus. Mending a weak financial structure had meant taking some difficult actions through the years, like reducing city staffing levels. At times, the staff reductions had led to confrontation with organized labor (Dover's full-time employees— police, fire, and public works—were represented by the International Brotherhood of Teamsters), but in the preceding couple of years the relations between management and labor had stabilized, new contracts had been negotiated, and life between management and labor was relatively peaceful.

At the time of this case, one of Spanning's priorities was an expansion of the community's economic base to stabilize taxes and to allow both for an increase in municipal services and for capital improvements. A number of positive signs indicated that Spanning's economic development strategies might pay off. The city had received several hefty state and federal grants, the city's business district was being spruced up, and a new wood products manufacturing plant had announced plans to create 130 new jobs for Dover residents.

The police department

The largest police agency within a seventy-five-mile radius, the ten-officer Dover department was also recognized as the most professional force in the area. However, it had experienced its share of difficulties over the years. For almost a decade before Spanning's arrival, the department had been commanded by a strong-willed and conservative police executive who had succeeded in shaping the department into an almost autonomous organization, largely exempted from the oversight usually exercised over police departments by local government managers.

Soon after Spanning's appointment as city manager, the chief resigned. After a comprehensive selection process, Spanning appointed the deputy chief to fill the position. This choice soon proved ill advised, for while the new chief had been an outstanding young police supervisor, he was not prepared to deal with the stress of managing an active department with a strong union presence. After only a year in the position, he, too, resigned, and Spanning again faced the task of selecting a new leader for the department.

Confronted with a dismal response to the city's advertisement for the position, Spanning was directed by the assistant district attorney toward Charles Johnson, a young but well-educated and well-trained supervisor with the county sheriff's department. Recognizing the challenge and opportunity presented by the Dover chief's position, Johnson agreed to accept the job.

Over the next four years, the relationship between Spanning and Johnson developed into one of mutual trust and respect. While at first very cautious about granting Johnson the authority to make major decisions, Spanning saw that the young police chief learned quickly to cope with the pressures of the job and displayed a willingness to explore nontraditional approaches to the police department's problems.

In contrast to previous Dover police chiefs, Johnson recognized the inevitability of budgetary constraints and implemented required staffing reductions while maintaining the level of services expected by the community. Recognizing that the city had relinquished too many management prerogatives in its first two attempts at collective bargaining with its public safety employees, Spanning and Johnson presented a united front in subsequent contract negotiations and managed to reverse the situation in several key areas.

Finally, the most critical dimension of the relationship between Spanning and Johnson was their firm commitment to work together to prevent other actors within the municipal structure from playing the police chief and the city manager against each other. In the past, Dover police chiefs and managers had developed separate power bases within the city council and had sometimes battled publicly over issues and resources. Spanning and Johnson elected not to operate in this fashion. The Dover city charter contained a specific noninterference clause that prohibited council members from exercising direct control over city departments. Whenever a council member would "stop by" the police station to discuss a matter with the chief, Johnson would invariably begin the conversation by subtly referring to the charter clause. Following the conversation, Johnson would immediately communicate the details to Spanning, ensuring that end-around plays were impossible. Similarly, Spanning communicated to Johnson about all matters, whether of a police nature or not, that might have a bearing on either one's ability to perform as a part of the senior management staff of the city. Communicating completely, Spanning and Johnson presented a strong, unified front to political forces that otherwise might have prospered.

At the time this case begins, in early spring, Dover Police Chief Charles Johnson notified Spanning that he had been accepted into a prestigious M.P.A/M.B.A. program and would be resigning his position in time to enroll as a full-time student in September.

Johnson's resignation left Spanning with the disappointment of losing a trusted department head as well as a confidant and friend. Happy for Johnson's career advancement, he knew that replacing the police chief would be difficult and would require a careful and thorough approach. He resolved to follow a process that had worked well for him in making other senior-level appointments. Furthermore, he expected to take advantage of Johnson's resignation announcement early to minimize the transition gap.

Dover's city government

Like other city charters in New England, Dover's enabling act contains language that establishes the city council as the body authorized to make policy on every aspect of city affairs. The charter also empowers the council to retain a manager, hired on the basis of education and experience, to serve as the city's chief administrative officer with the authority to carry out the policy directives of the council. That authority includes the power to hire and fire all city employees. In return, the council makes the manager fully accountable for the manner in which city employees implement council policies.

While giving the manager the power to hire and fire city employees, however, the Dover charter reserves to the council the power to confirm, or advise and consent to, the manager's appointment of city department heads.

Under the charter, Dover is governed by a seven-member city council, elected at large for three-year terms. Each year, two seats become vacant on the council so that, in effect, a new council is organized every January with five continuing members and two reelected incumbents or newcomers, as the case may be. From among themselves, the council members elect a mayor to serve as the council chairperson.

The council in place during the spring of Chief Johnson's resignation was a split group, with two distinctly different philosophies on most issues. One group of three Spanning regarded as personal and less objective in its decision making; a second group of three was readier to decide issues solely on their merits; and the seventh member was unpredictable: he wanted to be perceived as objective but was politically ambitious (then running for a seat in the state legislature) and therefore sensitive to pressure from various local constituencies.

The case

When Chief Johnson's resignation became public, Spanning informed the council that he would forthwith begin advertising the position statewide and place notices in appropriate national police journals. Knowing the temptation of some councils and some individual council members to try to be more "appointers" than "confirmers," Spanning designed the recruitment process carefully, hoping to ensure that politics played no role in this critical appointment.

Spanning set up a four-stage screening process. First, he would screen the respondents and invite the several most promising ones to appear before a specially created five-member professional review board. Second, the review board would conduct in-depth interviews and rank the candidates, by consensus, from best to worst. Third, Spanning would interview the top choice and determine whether he and that individual were compatible and whether the candidate could accept the city's compensation package. If the answers were affirmative, Spanning would authorize a thorough background check of that finalist and, all going well, would offer that person the position. Fourth, he would arrange for the council to meet, interview, and confirm his appointment.

Spanning also let it be known that rejection of a candidate by the council would not mean going down the list until someone the council preferred was chosen. Rather, rejection would trigger a new search, starting the entire process over again.

Finally, and most important, he placed on the five-member review panel well-respected police and management professionals from other similar communities and offered the chairmanship of the panel to one of the community's most respected lawyers, C. Abbot White, who had served as part-time city solicitor for thirty years in addition to conducting his private practice. White was noted for his impartiality and good judgment. A life-long resident of Dover, he ensured high-quality local representation on the panel and added credibility to a process still rather foreign in Dover.

It was at this point that the problems began.

Shortly after Spanning announced his selection process, he was visited in his office by Councilman Arnold Fornby, a member of the group that Spanning felt lacked objectivity. Fornby and the other members of his group on the council shared certain characteristics. None had the advantage of any formal education beyond secondary or trade school, all were lifelong residents of Dover who had

had little exposure to the outside world (with the possible exception of military service), and—probably most important—all had, over the years, seen friends and family members leave the area in search of economic opportunity because such opportunity was so limited in Dover. Raised in poverty, scrapping for what status they had achieved in Dover during their lifetimes, their perspective on who should get good local jobs—and how they should be picked—was certainly different from that of a professional manager. The group's view was supported by many local voters who came from similar backgrounds.

At this meeting with Spanning, Fornby bluntly stated that Spanning's elaborate selection process was unnecessary, and that he and three other members of the council (a majority) had identified a local candidate they liked who they believed should have the job. They felt so strongly about it, Fornby added, that if need be, they would subvert Spanning's selection process to gain their choice. Furthermore, though it was not made openly, Spanning perceived a veiled threat that failure to concede to this pressure would jeopardize his position. (Like most local government managers, Dover's chief executive was subject to removal at any time by a majority vote of the council.)

Spanning knew that some council members supported his use of a professional selection process, and he knew that there was a good deal of respect for him within the community. He recognized, however, that this issue could become the most serious personal crisis he had faced in five years in Dover. He decided to forge ahead with the process.

The candidates

In contrast to the meager fruits of his efforts four years earlier, Spanning was rewarded with several excellent applicants for the upcoming vacancy for police chief. He and Chief Johnson reviewed the applicants' resumes and ranked them on the basis of experience, education, and training. Three candidates emerged clearly from the pack. All had at least a decade of experience, having progressed through supervisory to management positions within law enforcement:

Chip Durning   With twelve years of law enforcement experience, a bachelor's degree in psychology, and extensive training credits, his current position was chief deputy of a large sheriff's department in the state.

Tom Boyd   With eleven years of law enforcement experience in various capacities with the same police department, Boyd had risen to the rank of deputy chief. Along the way, he had obtained a bachelor's degree in criminal justice and attended a large variety of law enforcement training sessions. The similarities between Boyd's current department and Dover's added to his attractiveness.

Sam Warren   Recently retired from the Boston Police Department (B.P.D.), Warren had risen to the rank of lieutenant and had commanded the personnel office of that department. A master's degree in public administration, coupled with high recommendations from the senior management of the B.P.D., enhanced his attractiveness as a candidate for the Dover position.

Councilman Fornby's local candidate was, of course, also an applicant. He was State Police Trooper Jim Waterhouse. Amiable and a passing acquaintance of Spanning's, Waterhouse had a variety of social and community connections to several members of the city council. As a rural patrol officer stationed in Dover for the previous ten years, he also was popular with a number of local residents. His only law enforcement supervisory experience, however, was as a field training officer for new state police recruits, and he had received no supervisory training since becoming a state police officer. Trooper Waterhouse had not chosen to pursue his formal education beyond high school. This lack of supervisory experience and higher education made Waterhouse a poor comparison to the other applicants.

Beyond that, Spanning learned through the local grapevine that Trooper Waterhouse had a very special relationship with a powerful local interest—the O'Hara Transport Company.

Big fish, small pond

In the modest-sized working-class community of Dover, there thrived a large, influential, family-owned company that employed, on the average, 150 area residents. O'Hara Transport Company was controlled by the members of a large family whose personal and corporate interests were intertwined. The corporation had been started by an Irish firebrand named Frank O'Hara, who came to Dover during the depression and gained fame for his ability to get his one truck to its downstate destination—on time and cargo intact—regardless of weather, mechanical difficulties, or personal health.

Through a combination of hard work, six tough and loyal sons, shrewd politics, and a cynicism regarding the law where it hindered business interests, O'Hara Transport was, at the time of Frank's death, the major employer in Dover. Still family run by the six sons and their progeny, the company had grown very large (125 trucks), and diverse and was tightly controlled by the six brothers. A variety of spin-off operations like O'Hara Sand and Gravel, Erie Land Development Corporation, Dover Cadillac/Olds, and Dover Orchards were run by various family members and employed numerous area residents. The six brothers met every morning at the same restaurant in which their mother had waited on tables many years earlier, to coordinate the business of the day.

By and large, the O'Haras lived in an affluent subdivision constructed twenty years earlier by Erie Land Development Corporation. When the third generation began rearing its own families, the "compound" expanded, but a number of the thirty or so grandchildren of Frank O'Hara also dispersed throughout the residential neighborhoods of the city. Many went away to college (the first O'Haras to do so), but all returned to the financial security of the family business in Dover.

The O'Hara family realized fully the power that comes with maintaining a cohesive family unit, and the six brothers used the leverage of their economic success to command the strict loyalty of family members and employees. They sponsored representatives to the legislature, contributed heavily to both state political parties, held court for state politicians when they came to Dover, and had exercised virtually unchallenged control of the local government. This power resulted from the sheer numbers of votes controlled by family and employees, three generations of "favors" to area residents, and a steadfast willingness to coldly punish any individual or local business that might oppose them.

Council politics

Without old Frank's force of will, with waning influence in state government as the rest of the state changed and grew, and with an influx to Dover of new residents, city government had become reasonably independent of the O'Hara family, but not entirely so. Several members of the seven-member city council were "connected." Michael O'Hara, a past mayor, was a grandson of Frank and manager of Erie Land Development Corporation. Kevin Beal worked for a local auto parts store that valued O'Hara business; he had spent his childhood as a playmate of the O'Hara compound kids. Arnold Fornby, a master mechanic and union shop steward at Brace Machine Corporation, a large independent employer some twenty miles from Dover, had played local politics for forty years, knew where all the skeletons were buried, and regularly joined the O'Haras for breakfast (toward the end of their morning sessions). He bragged about his political independence but belied that brag with an ever-present willingness to cut a deal with the O'Haras if there was something of political value in it for him.

Not surprisingly, these three council members constituted the solid opposition to Spanning's police chief selection process.

Four years after joining the state police, Trooper Waterhouse had transferred to the Dover area. Two years later, after meeting several members of the O'Hara family who were friends of his wife's family, Waterhouse was offered a part-time job as "safety officer" with O'Hara Transport. In accordance with state police policy, Waterhouse applied for and received permission to accept this form of employment with the O'Haras. As "safety officer," Waterhouse's responsibilities consisted primarily of ensuring that the company's vehicles were properly equipped for safe highway travel. Depending on perspective, this was a responsibility that either closely paralleled or directly conflicted with his duties as a state police officer and enforcer of highway laws. Like other trusted O'Hara employees, Waterhouse had accepted "special" company benefits—for example, no-interest housing loans and low-cost construction improvements, such as landscaping and driveway paving.

Spanning knew that Waterhouse's mediocre qualifications and dubious connections with the O'Haras dictated against seriously considering him to fill Johnson's job. Seeking a compromise, however, and hoping to allay criticism that city managers "from away" gave no credence to local talent, Spanning opted to include Waterhouse with the three other finalists to be rated by the review panel. This decision had the effect of quieting things temporarily. The Waterhouse group thought perhaps Spanning was capitulating in a face-saving way (by maneuvering Waterhouse through the process), and they ceased to pressure him for the moment. Council members Jim Dixon (a schoolteacher), Marion McQueen (a government accountant), and Jack Redmond (a semiretired manufacturer's representative) strongly supported Spanning and encouraged him to proceed with the recruitment in his own way despite pressure from the others.

Council member Steve Nicholson was the wild card. Young, aggressive, hard working, and politically ambitious, he had long set his sights on high elective office. He was a member of the council that had hired Spanning, and the two had a relationship that ran hot and cold. In years when Nicholson's political ambitions were dormant, Spanning relied on Nicholson's persuasive personality to help carry difficult issues in council. Now, however, Nicholson had a legislative seat within his reach and was devoting more time to politics. As a result, Spanning had increased difficulty working with him. The timing of the police chief selection process brought potential conflict between the two to a head.

Before the review panel met to fulfill its mandate, Nicholson sought a meeting with Spanning and made clear his support of "a local candidate" for the police chief's job, because "it's critical that the person understand our community." No mention was made of Waterhouse or of the hundreds of votes the O'Haras could deliver to Nicholson in the fall. No threats were made, but the point was clear: this item was of critical importance to Nicholson.

The selection process

Attorney White convened his panel, and, through the course of a beautiful spring day, they thoroughly questioned the four candidates who had emerged from a field of fifty-three applicants. At day's end, as Spanning treated the panel to a good steak for their trouble, they ranked their choices. The panel was unanimous: Boston Police Lieutenant Sam Warren was ranked number one, and Trooper Jim Waterhouse was ranked number four. The panelists even teased

Spanning a little at dinner over the obvious differences between Waterhouse and the rest; they suggested that Waterhouse must have been a long-lost relative of Spanning's to make the final cut.

Meeting Sam Warren, Spanning took to him immediately. Confident, quick witted, and soft spoken, Warren soon convinced Spanning that he would adjust easily to Dover. Even what Dover paid a city manager would have been a significant pay cut for a Boston police lieutenant with twenty-four years of service. However, the combination of Warren's pension from the Boston Police Department and the Dover police chief's salary would keep Warren and his family comfortable. Warren's wife had come from farm country and loved the idea of returning to it, and Warren had spent his nine years of patrol duty with Boston's mounted patrol. The sale of their house in suburban Boston would more than pay for a comfortable country home, complete with barn and pastures, in the Dover area, thus allowing Warren his long-desired indulgence of raising horses.

Spanning sensed instinctively that Warren would quickly earn the respect of the Dover Police Department and, probably soon thereafter, the community. His pronounced Boston accent would be a standout in "Yankee Dovah," to be sure, but his sterling record of police work, awards of merit, and recognized leadership abilities with the Boston Police Department would soon be known in Dover and would clear the way for his acceptance.

On a handshake, Spanning and Warren agreed that Spanning would appoint Warren and seek council confirmation within a few weeks. Spanning explained clearly to Warren the problems he faced regarding confirmation, and Warren, smiling encouragingly, indicated that it was surely worth a try.

Preconfirmation problems

Sensing that most residents were unaware of the dynamics of the selection process and that some counterbalance of political pressure might sway Councilman Nicholson, Spanning crafted a detailed press release that announced his appointment of Warren, elaborated on the review panel and its expertise, and chronicled the superb qualifications of Sam Warren. Spanning counted on an independent press in Dover to report the story accurately, well in advance of the council meeting set to confirm Warren. He judged correctly that council members—including Nicholson—were hard pressed after its release to find fault with Spanning's appointee. Three council members, locked into their predetermined choice, avoided discussion of the topic, except among themselves. Their strategy would still be to vote down Spanning's choice. Nicholson made no public comments prior to the meeting, leaning neither one way nor the other. The remaining three council members supported Spanning whenever their opinions were asked.

And so it came down to the day of the council meeting, and Spanning sat in his office, drinking his morning coffee, contemplating the evening session and his future in Dover. About the last thing in the world he expected was the phone call he received from outgoing Chief Johnson.

"Are you sitting down, Will?" the chief began.

"This is a bad day for that kind of question, Charlie," Spanning responded. "What's up?"

"It's about Councilman Redmond's son, Randy. He's going to be arrested this morning on arson charges."

"Oh, no!"

Spanning had known that young Randy Redmond was a problem for his father. The boy had dropped out of school and had had several minor brushes with the law. The senior Redmond, one of Spanning's supporters on the council, was a proud man who never talked to Spanning about his son's problems. Though Spanning sensed a strength of character in Redmond, he worried about what effect the arrest would have on him at that evening's council meeting. Because the arson arrest was a result of a joint police effort between Dover and state police, Spanning also cynically marveled at the timing. After some thought, he resisted the temptation to seek to have the arrest delayed until the following day.

Things went from bad to worse that afternoon, when Redmond's wife, Mary, emotionally distraught over her son's felony arrest, telephoned the state's prime witness against her son, attempting to influence him to alter his version of the circumstance of the crime. To prevent deterioration of the state's case, the arson task force, in consultation with the district attorney, elected to charge Mrs. Redmond with tampering with a witness. Mrs. Redmond was arrested, booked, and released on her own recognizance just hours before the council confirmation hearing. Would Redmond appear in the face of this family scandal? Could he still support Spanning after the day's events? Spanning skipped supper and anxiously waited for the meeting to begin.

The decision problem

Just a few weeks earlier, Spanning had been happy and comfortable in his job. Now he was on the verge of provoking a majority of his city council into firing him as the result of an emotionally charged dispute complicated by intricate power plays. To pursue this issue and lose could very well set the stage for continual conflict that could only lead to Spanning's ultimate departure—voluntary or otherwise. With the severe complication of the arrest of the son of a sympathetic council member, Spanning was forced to take stock quickly of the whole issue and decide how to proceed.

He sat at his desk pondering his problem. As he saw the matter, he had several options:

1. Committed to a course of action that had led to a council meeting scheduled that evening to confirm Sam Warren, Spanning could hold fast, let events take their course, and live with the results. What—if anything—might he do in the few hours before the meeting that would be of help to him?
2. Realizing the critical value of Councilman Redmond's vote, Spanning could attempt to intercede in the Redmond case. The assistant district attorney who was prosecuting the case had, four years before, recommended Johnson and understood the value of obtaining a good police chief and the politics of such a process.
3. To try to defuse the crisis, Spanning could contact the mayor, request a postponement of the confirmation meeting, and regroup to seek a compromise course of action that would somehow result in face saving for the council members and himself and still lead to the appointment of a qualified police chief.

The council would arrive shortly. Spanning had to make a very quick decision.

Discussion questions

1. What are the advantages and risks involved in pursuing Spanning's recruitment plan?

2. As city manager, Spanning exercised administrative authority over Police Chief Johnson. Would it have been proper for Spanning to seek to delay the arrest of Randy Redmond until after that night's council meeting? What are the benefits and risks of such a strategy?

3. What, if any, would be the ethical implications of action to defer Redmond's arrest? Given the existing threat to Spanning's effectiveness as city manager, if not to his job, would it be appropriate to put any ethical concerns aside? Given the importance of the appointment to the community's welfare, would it be appropriate to put these ethical considerations aside to secure Warren's appointment?

4. Apart from any action on the arrest, should Spanning have contacted Redmond prior to the meeting to discuss his family's problems?

5. If Spanning decided to delay the council meeting and seek a compromise, what kind of compromise might achieve his purposes and be acceptable to the council?

6. How might a compromise be initiated by Spanning? What would he need to do to execute a compromise without appearing weak or contradictory in the public eye?

7. What would be the long-term effect on Spanning's management ability and his authority if he sought a compromise at this point?

8. What should Spanning do? Why?

The aftermath

The overflow crowd that arrived at city hall for the one-item agenda that evening forced Spanning to relocate the session to the more expansive accommodations of the senior citizens' hall next door. There, on an evening of record-setting temperatures and humidity, without the benefit of air conditioning, over one hundred of Trooper Jim Waterhouse's friends and supporters gathered to demonstrate to their city council how they felt. Included in that group were off-duty Dover police officers and firefighters, a number of influential businesspeople (some named O'Hara), a sampling of former council members, and Jim Waterhouse himself. In the front row, eyes ahead and perhaps wondering if they were doing the right thing, were Sam and Mary Warren. Ten feet away, at two folding tables facing the crowd, were six of the seven members of the council and City Manager Spanning.

At the appointed time of 7:30, word was received that Councilman Nicholson had been delayed unavoidably until 8 p.m., and a resulting short recess added to the sense of anticipation. At 8 p.m., Nicholson arrived and the meeting began, only to be disrupted again when one of Frank O'Hara's nephews, overcome with the heat, slipped from his chair in a faint and had to be revived and assisted from the hall. Only then could Spanning endorse his appointee for chief of police, summarize his position, and present Sam Warren to the group for questioning.

That completed in fairly short order, a vote was taken. Three in favor, three opposed, and Councilman Nicholson's turn.

Remarking on his strong disappointment in Spanning for allowing the selection of a police chief to polarize the community, Nicholson stated that he must nevertheless vote to confirm Sam Warren in light of Warren's strong credentials. He closed his remarks by promising to revisit at a later time the issue of the city manager's press releases and other concerns he had with the process.

Dover had a new police chief on a 4-to-3 vote (including that of Redmond, who made no mention to anyone of his family troubles), and all seven council members immediately adjourned to congratulate Warren and begin becoming acquainted with the new chief.

During his career Spanning had often been called on to make difficult decisions. Over the years he had heard other managers tell stories that reinforced for him the idea that city managers frequently faced tough challenges. His old boss had told him often that the time would come when he would be called on to stick to the ethical standards of his calling, to fight to preserve his proper authority, and to execute his duty to the community he served to ensure that it received competent, honest government. Going home that night, he felt he had done so. But he also knew he had done so at a price.

During the months that followed, Spanning noted that a four-member majority of the council were frequently critical of him. His policy recommendations were often rejected—usually 4 to 3—and Spanning knew this was usually because he had made them. When Spanning failed to convince a majority of the council that participation in a model economic development project sponsored by the state was worth an up-front investment by the city, he knew he had lost his effectiveness. Six months after the confirmation hearing, when the new budget was adopted on a 4-to-3 vote and no raise was offered to the city manager for the first time in six years, Spanning offered his resignation.

Warren established himself quite well in Dover, as Spanning and the review panel had predicted. Nicholson lost a close race for the legislature, a loss generally acknowledged to be attributable to opposition from the O'Hara family. Fornby was elected mayor the following year, and Redmond chose not to seek reelection. A new city manager was selected a few months after Spanning's departure, and the community moved on to face other issues.

Final discussion questions

1. Did Spanning make a mistake in judgment by including Trooper Waterhouse as a final candidate for assessment by the review panel? Why or why not?

2. Should Spanning have put a member of his political opposition, such as Councilman O'Hara or one of the O'Hara brothers, on the selection panel? What would have been the benefits, the risks, and the likely result of such a move?

3. How should a manager react when the council seems intent on usurping some of the manager's legal authority? Are there times when it is better to cooperate with the questionable desires of a council than to resist them? Was this case such a circumstance?

4. In this state the council-manager enabling legislation clearly indicates that the manager is the agent of the city council and is charged to assist it in the development of policy and to oversee the execution of that policy. He or she has a professional responsibility to faithfully serve the council by providing it with complete and timely information. In this light, was it appropriate for Spanning to use the local media as a means of bringing pressure to bear on the council to decide the question of confirmation in his favor? Would it have been more appropriate for him to withhold announcement of his candidate until the council had met? How should the public's right to know be weighed against the need for confidentiality of personnel selection processes?

5. Spanning's actions in recruiting a new police chief led, eventually, to his perception that his overall effectiveness had been undermined, and,

therefore, he resigned. Should he have resigned when he did? Should he have resigned sooner? Should he have waited until after the next council election to see if the council composition changed significantly? Give reasons for your answers.

6. Should Spanning have issued a press release setting forth in detail the events that had occurred in the police chief selection process and his reasons for resigning? Why or why not?

7. In explaining his actions and his resignation to future councils from whom he might be seeking appointment to a new position, how should Spanning relate these experiences?

2

The resource recovery authority

Stephen A. Staub

Editor's introduction

In seeking to solve its solid waste disposal problem through the use of a special authority, the community in this case learned that professional public administrators perform a valuable role even when administrative responsibility is contracted out to a private firm. It was not until the community hired its own *public* administrator to oversee the private contractor's work, and to formulate policy proposals with the public's needs uppermost in mind, that the events in this case began to move toward a solution.

The search for that solution, which is the subject of this case, portrays the intricacies of both the public-private partnership and the use of special districts to provide public services. The decision facing the public administrator involves legal questions, intergovernmental considerations, financial strategies, questions of principle in cost allocation, and the wisdom and practicality of using private firms to provide public services. Overriding the whole issue are pressing environmental considerations—considerations that will face almost all cities and counties before the turn of the century.

The events of this case stem from a regional decision to use a special authority to address issues of solid waste disposal, recycling, and resource recovery. That problems were encountered in using this alternative is not a fault of the alternative itself; such problems are a natural outgrowth of any complex solution to a pressing problem. It is the inevitability of such problems that makes the use of experienced and skilled professional administrators an essential part of the local governing process.

Case 2
The resource recovery authority

Background

The beginnings of the Resource Recovery Authority (RRA) were auspicious enough. The RRA was to take advantage of a relatively novel technology for solid waste disposal (incineration) and new intergovernmental relationships for dealing with solid waste disposal in the Niles County metropolitan area.

Southridge Mayor Albert Linn had taken the lead in creating awareness that solid waste disposal was an areawide problem. Officials in nearby Riverton and the commissioners of Niles County were supportive, given that the single landfill used by all of these governments was rapidly approaching the end of its useful life. Convinced that incineration was a feasible and more attractive alternative to conventional landfills, Mayor Linn worked with other local officials and state legislators to address the problem—in particular, the use of incineration as a method of waste disposal and the recovery of steam as a salable by-product.

At about that time the state legislature passed a bill permitting municipalities to establish waste recovery authorities. Under the terms of the act, such authorities were granted the usual powers of an authority, including the power to enter into contracts, to sue and be sued, and to borrow money for the purpose of design, construction, and operation of a solid waste disposal/recovery facility. The law also provided such authorities with the power "to do any and all things, whether or not specifically authorized in this section, not otherwise prohibited by law, that are necessary or convenient in attaining the objectives of this act." Specific provisions in the law exempted any authority from the state competitive bid law, the sunshine act, the usury law, and the ethics act.

The case

Mayor Linn and the Southridge City Council moved expeditiously on the resource recovery plan and, within the first year after the enabling legislation was passed, incorporated the authority and appointed its three-member governing board.

The contrast between Mayor Linn and the person he chose to head the RRA, Roger Tarlton, could not have been more striking. Tarlton was a native of Southridge, a prominent businessman, who had no background in local politics or government, although he had been active in community affairs. Linn was a rarity in a local culture that placed strong emphasis on being a native. Linn was born out of state, and his speech confirmed his origins. Also, Linn had come into mayoral office through an unconventional route: twenty-five years of service in the city planning department in a variety of roles, including serving as director of planning for almost a decade. All that the two men shared were graduation from the same public university and their responsibilities for the RRA. These responsibilities Tarlton initiated with vigor.

Under Tarlton's leadership, the RRA Board began planning for the construction of an incinerator facility, visiting several such facilities in cities of similar size. Having no professional staff with expertise in this field, the RRA Board decided to engage the services of Recom, Inc., a firm that was actively involved in the resource recovery field and that, in fact, had designed and operated incinerator plants for a number of cities in other states.

The contract with Recom called for the design, construction, and operation of the incinerator facility on a cost-plus-10-percent basis. It was the first of a series of contractual arrangements involving the authority with area governments and private parties. The cities of Southridge and adjacent Riverton, along with Niles County, committed to use the facility for the disposal of their solid waste for a "tipping" fee of $9 per ton. The tipping fee was to remain fixed at the $9 rate for the first dozen years of the incinerator's operation. Contracts between the authority and private waste companies or individual firms needing to dispose of solid waste contained similar terms. Although the RRA was to enjoy a public monopoly over solid waste disposal, none of the government or private parties appeared to consider these terms anything other than favorable.

The RRA was expected to be a self-financing enterprise. Combined revenues from tipping fees and sales of steam generated as a by-product of waste incineration were projected to cover the construction, operation, and debt service of the authority over a ten-year period. The local plant of a national manufacturer, the ABX corporation, had been identified as a prospective user of steam energy. When approached in the early planning stages, the ABX plant management reacted favorably. Indeed, ABX agreed to donate a construction site on their property, partly for technical reasons such as the distance and rights of way for steam lines and partly because of their desire to facilitate the construction of the waste recovery unit. Further, ABX agreed to purchase $21 million of steam from the authority over the next ten years.

To finance construction of the incinerator, the RRA issued $8.5 million in revenue bonds. These bonds were sold through the Fidelity Bank of Southridge. RRA chairman Tarlton asserted that quick action on the bond sale was necessary to take advantage of favorable interest rates. Interest rates were forecast to increase early the next year.

Precipitator problems

Construction of the incinerator facility was well under way when the first major problem arose: the design and the construction cost estimate, which had been the basis for the $8.5 million bond sale, had not included an electrostatic precipitator and some other start-up equipment. The precipitator, an air pollution control device to remove particulate matter from the smoke of the incinerator, was revealed to be an expensive and especially important piece of equipment: it would enable the incinerator to pass a battery of emission tests so that the plant could obtain an operating permit from the state Department of Environmental Management (DEM). The reason for the omission of such critical equipment from the project design and cost estimate was to remain cloudy. Recom's extensive experience in resource recovery made simple oversight a questionable explanation. Other speculation noted that without the cost of the precipitator, the cost estimate of $8.5 million was "coincidentally" the maximum amount of financing that the RRA had been able to secure in its haste to take advantage of favorable interest rates.

Another issue surfaced in conjunction with the problem of the precipitator: lack of access by the press to RRA Board meetings. Under the state sunshine law, representatives of the press were accustomed to broad access to meetings of public officials, and they were reluctant to accept the closed meetings of the RRA Board. The controversy over access to board meetings added to the suspicion and mistrust surrounding the RRA and ultimately contributed to friction that was developing between the authority and other public officials.

Faced with the serious problem of an incomplete incinerator plant and no source of funding for the precipitator, Tarlton and the other board members sought the assistance of Mayor Linn. In the meetings that followed, Linn was apprised of the problem and agreed to help in whatever way he could. Linn's political skills were soon revealed as he obtained approval from the Southridge Council for a $750,000 loan to the RRA to complete the incinerator plant. Unfortunately, the RRA's precipitator problems were not to end with the completion of the plant.

Plant certification and community protest

After test burning to cure the ceramic tiles lining the incinerator furnace, the authority obtained a temporary operating permit from the state DEM, and commercial burning began at the facility in the late winter. The RRA's next priority was to obtain a permanent operating permit to replace the temporary permit, which would expire ten months later. In order for the RRA to secure the permanent permit, the incinerator would have to meet DEM-mandated emission standards during the ten-month period.

Two problems relating to emissions from the incinerator arose after a few months of operation. First, the incinerator failed early DEM tests for particulate emissions because of operational problems with the electrostatic precipitator, and Recom became continuously involved in modifications and adjustments to the precipitator in its effort to meet DEM standards. Second, residents in Woodgrove, a nearby residential area, were complaining of smoke and odor emissions from the plant.

John Rayford was among three hundred Woodgrove residents who petitioned the DEM, alleging that smoke and odor emissions were causing health problems.

Rayford described the odor as strong for about a one-mile radius around the facility. According to Rayford, the offensive odor "smelled like a hog pen or raw sewage."

These complaints prompted the DEM to conduct several site inspections in the fall. The DEM staff reported that, although their site inspections found only a "faint odor," they did "perceive an ash emission problem." The DEM ordered the authority to correct the emission problem and, further, to discontinue the practice of ventilating the building on weekends, when raw garbage was stored pending resumption of steam production for ABX on Monday. A consulting engineer employed by the authority asserted that the smoke and the odor were separate issues and that the RRA would "bend over backwards" to solve the problems raised by the DEM and area residents.

Another episode involving plant emissions continued the focus of negative publicity on the authority. A necessary operating practice of the plant, dictated by the design of the precipitator, required that garbage be burned only when ABX was in operation. This meant that burning was halted on Friday of each week and resumed again on Monday to coincide with ABX's production schedule. Any solid waste that was not incinerated at the end of the week, or any garbage delivered to the plant before burning began Monday, was stored inside the incinerator building. When ABX closed for the New Year holiday, the impact on the incinerator facility was not adequately considered, especially since the holiday period typically produced a peak level of solid waste.

The volume of waste delivered to the facility during this time far exceeded the internal capacity of the incinerator building, and several hundred tons of garbage were dumped outside. When Recom's plant manager informed authority chairman Tarlton about the problem, most of the deliveries had already been made for the day. Nevertheless, Tarlton acted to get the city crews to keep their last loads of garbage in their trucks rather than dump them at the incinerator.

Tarlton and the plant manager agreed that burning the garbage without using the precipitator was better than leaving the raw garbage outside the building for several days. Almost immediately, however, the firing of the incinerator produced a number of complaints to the DEM from nearby residents, and the next day the DEM issued the authority a notice of violation, citing both the storage of garbage outside the building and the operation of the incinerator without the precipitator.

Tarlton and officials at the DEM agreed that the primary cause of the incident was "the absence of good planning in linking the operations of the RRA with the production schedule of ABX." In the RRA's response to the violation, Tarlton stressed that administrative steps would be taken to prevent such incidents in the future. While this incident did no consequential damage to the authority's quest for a permanent operating permit—the RRA obtained the permit several months later—it did evoke further criticism of Roger Tarlton, specifically, and the RRA Board, in general, regarding the operation of the incinerator plant. Speculations were voiced that Tarlton might be approaching the end of his tenure as head of the RRA.

Financial pressures and a labor strike

During the plant's second year of operation, continuing financial problems compounded by a labor strike were to aggravate growing suspicion and mistrust among the institutions linked to the RRA and to erode the working relationships among the officials involved.

In April the authority released the report of an internal audit, which disclosed losses of $505,000 for the previous year. Subsequent efforts at damage control by the RRA were ineffective. One board member, in an interview with local news media, claimed that if depreciation were taken into account, the loss was only $147,000 and that original projections for the project had forecast losses for the first three or four years. The latter assertion was widely viewed as lacking credibility in light of the self-financing character of the RRA. In any event, efforts to downplay the audit did not alter the seriousness of the basic problem: the authority did not have sufficient revenues in excess of operating costs to meet the scheduled bond payments.

Linn and other officials in Riverton and Niles County knew that unless the RRA began to generate more revenues or to contain operating costs, the only alternative was a bailout by the area governments. Contracts between the authority and the governments using the incinerator provided that "any financial losses of the RRA become the responsibility of users in proportion to their usage of the incinerator facility." This obligation escalated the concerns of local public officials and renewed questions about Recom's management and the authority's oversight of the plant.

Several officials were openly critical of the RRA's unresponsiveness to their need for information to assess the financial liability of their respective governments. James Everly, chairman of the Niles County Commission, spoke for several elected officials when he complained of the failure of the RRA Board to appreciate the situation faced by area governments. None of these governments had contingency funds or budget lines to cover financial shortfalls of the authority. "They've got to realize that when we make a budget, we make a budget," said Everly, speaking of the financial constraints confronting local governments.

In response to the growing criticism of the RRA by user governments, the authority held a series of meetings in early summer. These closed meetings of all public officials working with the authority were designed to satisfy their demands for more complete disclosure of the RRA's internal affairs. But these meetings neither produced the desired understanding nor moderated the growing schism between the authority and area governments.

In this atmosphere, the plant workers' strike on June 8 could not have been more ill timed for the authority. Garbage deliveries were interrupted for several weeks as city workers honored picket lines, and the existing landfill was again pressed into use. To minimize the strike's impact on incinerator operations, Recom brought in out-of-state workers to operate the plant, and the Southridge Council hired off-duty police officers to drive city garbage trucks.

While negotiations were taking place to resolve the strike, Tarlton announced his immediate resignation as RRA chairman for "personal reasons." This was followed a month later by the decision of another board member to resign "on the appointment of a successor or October 1, whichever comes first."

As the strike continued, pressures mounted for a more complete accounting of the authority's operations and performance. Mayor Linn requested the city attorney to undertake an investigation at about the same time that the county commissioners requested state auditors to conduct a full audit of the RRA. When Linn released details of the city attorney's report, he acknowledged that further questions had been raised in the investigation, and he intimated that an independent audit might be required. The report also raised questions about the absence of oversight of Recom's operating expenses.

The inability of the authority to satisfy public officials about its oversight of Recom and the imminence of another bond payment shifted the necessity for action to Mayor Linn and the Southridge City Council. In a period of two weeks at the end of July, the city council approved another loan, for $377,000, to the authority and passed a resolution calling for an independent investigation. There was no joy in this decision; at best, it bought some additional time for officials to wrestle with the problems of the troubled authority.

Strained relations with Recom

During the planning, building, and start-up of the incinerator, the RRA was occupied largely with community and governmental relations. Now that the incinerator facility was operational, the authority became increasingly involved with its internal management.

After the settlement of the labor dispute in late summer, Mayor Linn appointed two new board members to fill the vacancies created by the two resignations. This time, Linn selected a former member of the Southridge City Council, Ray Gunther, to head the authority. In addition to having held public office, Gunther possessed considerable executive experience, and, under his leadership, the authority began to take a more active role in supervising routine operations of the plant and in overseeing Recom's performance. This more active, "hands-on" approach was not well received by Recom's plant manager, Les Martin, who had been accustomed to less scrutiny by the previous administration.

Relations between Recom and the authority became increasingly strained. From Recom's perspective, there was the issue of the cost-plus contract, which had not been paid in full. Because of the RRA's financial problems, Recom had not demanded or received its 10 percent management fee; it had been paid only for operating expenses. However, Recom expected to receive full payment and was itself under pressure from the parent company to force the issue. On the other hand, the authority was dissatisfied with the management provided by Recom and raised questions about overruns in operating costs, substandard maintenance, and other administrative issues that the authority found to be unsatisfactorily resolved after months of effort by Recom officials. Gunther and the other board members became convinced that their long-term financial problems were in large measure a result of Recom's flawed plant design and management.

A management change

Reluctantly, the board members began to acknowledge their inherent inability to deal with the growing array of problems confronting the authority. A lay, part-time board might have been appropriate for overseeing a professionally managed, fiscally sound public enterprise, but it was ill equipped to provide either the attention or the expertise required to develop a coherent management plan for these difficult circumstances. Turnover on the board had reduced the continuity and experience it might otherwise have had and contributed to the feelings of some board members that events were out of control. Recognizing that it needed administrative help, the board decided, five years after its inception, to hire a full-time professional executive director for the RRA.

The board recruited Bob McAdams to fill the new position on a temporary basis. McAdams had over thirty years' experience in public-sector organizations. Those acquainted with McAdams regarded him as a competent and task-oriented administrator who especially enjoyed a challenging work environment. The RRA Board obliged by making it plain that McAdams should immediately begin to oversee the daily operations of the incinerator and to work on a "comprehensive study of the authority's operations, including any and all recommendations which would promote a fiscally sound authority."

When he accepted the position, McAdams was under no illusions about the seriousness of the problems he faced. In his first month as executive director of the authority, McAdams concluded that the central financial problem of the authority had three dimensions. One was legal. The law creating the authority and the contracts with area governments and private solid waste companies all created obligations and constraints upon the authority as a service provider. A second factor was political. The authority was only one of several actors in the intergovernmental arrangement that constituted the local solid waste industry. Plans for any action by the authority would need to take into account the impact on other actors. Finally, there was a managerial dimension. Had Recom managed the incinerator in the interest of the authority, with appropriate controls on operational costs? Furthermore, it appeared that these considerations were highly interdependent. Changes in any one of them produced consequences for the others.

Les Martin, who had managed the incinerator facility for Recom for two years, was not disposed to like the idea of reporting to the new executive director, since this ended his direct access to individual board members. Neither was he enthusiastic about the oversight and supervision that McAdams began to provide.

As McAdams reviewed internal documents—including financial reports that Martin reluctantly provided—he identified several cost-saving measures he thought Recom should adopt. For example, Recom carried a large and, in McAdams' judgment, excessive inventory of costly spare parts. McAdams estimated that reducing the parts inventory, together with reductions in some labor costs, would result in savings of four to five thousand dollars a month.

McAdams also discovered that some revenues were being lost because Recom operated its scales for only one eight-hour shift. During the time no scale operator was on duty, some truck drivers were failing to weigh their loads, thereby avoiding any tipping fees. There was no firm figure for the magnitude of these revenue losses, but McAdams estimated that they could run as high as two thousand dollars per month.

McAdams discussed these items with Martin on several occasions. In these meetings, Martin expressed the opinion that he and Recom had done a satisfactory job of managing the incinerator and criticized the authority for failing to pay Recom the 10 percent management fee for which provision had been made in the original contract. Although acknowledging that the proposed measures would save some money, Martin asserted that the savings would not substantially contribute to solving the authority's financial problems.

In the weeks that followed, the relationship between McAdams and Martin worsened. Officials from Recom's headquarters office made several trips to the RRA incinerator to confer with both Martin and McAdams. These visits only served to widen the gap between the authority and Recom, and they resulted in veiled threats by one of Recom's headquarters officers that Recom might sue the authority for its management fee. McAdams reported these developments to the board, along with his concern that the attitude of Recom officials was not conducive to a satisfactory long-term relationship.

The decision problem

Among the uncertainties faced by McAdams as he prepared to make his full recommendations to the board was whether the authority and Recom could come to any mutual accommodation or whether the authority should seek legal termination of its contract. Clearly, one of the sticking points was the issue of the management fee. McAdams felt that the cost-plus feature of the management contract discouraged Recom from holding down operational costs and was itself part of the problem. Another was the issue of Recom's responsibility for design and construction faults. Some expensive modifications in the facility were still necessary. Most pressing was the design and installation of a bypass system that would allow the incinerator to operate when ABX was closed. Preliminary cost estimates for a bypass system obtained by McAdams ranged as high as $500,000. The authority did not have any cash reserves to cover such an outlay, nor could it seek new loans in its current financial straits.

McAdams was slightly more optimistic about the political and legal issues that surrounded the authority, primarily because they overlapped in so many ways.

Although the cost overruns of the incinerator had produced growing criticism of the authority, the authority had enjoyed the support of area governments in the past. Indeed, only the financial help provided by the city of Southridge had kept the RRA from defaulting on the revenue bonds. It was also clear that failure of area governments to meet bond payments by covering any revenue shortfalls of the incinerator operation would most likely result in Fidelity State Bank's declaring the authority in default. Though McAdams knew that these decisions were ultimately beyond the control of the authority, default seemed to him unlikely, except as a last resort, because default would have serious repercussions on the bank and local bondholders. Similarly, the users of the incinerator would lose the means of solving their solid waste problems if the authority were forced to default because of insufficient revenues. These considerations led McAdams to believe that the contractual obligations between the authority and its clients might be subject to renegotiation on terms more favorable to the authority's cost/revenue balance sheet.

In the short term, the authority needed to strengthen its financial condition. The eighty thousand dollars or so of annual cost savings that McAdams had identified would not be sufficient. However, a combination of cost savings, increased revenues, and some concessions from Recom might be adequate to place the authority on a secure financial basis.

What recommendations should McAdams make to the board?

Discussion questions

1. Given the roles played by the other governmental participants up to this point, what level of involvement should McAdams have with Southridge, with Southridge Mayor Linn, with Riverton, with Niles County?

2. The authority has several options vis-à-vis Recom. For example, it can seek to terminate the existing contract, renegotiate the contract under revised terms, and/or take legal action. What factors should be considered in making these decisions? What should McAdams recommend?

3. What should the authority's strategy be in light of Recom's veiled threat to sue for the unpaid management fee?

4. If the Recom contract is terminated, the authority could contract with another firm to manage the incinerator, seek to turn management responsibility over to Southridge, or manage the plant itself. What factors should be considered in making this decision? What should McAdams recommend?

5. If Recom is to be retained as the plant manager, how could Recom's cooperation in cost-saving efforts be secured?

6. Assuming it is legal, should operation of the incinerator facility be privatized? What would be the advantages and disadvantages of such a move, both in general and in relation to the specific circumstances of this case?

7. One option in this case would be for the area governments to abandon the concept of a self-financing enterprise and simply budget funds to cover the imbalance between the authority's expenses and revenues.

Another option would be to renegotiate the tipping fees charged to users. What are the advantages and disadvantages of each option?

8. What strategy should be adopted to deal with bondholders?

9. What concessions should the authority be willing to make regarding the cost considerations, the Recom contract, the management issues, and the concerns of the other units of government?

The aftermath

The authority's first act based on McAdams' recommendations was to file a $20 million lawsuit against Recom for fraud, negligence, and breach of contract in the design, construction, and operation of the incinerator. Next, the RRA took steps to remove Recom as manager of the incinerator plant. Notice was sent to Recom informing Recom of the immediate termination of its services. Recom reacted by filing a $224,000 countersuit against the authority seeking temporary and permanent injunctive relief from the authority's interference in plant operations.

Three major subsequent developments summarize the outcome in the RRA case. First, the authority and Recom ended their legal battle through a negotiated agreement. Under the terms of the agreement, the earlier cost-plus contract was abandoned in favor of an incentive contract. Recom agreed to a fixed-cost operation fee that it would receive whenever it produced steam or burned garbage. Any additional operating costs would be absorbed by Recom. Further, Recom agreed to make $700,000 in design changes and improvements at the plant, including the bypass system that would allow the incinerator to operate seven days a week. Second, the tipping fees charged to users of the incinerator plant were revised. The earlier fee of $9 per ton was increased to $13 per ton for municipalities and to $18 per ton for commercial users. Third, the authority retained McAdams as executive director on a permanent basis.

An audit for the next year revealed that the authority completed its first year in the black, and the following year it signed an additional contract with Recom to operate the incinerator seven days a week instead of five.

Final discussion questions

1. Did the authority's action in filing a lawsuit simply contribute to the general trend toward making the United States a "litigious society"? Under what circumstances is the use of a lawsuit justified as a means of resolving a public policy question or as an administrative tactic?

2. To what extent did environmental considerations enter into the decision-making process? To what extent should they have been a consideration? What should have been done differently to protect the environment?

3. A part of the solution was the abandonment of the cost-plus contract with Recom. Do cost-plus contracts have an appropriate use? If so, under what circumstances? If not, why are they used? How can the use of such contracts be discouraged or limited to appropriate circumstances?

4. What negotiating strategies would you recommend for getting Recom to agree to make the $700,000-worth of design changes and improvements?

3 What to do about housing?

Mark Etling

Editor's introduction

The oldest charge against professional management in local government is that the use of "professionals" gives control of the community to "outsiders" and reduces local control over local affairs. Advocates of professional management point out that professional administrators are "servants of their elected bosses" and must be responsive to electoral politics even though they are not, themselves, elected to office.

This case describes the dilemma of a professional manager who finds his efforts to address local housing issues held hostage both to the outcome of a local election and to the policy preferences of newly elected council members whose views on the housing issue have not been clearly articulated. At issue here is a key question: How should the manager adjust his efforts in the area of housing to changes occurring in the community's political climate and leadership?

Also involved in his decision is the need for sensitivity to a local citizens' group actively opposing any new city housing initiative. The group poses no direct threat to the manager, but it does affect the political climate within which the manager works, and it can influence the council, whose support for any new housing effort is essential.

In describing the politics of housing (often a sensitive local issue) the case also focuses on the role of the professional administrator as a leader in the policy-making process. First, it describes the administrator's role in bringing policy problems to the attention of the elected leadership—the kind of staff work that is the core of the professional administrator's policy responsibility. Second, it shows the kind of decisions administrators must make as they try to balance their sense of community needs with the political realities of the communities they serve.

In working its way through these political complexities, the case also follows the evolution of a key administrative decision regarding the community's housing needs and the formulation of an appropriate housing policy for a community whose aging housing stock threatens to decline in value and quality.

Case 3
What to do about housing?

Background

When the Clarkville City Council authorized the hiring of an administrative assistant to deal with housing issues, it reopened a question that had been of interest in the community for several years. During that time the council had been considering what to do about the city's perceived housing problems. The time now seemed right to confront the issue head-on.

Clarkville sprang up in the 1850s as a whistle-stop community several miles from a major midwestern city. Incorporated in 1894, it evolved into a middle-ring suburb of 24,500 residents located within a metropolitan area with a population of 2.5 million. Like many other suburban communities nationwide, Clarkville experienced rapid growth after the Second World War: its population jumped from 11,500 in 1950 to a peak of 29,000 in 1970.

Clarkville's seven thousand units of single-family housing spread in all directions around a core of original homes and a central shopping district; the city became a patchwork of subdivisions and annexation areas.

Over the years the city developed a proud tradition of autonomy and active citizen participation in local government. The council-manager form of government was adopted in the 1950s, and well over 150 citizens serve on a variety of boards and commissions. The seven-member council, though composed of independent-minded individuals, has demonstrated a high degree of solidarity on most issues in recent years.

By the mid-1980s, when this case begins, a set of perceptions had developed about the city's housing market that troubled several members of the city council. Some early signs of housing deterioration were evident in parts of the city, particularly near the border between Clarkville and Cozens, a poverty-stricken community to the west. Some residents observed that homes in Clarkville seemed to be undervalued by as much as 10 to 20 percent. There was an informal consensus that major corporations in or near Clarkville were directing their relocated employees to homes in other parts of the metropolitan area. Many people wondered whether the "white flight" that had occurred in much of the northern part of the county in the 1960s and 1970s was now affecting Clarkville as well.

These perceptions persisted despite the fact that the city had taken some steps to address them. For several years the local community development office had been administering Community Development Block Grant (CDBG) funds in the form of home improvement grants and rebates, a paint program, and urban homesteading. A minimum exterior-appearance housing code was enacted in the early 1980s over a storm of protest and after an unsuccessful referendum.

Still, it took time for consensus to emerge among the council members about the need for more comprehensive and direct intervention in the housing market. Long-time mayor John Keane had, over the course of many years, become more and more convinced of the need for direct city intervention. Two other council members, Fred Castoria and Ted Bunker, also were thought to be solid, if not staunch, believers in greater housing activity by the city. Three members—Janet Johnson, Carl Barth, and Carol Marx—had vigorously supported a more active approach for several years. The seventh city council member, Richard Hall, was considered part of the group favoring greater intervention, but he was in the midst of a campaign for a seat on the county council. Ken Calm, the city manager for three years, had helped build consensus on the issue by consistently advocating a higher priority for the housing issue.

The council would have to overcome a major political hurdle if it decided to take a more aggressive approach to housing. A small but vocal group of residents would almost certainly fight any new housing ordinance or program. This group embraced the philosophy that city government should be only minimally involved in people's lives, and they were opposed to the concept of any city intervention in housing. In the recent past they had attempted to block the exterior housing code and the CDBG-funded programs. They would almost certainly try to put a stop to any new form of housing activity.

Another factor looming on the political horizon was an impending mayoral race. Retiring Mayor Keane's seat was expected to be contested by Janet Johnson—one of the outspoken supporters of greater housing intervention and a loser to Keane in a close race in the previous election—and Fred Castoria, whose support for more housing activity was considered solid but not as strong as Johnson's.

The case

The city council took a first step toward the possibility of increased intervention when, at a June budget hearing, it voted to authorize City Manager Calm to hire an administrative assistant for housing issues. Cecil Roberts, a former newspaper reporter with several years' experience in housing issues, was hired in mid-September, and Calm gave his new administrative assistant two directives: (1) to research the housing situation in Clarkville thoroughly, and (2) to write a report to the council listing a range of viable options for possible housing activity.

During his first three months on the job, Roberts gathered relevant data about the housing market in Clarkville, using several research methods:

He compiled and analyzed demographic, socioeconomic, and housing data, using Census material and data previously gathered by the city and by the urban information center of a nearby university.

In cooperation with the chief housing inspector, he conducted an informal windshield survey of the city to determine the extent of exterior deterioration of the housing stock.

He gathered information about housing agencies in the local metropolitan area and in other cities around the country.

He investigated potential funding sources for housing programs in both the public and the private sectors.

He interviewed community leaders in the real estate and banking industries to learn their impressions of the condition of the housing market in Clarkville.

The housing report

By the start of the new year, Roberts had completed a lengthy report. He presented his findings formally to the council and the public at a regular council meeting in February. His analysis of the data led him to draw two basic conclusions: first, that the housing market in Clarkville was fundamentally viable and self-sustaining, and second, that some negative conditions existed that warranted the attention of the city. Several factors substantiated the claim that the housing market was basically self-sustaining.

First, homes were found to be available in many styles, sizes, and prices. The variety of housing in Clarkville included everything from modest brick or frame bungalows and ranch-style homes to luxury subdivisions and historic homes built a century or more ago. The price range of homes in the city was roughly $30,000 to $160,000.

Second, the rate of housing turnover was low—4.1 percent in the preceding year and an average of just 5.3 percent over the previous ten years.

Third, the population base was heterogeneous but stable. The 1980 Census reported a 14.4 percent minority population in Clarkville. At the same time, the Census indicated that 57 percent of Clarkville residents had lived in the city at least eleven years. Apparently the minority population was being integrated into the community gradually and peacefully, and any fears of "white flight" were misplaced.

Fourth, homes were appreciating steadily in value. In the preceding year the median value of a house in the city was $46,105, a 30.2 percent increase over the median value of $35,400 seven years earlier.

Fifth, there was a surge of new housing construction in the city. After a ten-year lull in construction activity, ground had been broken for some forty-seven single-family units and ninety-two condominiums in the preceding year alone.

Sixth, home mortgage financing and homeowner's insurance were readily available to Clarkville homebuyers.

Finally, the city's housing stock was, overall, well maintained.

Roberts' report went on to state the adverse housing-related conditions in the city.

Knowledge was generally lacking in the metropolitan area about the quality of housing in Clarkville. Although several major corporations were located either within or just minutes away from Clarkville, they routinely directed their relocated employees to housing in other parts of the metropolitan area considered more "desirable." Several persons interviewed during the preparation of the report noted that Clarkville was "too well-kept a secret" and needed to be marketed more systematically and aggressively.

Furthermore, there was a misperception that Clarkville was racially segregated. Much of the area to the south and west of the city had either traditionally housed a minority population or had experienced racial turnover in the 1960s and 1970s. Clarkville, however, had assimilated its minority population gradually over the preceding fifteen years without the upheaval in housing values caused by "white flight." Although race was not a significant factor in Clarkville's housing market, this fact was not generally known in the metropolitan area.

Largely as a result of the first two factors, housing in Clarkville tended to be undervalued and was not appreciating at the same rate as comparable housing elsewhere in the metropolitan area. The 30.2 percent rate of appreciation in Clarkville over the preceding seven years, although respectable, still lagged behind such cities as Rosebud (37.1 percent) and Churchtown (37.8 percent) in the southwestern part of the county.

The number of homes showing signs of deferred maintenance was slowly but steadily increasing. Although Clarkville's over-all rate of substandard units (4 percent) was significantly lower than the national average of 8 percent, the number of substandard units in the city had doubled in the preceding twenty-one years. In some parts of the city, the owner-occupancy rate had declined in recent years, as investor-owners converted single-family units into rental property. This situation was exacerbating home maintenance problems and holding down property values.

There were a few eyesore properties in various parts of the city. These properties—each of which had a dramatically negative effect on an entire block—had deteriorated to the point where the conventional housing industry had given up on them.

The report pointed out that these conditions did not pose an immediate threat to the viability of the housing market in Clarkville but that "if these adverse factors are not addressed, a cycle of lower appraisals, deferred maintenance, and more eyesore properties could be created, resulting in a depressed housing market in Clarkville."

Recommendations

Roberts' report spelled out four viable courses of action that were open to the council:

1. No intervention in the housing market. A "do-nothing" approach would acknowledge that Clarkville's housing market was fundamentally

self-sustaining and would allow the market to continue to be entirely self-directing.

2. A modest level of city intervention. The council could authorize low-key activities such as conducting ongoing research and gathering data about the housing market, monitoring real estate and lending activity, and marketing the city to major corporations. These activities could be conducted without the hiring of any new staff.

3. A moderate level of intervention, such as the creation of either a housing corporation or a city housing department. This type of housing agency could acquire, rehabilitate, and sell eyesore properties and give the local realtors a role by listing rehabilitated homes with them. The agency could acquire and demolish seriously substandard homes. It might offer home improvement loan counseling, technical assistance, and loan packaging to city residents.

4. A major level of intervention. The council could decide that the best approach to Clarkville's housing situation would be to make the city a competitive "player" in the conventional housing market by establishing a city-run real estate and mortgage finance agency. Such an agency could be empowered to engage in activities that a housing corporation or department could not engage in. It could acquire and dispose of real estate of all types, including, but not limited to, eyesore properties. It could offer permanent financing through federal and state programs. It could also seek funding and marketing support from major corporations.

After Roberts finished his presentation, Calm made his personal recommendation to the council: that the city establish a not-for-profit, tax-exempt housing corporation. The council agreed to take his recommendation under advisement and opened the floor to the public for discussion.

Several persons in the audience asked questions or made comments that suggested they wanted to know more about a housing corporation before making a commitment for or against it. Jim Bishop, a long-time local realtor and president of the Clarkville Business Association, was one of those who expressed some reservations about, although not outright opposition to, the proposal. As expected, representatives of the vocal opposition spoke out against the concept of a housing corporation. One of the group's leaders questioned Roberts at length about what a corporation could or could not do. It seemed certain from the tone of their questions that the opposition would try to stop a corporation from ever coming into being.

Politics and housing

By February 9, when the housing report was presented, the political landscape in Clarkville had changed considerably. Carl Barth, a staunchly prohousing council member, had announced that he would not seek reelection, and two other supporters, Carol Marx and Ted Bunker, were involved in hotly contested races against younger and better-funded opponents. It was not clear whether either the incumbents or their challengers would be eager to make housing a major campaign issue. In addition, former Clarkville council member Richard Hall had won a seat on the county council in December, and his appointed successor, Bud Adams, was a relative newcomer to Clarkville politics whose views on housing were not widely known. Calm wondered whether council action on the housing report might be delayed for several months or even indefinitely, depending on the outcome of the council races.

Public discussion on the housing report continued at the February 23 meeting. Then, at the meeting on March 8, the council unanimously voted to authorize

Calm to draft an ordinance enabling the formation of a not-for-profit housing corporation. The council also decided that the corporation would operate under a set of limitations designed to make it politically more palatable:

Its activities would be confined to just one area of the city—a neighborhood adjacent to Cozens—where the greatest concentration of eyesore and substandard homes had been identified.

It would be forbidden to exercise the power of eminent domain (a limitation already imposed by state statute).

Participation by city residents in any housing programs would be strictly voluntary.

The city would maintain a high degree of control through the council's appointment of a board of directors to oversee the operation of the corporation.

At its next meeting, on March 22, the council gave first reading to the ordinance. The political risks involved in this step were dramatized that night when a leader of the opposition announced that he was initiating a petition drive that would require that the corporation be brought to a referendum. With the election just two weeks away, a demonstration of the council's unanimity—or lack of it—on the issue would be an important symbol of its political will. That symbolic gesture was forthcoming: the motion to read the ordinance was supported unanimously by the council.

The outcome of the April 5 election cast considerable doubt on the status of the ordinance and the corporation. The moderate, although heretofore supportive, candidate Fred Castoria won the mayoral race by just twenty-four votes over the more vigorously prohousing candidate, Janet Johnson. Carol Marx and Ted Bunker, incumbents whose support for the corporation had been consistent, were defeated by Luke McCoy and Bill Reuther, two newcomers whose positions on housing were unknown. A local businessman named Dan McPherson was elected to the seat vacated by the retiring Carl Barth. Yet another opening on the council, created by Castoria's election as mayor, was filled by the appointment of Phil Jameson, another political newcomer who had served as McPherson's campaign manager.

The makeup of the council was now dramatically altered, with new members in five of the seven seats and a new mayor for the first time in fourteen years. Calm doubted seriously whether the new council would support the housing corporation with the nonpartisan unity that had characterized the outgoing council.

Two agendas were published for the council meeting of April 19: one for the outgoing and one for the incoming council. The scheduled second reading of the ordinance to set up a corporation appeared on the first agenda and would be considered by the outgoing council for final passage.

After hearing a request from an opposition spokesman to table the ordinance so that it could be taken up—and struck down, he hoped out loud—by the incoming council, the outgoing group made a parting gesture of support for the corporation: they passed the ordinance without dissent.

The decision problem

Even though Calm knew he now had the statutory authority to proceed with the formation of a housing corporation, he was reluctant to use that authority. If the membership of the city council had not changed so drastically, he would have seen the April 19 vote as a mandate to proceed with incorporation. But with five new members elected or appointed within the space of just four months, he knew that a reevaluation of the situation was in order.

To what extent, he wondered, would the new council try to establish an identity of its own, perhaps at the expense of existing programs and policies? What kind of group dynamic would emerge in the new council—would the members be cooperative or combative? What would their attitude toward city staff be? What opinion would they have of housing activity in general and of the embryonic housing corporation in particular?

With these considerations in mind, Calm pondered his options regarding how, or whether, to pursue the housing corporation with the new council. He reasoned that he could handle the issue in one of three ways.

His first option was a "hard-sell" approach. He could aggressively pursue the issue by proceeding full-speed with the implementation of the April 19 ordinance. He could direct Roberts to draft and submit suggested articles of incorporation and bylaws. His objective would be to capitalize on the momentum already generated by years of consensus building by the former council. If successful, he would head off the antihousing forces in the city before they could exert much pressure on the new council.

But this approach, with its potential for quick success, might also produce instant failure. Calm's aggressiveness might pressure the council into a defensive posture. They might feel that they were being "railroaded" on the housing issue and respond by rescinding the ordinance (as the opposition had already suggested) or by directing him to delay action on incorporation, perhaps indefinitely.

Calm's second option was a "low-key" approach that would give the council more time to consider the housing corporation. He could refrain from any immediate administrative action but keep the issue before the council by means of agenda items and the suggestion of a work session on the subject of housing. The council would then be free to dictate the pace of action. Calm could direct Roberts to distribute to the new council the informational report that he had submitted to the former council and to be available to answer the council's questions. Roberts could also make presentations before city boards and commissions and other groups of residents for the purposes of public education and positive consensus building.

With good information and without the pressure of having to make a quick decision, the council might come to view the housing issue in a favorable light. There was also a greater likelihood that the new council would assume "ownership" of the proposal if given the time to study and evaluate it.

However, Calm knew all too well that the ancient Greek adage "to know the good is to do the good" did not always hold true in the real world of politics. And he was sure that the opposition would take advantage of the time factor by pressuring the council to abandon the issue.

Calm's third option, as he viewed it, was a "hands-off" approach. He could simply let the issue go and wait to see when the council would take it up again. He could direct Roberts to "lay low," so as not to pressure the council in any way.

If he chose this approach, Calm would, of course, be giving the council maximum latitude to act or not act on the corporation. That approach might ultimately prove to be most effective, because the new council might arrive at its own consensus about the need for the corporation or at least for some type of new housing activity. The council would then feel a high degree of "ownership" of the decision. Besides, Calm knew that so far, none of the new council members had publicly expressed outright opposition to the corporation.

On the other hand, a do-nothing strategy might backfire. In the absence of impetus from city staff, the opposition might convince the council of its position. Or the housing corporation might get lost in the shuffle of a long list of issues facing the council that summer.

Calm knew he must choose a tactic.

Discussion questions

1. What are the key considerations, in addition to those stated in the case, that City Manager Calm must analyze as he selects his course of action regarding the proposed housing corporation? In particular, what information does he need from, and about the attitudes of, the individual council members regarding housing?

2. With whom should Calm consult before making his decision? How should he approach the mayor, individual council members, other administrators, persons opposing the proposed housing policy, others in the community?

3. Under what conditions should Calm work with individual council members on this issue? Under what conditions should he urge the mayor to take this leadership role? What should the manager do if the mayor refuses?

4. If Calm decides to consult with the council members, should he talk to them individually, collectively in work sessions, or both? Should he restrict himself to inquiries about their position, attempt to educate them about the development of the city's new housing policy, and/or attempt to convince them to support that housing policy?

5. How should Calm weigh the fact that the issue in question—housing—has major social policy implications and that the new housing program might provide the city with a vehicle through which help could be offered to those residents least able to afford adequate housing? What, if any, effect should this consideration have on the way Calm handles the issue? Why?

6. While the issue awaits resolution, Roberts will naturally be unsure of whether or not his job is in danger. How should Calm deal with Roberts at this time? What direction or advice should Calm give him?

7. Besides the three options generated by Calm, are there others he should have considered? If so, list and discuss them, citing management and political factors that make them worth considering.

8. Which approach would you choose? Why?

The aftermath

The more he thought about it, the more Calm came to believe that there were too many unknowns for him to take a hard-sell approach to the housing corporation. He wasn't sure where any of the new council members stood on the issue of housing or how high a priority they placed on additional city-sponsored housing activity. It was far too early to tell whether this council would accept the precedents of the previous council or would want to forge new policies and establish a separate identity.

On the other hand, Calm believed that the housing issue had progressed too far for him to adopt a "hands-off posture." Roberts had been hired; the housing report had been prepared and submitted; the proposal had been given considerable public exposure and discussion; and an enabling ordinance had even been passed. Calm concluded that if he were to let the issue lie dormant now, he might lose all that had been accomplished up to this point.

Therefore, Calm decided to take the middle course—a low-key but persistent stance. He would keep the issue alive by making sure that it came to the council's attention regularly, by making it a part of his report at council meetings, and by suggesting a council work session to study the proposal. But he would not pressure the council to make an immediate decision about the status of the housing corporation.

The housing issue resurfaced for the first time on the night of May 24, when a representative of the opposition announced at a council meeting that the petition drive to force a referendum had been called off. Still, the new council remained noncommittal on the issue and gave evidence of wanting to forge its own identity on policy matters.

In mid-June the council defeated a proposal to fund housing improvements in one part of the city through a tax increment finance agreement. On June 28 it postponed adoption of the budget at the urging of council member Luke McCoy, who reportedly was concerned because "there is money budgeted for a housing corporation, and we do not have a housing corporation." In mid-July the council held a work session at which they reached agreement on the budget but approved funds for the housing corporation, including Roberts' salary, for only ninety days. Further council discussion on the issue, while tentatively favorable, remained noncommittal. Finally, on September 12 the council canceled a four-year-old cross-training program for police officers and firefighters in response to opposition stemming from many of the same persons who opposed the housing corporation.

The final council session on the housing issue was held on September 26, just four days before the appropriation for housing funds and Roberts' salary were due to expire. At the session, council members endorsed the idea of the corporation, authorized its funding for the remainder of the fiscal year, named it the Clarkville Neighborhood Improvement Program, formed an eleven-member board of directors, and decided that all members of the council would serve as the agency's legal incorporators.

Calm's decision to take a low-key approach to the housing question had given council members time to study the issue, sound out their constituents, draw their own conclusions, and make the policy their own. The decision had involved risks and costs, but the result was that Calm met, and passed successfully, a crucial test with the new council.

Final discussion questions

1. Should Calm have relied more on the mayor for leadership? Why or why not?

2. In the council-manager form of government, what is the proper balance between the municipal administration and the council in proposing or advocating new programs?

3. Why was the "low-key" approach sucessful in this case? Would another approach have worked better? If so, which one and why?

4. If the opposition had sustained its level of political pressure, should Calm have changed his strategy? If so, how and why? What role should Calm have played if the issue had gone to a referendum?

5. If the housing corporation proposal had been defeated by the new council but the manager remained convinced that it was needed and feasible, how should the manager have proceeded in the aftermath of the defeat?

Part three: Community politics

Introduction to part three:
Community politics

Community politics—politics at the local government level—is the grass-roots politics that Thomas Jefferson so revered. It is the cradle of American democracy. The average American citizen has more diverse political involvement at the community level—voting, working in political campaigns, communicating with public officials, holding public office, running for election to office, testifying at public hearings—than at any other level of government. It is in local politics that most political leaders get their start; it is in local politics that most citizens have their personal involvement with government. It is in local politics—where elections are frequent and referenda are common—that the will of the voters is most evident, most easily measured, and most clearly felt by government decision-makers. In short, politics is the warp and woof of local government; it is the catalyst that makes local government work.

The presence of community politics in local government clearly affects the job of the local government administrator. More than anything else, it is what makes the job of the local government administrator different, not just from the job of the administrator in the private sector, but from that of the public administrator in state or national government. Local politics, because it is so close to the voters, is different from state and national politics; the local administrator deals with fewer representatives of large interest groups, but has much more contact with voters. Local administrators encounter constituents who wish to "talk business" in the office; at public meetings; in the stores, churches, and parks of the community; and even during the administrator's "off" hours at home. Local politics permeates all aspects of the local administrator's work and life in the community.

All the cases in this book deal in some measure with community politics. Such politics are a constant theme in local government management and decision making. The cases in Part Three have been selected for their diverse perspectives on community political processes and their reflections on appropriate responses by professional administrators to the local political climate.

The first case in this part, Case 4, links the mayor, the city manager, the police department, and important and vocal community groups in a dispute over the retention of a black police chief. It probes the difficulties involved in resolving complex problems to which there is neither a clear solution nor an obviously "right" one. Issues of race further complicate the picture, creating community support for the police chief even in the face of evidence of poor performance in the police department.

The next case presents a problem with a solution that appears "right"—it promotes economy and efficiency in government operations—but is vigorously opposed by a wide range of community groups. The issue at hand is an effort by the city and the manager to restructure local advisory boards and commissions in a way that would achieve greater administrative centralization and enhance the manager's ability to coordinate their input. The case poses a classic dilemma: a clash between popular control and administrative effectiveness.

Case 6 looks at political conflict between a constituent group seeking government support and the government's middle management administrators. The conflict involves fees for the use of park and recreation facilities; the citizens' group questions the government's administrative procedures as well as its fee structure.

All these cases give a sense of the texture as well as the significance of Jefferson's beloved grass-roots democracy in its contemporary manifestations.

Race, politics, and the police chief

Richard K. Ghere and Frederick R. Inscho

Editor's introduction

This is the classic "tough" case in local politics. It pits the officers in the police department against their chief; it embodies the prejudices and tensions so frequently associated with contemporary race relations and issues with a racial component; it demonstrates the varying political styles of elected mayors and the impact on the administration of a change in mayoral style; and it puts the manager in the "hot seat" of having to solve an emotion-laden political problem that has no obviously "right" solution.

Central to the case is a key issue: a lack of congruence between the administrative and political dimensions of the problem. That problem—poor performance by the police chief—has an obvious administrative solution: The police chief should be replaced. That solution, however, is politically unacceptable to vocal and influential segments of the community.

The case also demonstrates the episodic nature of many public-sector political decisions. It shows how the nature of the decision problem changes daily as events unfold. Over time, the problem posed in this case is affected by the resignation of the mayor and his replacement by a new mayor, a black man with a very different political style; by active political pressure from the Fraternal Order of Police; by the disclosure of an indiscretion by a senior police officer; by the actions, over time, of the police chief; and, most important, by the political actions and strategies of groups in the city's black community over which the manager could exert neither control nor significant influence.

Overriding all of this, and forcing a response by the manager, is the problem of poor performance and poor morale in the police department. No local chief executive can afford long-term poor performance in this critical function. In this case the members of the department themselves are demanding action. The manager has to act, but any action against the chief is certain to provoke an angry community response. Police operations are the manager's responsibility and the new mayor seems reluctant to get involved. Along with everything else, the manager must decide how proactive a professional administrator should become in promoting the resolution of a conflict that is more political than administrative in nature.

It is situations such as the one portrayed here that give full meaning to Karl Bosworth's assertion, "The manager is a politician."

Case 4
Race, politics, and the police chief

Background

Valley City Manager Bob Schmidt was faced with a difficult and distasteful decision. His chief of police, John Jones, was under serious fire from within his department. At the same time, Jones enjoyed strong support from important elements of the community. It seemed that whatever might be done regarding the situation, significant groups were likely to be offended, resulting in considerable damage to the city. As he contemplated his range of possible actions, Schmidt recalled the sequence of events that led to his present dilemma.

John Jones followed an unusual path to the leadership of the Valley City Police Department (VCPD). Not a sworn officer, he had been "loaned" to the police department seventeen years earlier by the Valley City Human Relations Commission, to serve as a civilian assistant to the incumbent chief. He quickly attracted favorable attention, both from his superiors and from the Fraternal Order of Police (FOP), the bargaining unit for the rank-and-file officers.

While still serving in this civilian position, he achieved recognition for his role in establishing and heading the department's conflict resolution group and began to establish himself as a black role model in law enforcement. After about two years, the city manager, in an effort to fully integrate the police department's command structure, proposed sweeping reforms that would have placed blacks at all levels of the department's command structure within eighteen months. Although not completely implemented (in part because of FOP opposition), the plan did result in Jones' being named a police major. With this move Jones became both a sworn officer and the first black on the force to rise above the rank of sergeant.

This partial implementation of the manager's plan was to have profound, long-term effects on the VCPD. While some of the department's rank-and-file may have resented the lateral appointment of a civilian to high police rank, this did not seem to be a serious problem at the time. Indeed, three years later Jones was named deputy chief under Chief Peter Flaherty. This position made Jones the "heir apparent" to Chief Flaherty.

On the other hand, the failure to implement the plan completely signaled to the city's black community that it faced continuing problems in moving into Valley City's mainstream. This concern was especially important in light of the city's precarious economic and political situation. A midwestern industrial center with a population of just under a quarter of a million, Valley City had a reputation for innovation and leadership in industry and in government. A pioneer in the city management movement and the site of several major manufacturing operations, the city had been known for decades as a prosperous and wellgoverned community. The governing body was a five-member city council, elected at large in elections that were nominally nonpartisan. In reality, however, political parties actively backed candidates for the council, and council members' partisan leanings were readily identifiable. Despite this variation in form, the city had a tradition of successful use of the council-manager form of government.

This prosperity and political peace began to change in the 1960s and early 1970s as the city experienced the industrial and economic decline that was affecting the entire region. Several major employers shut down, unemployment rose, and the corporate and business leadership that had once contributed to the city's success began to leave the area. Politically, the city began to change as its large black minority (roughly 40 percent of the total population) began to assert itself. Besides actively supporting candidates sympathetic to their interests, the city's blacks were concerned with the administration of the city government. This concern was especially acute in the case of the politically sensitive police department, since only 10 percent of its roughly five hundred officers were black.

Flaherty and Jones made something of an "odd couple" as the two highest-ranking persons on the force. Flaherty, a prototypical "street cop," had risen through the ranks until, after many years of service, he had achieved ultimate command. Blunt and outspoken, he was a forceful figure on the force and in city hall. Jones, on the other hand, was young, college educated, and experienced in human relations and conflict resolution, and he had an active off-the-job interest in art. In addition, he lacked formal administrative training and had little experience in managing paramilitary organizations. Vastly different from Flaherty, Jones was clearly a new type of police commander.

Either these personality differences or Jones' unusual route to the deputy chief position might explain the strained working relationship between the two men. A police chief in a city of Valley City's size would usually delegate major responsibilities to his deputy, but this did not seem to happen in Valley City. Although he was the second-ranking person on the force for the next eight years, Jones never appeared to be fully involved in citywide police operations and often seemed to be excluded from serious decision making. He did remain visible as a departmental spokesperson on affairs pertaining to the black community, retained his reputation as an innovative and effective human relations–oriented administrator, and continued to serve as a prominent black role model in law enforcement. He was also able to achieve some visibility outside the local area and eventually received serious consideration for a command position in a major metropolitan police force in the northern part of the state. Turning this offer down seemed to cement Jones' chances of succeeding to the leadership of Valley City's department. When Flaherty retired, Jones was named chief.

Shadows over Chief Jones

The "Jones era" in the Valley City police force was marked by two continuing realities. First, the city was politically dominated by its mayor, Hugh Marion, who brought an explicitly partisan political style to the city government. A long-time Democratic party activist and a former state legislator, Marion saw himself as a "strong mayor" who needed to demonstrate leadership and to concentrate power to be effective. Coming to office with an agenda that included establishing better working relationships with the business community and with the city's suburbs, Marion quickly established himself as the dominant force in city government, a role that his fellow council members appeared willing to concede to him.

Rumors of partisan control over administrative appointments were prevalent during Marion's tenure as mayor. Although those charges proved difficult to substantiate, it was clear that Marion's political strength eclipsed that of his only real opponent on the council—lone Republican Frank Ackerman. The only area politician with sufficient influence to rival Marion was Martin Plunkett, a state representative widely regarded as one of the state's most powerful black politicians. While focusing primarily on state-level issues, Plunkett enjoyed powerful local support and was capable of wielding considerable influence in Valley City politics—particularly on behalf of the black community.

By assuming the "strong mayor" role, Marion departed from the traditions of council-manager government in two ways. First, he assumed a highly visible position in controversial policy areas. As a political pragmatist, Marion moved to "cash in" politically on the opportunities available in the inevitable conflicts of a city experiencing major demographic change. By assuming this high-profile leadership position, the mayor accrued political support from Plunkett and others in the black community as well as from other groups (such as the FOP) with demands to make on the city government. This extended political involvement allowed Marion to enhance his direct influence over the municipal bureaucracy and to strengthen his ties with the black community (in general) and Martin Plunkett (in particular). It also carried the risk of touching off a political backlash from the FOP and white officers in the department.

Second, Marion departed from the traditional role of the mayor in council-manager government by involving himself in departmental personnel and operations decisions. In effect, the mayor became the police department's top-level decisionmaker. Although Jones was the titular head, the mayor viewed the chief and deputy chief more or less as equals in departmental management—the chief focusing on community relations and the deputy chief on operations. In addition, many city hall observers felt that subordinate police officers regularly answered to the mayor regarding day-to-day operations.

The second constant during Jones' tenure as Valley City police chief was turmoil in the department itself. Barely nine months after Jones' appointment as chief, the police department's vice squad conducted a raid in which one Donald Butler was killed. Amid widespread speculation that the raid had been bungled (indeed, Butler was not a suspect but a bystander on the scene), Harriet Butler, the widow, filed a wrongful-death lawsuit against the city. During the highly publicized trial, which dragged on for several years, Jones was criticized for giving conflicting testimony and for not having kept the vice squad under closer control.

Perhaps even more damaging was another vice-squad–related scandal that broke less than a year later. This one involved allegations of illegal surveillance and unauthorized deals between VCPD vice squad detectives and alleged drug dealers. A special prosecutor's grand jury investigation resulted in charges being filed against twenty current or former Valley City officers. As a result, a number of officers (including Jones' deputy chief) quit the force or were forced to resign.

The circumstances surrounding the investigation of police wrongdoing called out for strong executive action, but the chief did not move to fill the vacancies caused by the scandal (perhaps because he was spending the bulk of his time responding to the grand jury probe). Eventually the mayor went on record as being dissatisfied with the chief's failure to act. Six weeks after the mayor's statement, the chief responded by announcing a five-point reorganization plan that he described as "an action plan for excellence" (the plan apparently reflected specifications imposed by the mayor).

Finding appropriate candidates to fill the available positions in the department's command structure proved to be as problematic as dealing with the damage done by the dismissed officers. Acting against the advice of high-ranking friends in the city administration who urged him to act quickly to appoint officers from within, Jones delayed and opted for a national search. The delay may have been due in part to a request from Mayor Marion, who issued a press release suggesting such a search. During the search, the police force's command structure was further reduced by retirements, leaving vacant three of the force's four top command positions under Jones.

Eventually, the one remaining senior commander, Major Charles Westwood, was promoted to deputy chief, and the other senior command positions were filled. Two of the new senior commanders were "outsiders" who had been identified by the national search and brought to Valley City as police majors. One, Alvin Jackson, was a black man who had previously served as a commander of detectives in a large southern city. Jackson became the new superintendent of investigations, while the second outsider, Jane Meagher, a white woman with an advanced degree in education and a professional background in law enforcement training, was appointed as superintendent of professional standards. After Stan Spivak, a long-time Valley City officer, was promoted to major and named to fill the remaining senior command vacancy, three of the five most senior command positions on the force were held by persons who had not served as Valley City patrol officers.

Had the VCPD been able to put the scandals to rest after their first airing, the department might have been able to recover. Unfortunately, these fiascoes seemed to have a life of their own. The Butler wrongful-death lawsuit dragged on for several years until the court ruled in favor of Harriet Butler, granting her a multimillion dollar award. Faced with a huge financial loss and flagging public confidence in the police, the city responded by creating a Special Committee on Police Affairs to review departmental operations in light of the scandals. The Special Committee was to make recommendations to the chief, the city manager, and the council on methods for improving the force. Robert Carter, a local building contractor with considerable interest in downtown redevelopment, was named to head the Special Committee. The Special Committee submitted its report—which, among other things, suggested granting the chief considerably greater discretionary power over promotions—to Chief Jones and Manager Schmidt shortly before Christmas.

The case

After the next election, the city faced a major transition. Mayor Marion had been elected to statewide office and was leaving the city. His successor, Daniel Hayes, was a black man with a professional background in education and several years of service on the city council. Much quieter and less overtly political than Marion, Hayes represented a return to a more traditional Valley City mayoral style.

Police politics

Marion's departure necessitated a special election, held in the spring, that would have pronounced but cross-cutting effects upon Jones and the police department. First, the city's voters elected Peter Wilson, a maverick Democrat, to fill the council seat that Hayes had vacated when he succeeded Marion. Since Wilson (who had previous council experience) was more prone to ally with Frank Ackerman, the sole Republican, than with the other Democrats, his return effectively fragmented Marion's old power base on the council and formed a two-vote block with pro-FOP leanings on the five-member council.

Second, the voters rejected a ballot issue that would have overturned the city's residency rule. This rule, which required all city government employees to reside within the city limits, had been exceptionally unpopular with the unions representing city workers since its adoption nine years earlier. The FOP had been especially active in fighting the rule, both by supporting several unsuccessful lawsuits aimed at dismantling it and by pressuring council members to overturn it. The unions launched a major, but ultimately unsuccessful, campaign to defeat the residency rule in the spring election. The FOP contributed threefourths of the antiresidency campaign's funding—while some council members and senior administrators, including Jones, contributed to the proresidency campaign.

The residency vote was a significant factor in heightening racial tensions, as city employees demanded the "right of flight" from the city and the school district (widely viewed as deficient). The election campaign politically mobilized these employees (most visibly, police officers), and its failure left them disappointed and bitter. Not surprisingly, strong black support was instrumental to the residency rule's success. In the short term, an overwhelming black vote for residency provided strong support for top municipal management (which had actively backed residency). Over the longer term, heightened black political interest in the city government, especially in the police department, was to mobilize against City Manager Schmidt on behalf of the police chief.

Shortly after the special election, the public was again reminded of the Butler case and the vice squad scandal when a former principal in the drug case accused two detectives of having accepted bribes. The Valley City *Examiner* gave the story front-page coverage for several days; then the story again faded into the woodwork. A month later Jones and Schmidt announced that they were backing the Special Committee's report. Thus, little remained to be done before the council could formally adopt the committee's findings.

Rebellion in the police department

By summer the Valley City Police Department was under severe strain. Scandals, "bad press," departmental restructuring, the Special Committee report, the residency vote, and the lateral-entry approach to filling senior command positions all had devastating effects on police morale. The severity of this problem became evident in June, when all but two of the force's lieutenants refused to participate in a stress-management seminar supported by Jones. The letter announcing this action (the "lieutenants' letter") was widely interpreted as a sign of dissatisfaction within the force's mid-level management. Newspaper accounts of the incident suggested that there was more to the protest than a simple dislike of the prospective seminar. Published reports spoke of complaints of poor communication between senior commanders and mid-level managers, low morale on the force, and simple mismanagement.

A second challenge to the department's leadership emerged at virtually the same time as the "lieutenants' letter," when the FOP announced its concern over the Special Committee's recommendations, especially those giving Jones greater discretionary powers over promotions. This forced Jones and Schmidt to meet with the FOP before presenting their report on the proposals to the council. When Schmidt was finally able to make his presentation, he accompanied it with a strong statement of support for both Jones and the force. After hearing the proposals (and having previously met with the FOP), the council members deferred action, stating that they believed that the proposals needed to provide greater detail regarding implementation.

In early July the Valley City *Examiner* showed the extent to which the police department's troubles had became a matter of public concern when it editorialized on the department's problems, directing mild criticism at both Jones and his critics. The chief was faulted for not listening sufficiently to his subordinates' complaints and for relying on weak senior commanders. The critics were reminded that Jones wasn't responsible for most of the department's scandal-related problems, which had developed while he was still Peter Flaherty's deputy.

Three days after this editorial, Jones faced the third major challenge to his leadership within as many weeks when a group of sergeants and lieutenants sued him, Schmidt, and the city over the department's merit-pay plan. This plan, which had been in place for several years, was designed to link a manager's annual salary increase with his performance through a type of management by objectives. The thrust of the suit was that the merit pay system was being unfairly manipulated through the establishment of unreasonable and unattainable objectives.

Faced with a virtual revolt by the department's mid-level managers, Schmidt opted to involve the city's director of management and budget, Bob Markham, in the deteriorating situation. Markham was directed to consult with Jones and Deputy Chief Westwood concerning existing management procedures and then to report back on methods for improving the department. Originally off the record, Markham's assignment was made public by Mayor Hayes on July 30—shortly after fifty-seven of the department's sixty-two sergeants signed a letter supporting the lieutenants.

As Markham worked at his assignment, attention began to focus on the two "outside" majors appointed in the wake of the vice squad scandal. Alvin Jackson and Jane Meagher were publicly identified as the "weak" command officers previously described by the *Examiner*. Westwood, on the other hand, appeared to enjoy a strong following among the mid-level managers and seemed to command greater respect among the department's rank-and-file than did Jackson, Meagher, or, for that matter, Jones himself.

Schmidt met with Jones and Westwood to discuss the situation on August 7. The next day, amid speculation that he had asked Jones to fire the two majors (but had been refused), Schmidt announced another departmental reorganization. Westwood (while still reporting to Jones) was to be given considerably expanded authority, with all departmental divisions reporting to him. Even more significantly, Jones and Westwood were now to be treated as a team, that is, they would "rise or fall together." Nothing was said about other possible changes in the department, including the fate of the two majors.

In the wake of these announcements, some observers speculated that Martin Plunkett, the state representative, possibly concerned that recent events had undermined Jones' position, had contacted key council members on Jones' behalf. Several days after the meeting of Schmidt, Jones, and Westwood, a group representing various civil rights and church groups announced its public support of Jones and warned of the dangers of "racial polarization" in the department.

The final crises

The brief respite given to the police department by the August 7 announcements ended when Meagher was involved in a minor traffic accident on August 17. Seemingly insignificant at first, the incident became front-page news several days later when it was discovered that she was driving on an out-of-state license at the time of the accident. State law requires that all residents, including police officers, obtain a valid license within a "reasonable period" (usually considered to be thirty days) after moving into the state, and Meagher had been in Valley City for eighteen months. Things became even more complicated when it was discovered that Meagher had obtained a valid in-state license the day after the accident and that the accident report had been altered to reflect her new license number. Ironically, Jackson also obtained his in-state driver's license following Meagher's accident.

These "revelations" provided front-page news stories for several days in the late summer and furnished further material for the majors' departmental critics. Deputy Chief Westwood was rather low-key, expressing understanding of the personal and professional pressures that might lead a person to forget a driver's license. Other less accommodating supervisors cited the cumulative effect of this affair added to other recent events and raised questions about the majors' basic competence. Most council members treated the flap as an administrative matter, with the exception of Frank Ackerman, who was quoted as saying that the police department was in "a crisis."

Although the uproar over Meagher's woes had waned by the end of August, her fate (as well as that of Jackson) was still very much in question. Finally, on Friday, September 19, the end appeared to have come. Early that afternoon, Jones asked each of the majors into his office, informed them that he had been instructed to fire them, and asked each of them to resign by 5 p.m. or be terminated. Each refused to resign, leaving the next move up to the chief. At the same time, a special, closed-door council meeting was scheduled for the following Monday.

It soon became apparent that the managerial script for a straightforward resolution of the police department's problems would not be played out as written. By late Friday afternoon Jackson and Meagher were meeting with the Christian Ministers' Association (CMA), a group of politically active black ministers, and with State Representative Martin Plunkett. Plunkett denounced the move to dismiss the two majors, saying, "It comes down to racism. The FOP is running the city manager, and that means that the FOP is running the city." A delegation left the meeting to meet with Jones and requested that he hold off any final action on the majors until Monday. Following this meeting (at about 6:30 p.m.), Jones announced that "discussions" regarding the majors' status were under way and that he would have a statement on Monday.

The CMA met again over the weekend to lay plans for a Monday morning rally at city hall in support of the majors. The rally was timed to coincide with the previously announced council meeting. A CMA spokesman indicated that the ministers feared that the move to dismiss Jackson and Meagher was an overt threat to Jones' status as chief. Reverend Henry Howard, a long-time community activist, related that he had met with Jones several months previously, at which time the chief had expressed satisfaction with the majors' performance. Howard reasoned that since Jones' appointees were on the block, the chief was very likely in jeopardy as well. In a separate statement, Plunkett conveyed his belief that the firing of the majors was indeed a threat to Jones.

As the city's official spokespersons, Mayor Hayes and Manager Schmidt maintained a discreet silence over the weekend. In contrast, council members George Costantino and Charles Davis issued statements on Sunday denying that the move to dismiss the majors was a racially motivated maneuver (against Jones) and reiterating the council's previous statements supporting the chief. These comments, made by a pair of council members usually considered to be among Jones' supporters, suggested that the chief still retained the core of his council backing.

When the city council met on Monday, it confronted a remarkable scene. An angry crowd of three hundred people filled the council chambers and spilled out into the hallways. Chanting, shouting, and singing "We Shall Overcome," the crowd made its displeasure known. Plunkett, acting as one of the crowd's spokespersons, attacked Costantino and Davis for denying that racism was the motive for forcing the majors' dismissal. He further charged that the FOP, Schmidt, and Council Member Ackerman were acting together in an effort to undermine Jones. Various other spokespersons lectured on the evils of racism and threatened to turn the coming November election into a referendum on the council's treatment of Jones. Faced with an uncontrollable and potentially explosive situation, the council members retreated into a closed-door session to discuss the situation with Jones.

The chief's statement to the council was a bombshell. Rather than announce that Jackson and Meagher had been dismissed, Jones stated that he had changed his mind—he was retaining them! Denying that he had been swayed by the demonstration, Jones insisted that he had made the move entirely on his own, having arrived at his final decision late Sunday night. In the days following the reversal, news reports suggested that an inconclusive confrontation between the chief and the city manager had taken place during Sunday's wee hours. Allegedly, the chief had argued that he could not in good conscience fire the majors, whom he had himself recruited (within specifications set by the previous mayor).

The announcement of this decision to the crowd produced mass confusion. Plunkett, the ministers, and the rest of the audience were delighted. Some council members, perhaps trying to put the best face on a bad situation, characterized the reversal as proof that indeed Jones, not the FOP or the council, was actually running the police department. Other council members bitterly charged that the day's events had made them "look like fools" and that the city's credibility had been damaged.

By the end of the week, it was all too clear that the more outraged council members had been correct. The situation deteriorated rapidly following Monday's tumultuous events. Schmidt issued his first public criticism of the chief on Wednesday, apologizing for the events and characterizing the chief's handling of the abortive firings as "unacceptable." To make the point even more firmly, the "linkage" between Jones and Westwood, which had been created in early August, was severed. The council, having borne the brunt of Monday's attack, began to reassess its previous support for the chief. The FOP cast a vote of "no confidence" in the chief on Thursday and called on Schmidt and the council to dismiss him. Although the department's mid-level managers (the sergeants and lieutenants) did not take a formal public stand, it was likely that the FOP's position reflected their own. The *Examiner* retreated from its generally favorable stance toward the chief in an editorial asserting that the time had come to recognize Jones' "deficiencies as a manager" and to dismiss him.

Sensing the seriousness of the situation, Jones' supporters were far from idle. Their strategy for protecting the chief soon became clear. Rather than allow any decision over the chief's future to be handled as a purely internal personnel decision, Plunkett and the other supporters were determined to transform the debate into a broader one over allegations of racism in Valley City law enforcement. Their tactics would include questioning the force's racial composition and personnel procedures and, most generally, the political role of blacks in Valley City. On another front, rumors surfaced that Jones would sue the city if he were dismissed.

Despite the tension inherent in the situation, no immediate solution seemed likely. Amid a spate of overwhelmingly bad press about the chief, a newspaper survey (conducted by independent pollsters) indicated widespread sympathy for Jones—among both blacks (where support was nearly unanimous) and whites. In addition, another city council election was to be held in November. In this one, Frank Ackerman, the incumbent Republican city council member most closely aligned with the FOP, faced a serious challenge from Odetta Devon, a black woman with close ties to Plunkett. (Some observers speculated that a Devon victory would pose a threat to Schmidt's tenure as city manager.) Both the council and Schmidt wanted to prevent the police controversy from becoming a factor in the November election.

The decision problem

By the end of September, Bob Schmidt was a man with a problem. Troubled by scandals and embarrassing publicity for years, his city's police department had become nearly unmanageable during the previous seven months. Whatever the legitimacy of the FOP's and mid-level managers' complaints, the chief had seriously hurt his own cause by flip-flopping on the decision to dismiss Jackson and Meagher and by allowing the council (and Schmidt) to endure the demonstration after having decided to reverse the firings. This incident seemed to destroy whatever support for Jones had remained in the department and led the council to reassess its position regarding the chief. It was hard to see how the department could be returned to good health under the current management.

The Valley City Charter gave the city manager the power to hire and fire the chief of police. Nonetheless, it was clear that the decision could not be made on exclusively managerial grounds. Plunkett and the CMA had successfully transformed the question into a very public, and very volatile, debate over race relations in the city. This occurred at an exceptionally delicate time in the city's history, since many persons felt that the appearance of serious racial divisions in the city would make it even more difficult for the city's political and business leadership to successfully implement their plans for dealing with the city's economic problems. Dismissing the chief along with the two majors could touch off a firestorm of racial protest that Schmidt was extremely reluctant to face.

With an election coming up, and without former mayor Marion's presence, the council seemed content to see Schmidt "out front" with the Jones situation. Lacking Marion's political savvy, without access to the former mayor's guidance, embroiled in an unfamiliar and uncomfortable public political debate, and with pressure mounting to do *something*, Schmidt faced his dilemma. Should he dismiss the chief, thereby satisfying the department's membership but possibly touching off a bitter community political power struggle? Or should he retain Jones, thus mollifying the black community but further outraging a rebellious police force and an increasingly disenchanted council?

In contemplating the situation, Schmidt knew well that his current options had been shaped by previous decisions he had made concerning Jones and the department. So it was only natural for him to second-guess his past actions in view of the decision-forcing events discussed earlier.

When Schmidt's thoughts returned to the situation at hand, he realized that the heightened level of controversy over Jones' about-face regarding the majors clearly required decisive action from the city manager. To allow the situation in the police department to continue without strong intervention of some sort would only invite further, possibly even more disruptive, actions by the FOP, by the department's mid-level managers, or by Plunkett and the CMA. Clearly something had to be done, but what, and when?

Discussion questions

1. Should Schmidt have taken a stronger role in resolving community conflict? If so, how?

2. What strategies could Schmidt have employed earlier to address the concerns of rank-and-file police without further alienating the black community?

3. What steps might Schmidt have taken to retain greater administrative control over departmental affairs in general—and the majors' fate in particular?

4. At this point Schmidt could fire the chief summarily; resign, himself; begin negotiating behind the scenes to induce the chief to resign voluntarily; or come up with another strategy. What should he do, and why?

5. How should Schmidt time his moves in relation to the election?

6. Should Schmidt involve other actors in solving this problem? If so, whom, and how?

The aftermath

By early October most parties inside the city government had decided that Jones had to go. The key question was how to arrange for his departure without further traumatizing the city.

The first order of business was to get past the November election. Apparently by mutual agreement among the various candidates for council, the police crisis was put on the back burner during the campaign. Immediately following the election (in which Ackerman was reelected), Schmidt and Hayes began to move. Hayes, in a departure from his usual low-key approach, took the lead in cooling racial tensions. His primary tool for doing so was a tried-and-true tool, the special commission. Shortly after the election, he established a committee of local notables to study various police issues and to recommend methods for reducing racial tensions in the city. Eventually, the city would pledge to improve minority recruitment for the police force and would encourage a "friendly" lawsuit—possibly to be brought by the CMA—to work around restrictive civil service hiring and promotion rules.

While Hayes was working to defuse public racial tensions, Schmidt worked quietly to arrange for Jones' departure. His primary problem was to find a formula that would allow Jones to leave without feeling that he had been publicly disgraced. The Valley City business community, which had begun to fear that increased racial tension posed a threat to the city's efforts to promote economic development, provided key assistance in this quest. Robert Carter, the local contractor who had been a key actor on the Special Committee, offered to donate a substantial sum of money to a severance package for the chief and to solicit additional donations from other business leaders. It was anticipated that this package, which grew to well over $150,000, would provide seed money for Jones' ambition to establish a law enforcement training institute for minorities at a local university. This private-sector contribution provided the formula that Schmidt was seeking to facilitate a nonconfrontational departure for Jones. His early-December resignation was quickly followed by Westwood's promotion to chief and Meagher's resignation.

Final discussion questions

1. Are there other strategies that could have been used to encourage Jones to resign? If so, what are they and how well might they have worked?

2. Were there any ethical questions that could be raised about the method that was used to secure Jones' resignation? What are they?

3. What kind of risk did Schmidt take when he postponed action until after the election? Would it have been appropriate for Schmidt to meet with the candidates prior to the election in an effort to keep the police crisis from becoming a campaign issue?

4. If the police crisis had been a major issue in the campaign, what options would have been open to Schmidt? What should he have done?

5. What can managers in similar circumstances do to defuse racism as an issue? What could have been done to have kept it from becoming an issue in this instance? What can a manager do when confronted by charges of racism in his or her administration?

5

Efficiency, effectiveness, and patronage

Joe P. Pisciotte

Editor's introduction

Few themes are more commonly articulated in local political campaigns than the need for economy and efficiency in government operations. Presumably, the public is committed to these values and expects both the structure and the processes of government to promote them.

As with other values, however, the public's concern for economy and efficiency must be reconciled with other, sometimes competing, priorities. As a result, what the public wants, and consequently what the public gets, is not always so clear and unambiguous.

This case shows the impact of competing values on one community's attempt to modernize its governmental structure so that its operations can be made more efficient, with immediate budgetary savings.

As the case unfolds and reaches a decision point, a classic contemporary political paradox emerges. Every citizen wants reductions in government expenditures; yet no citizen wants cuts that are likely to affect his or her political influence or material well-being. The case also highlights another reality of contemporary politics: The citizens who take an active role in a political issue are those with a personal stake in the outcome. Citizens who will benefit only from better and more efficient government seldom make their voices heard, with the result that political pressures, and ultimately political decisions, tend to be self-serving for those personally affected and involved.

In such an environment, the manager in this case is faced with a dual task—first to frame a set of recommendations to solve a budgetary crisis and then to determine how to sell them politically to the community. The political salesmanship is not made easier by the fact that the recommended changes are intended to promote efficiency by consolidating public functions under the council and manager, thereby increasing the administrative influence of the manager's office.

Finally, the case highlights questions of strategy. It poses directly to the manager the task of formulating a strategy that will result in the desired change. Of greater importance, it poses the question of whether the manager could have achieved better results by pursuing a more politically sophisticated strategy from the beginning. Is it really the responsibility of the manager to be so politically sophisticated? Is this what the public expects of its professional administrator?

Case 5
Efficiency, effectiveness, and patronage

Background

River City could be viewed as a textbook model of council-manager government. A historically conservative, midsized, midwestern community, River City has operated under the council-manager form of government for over seventy years. The community values highly the "reform" elements of its government, that is, a part-time, nonpartisan elected city council that appoints the city manager as chief administrative officer. The mayor is selected from among the city council members on a one-year rotating basis; the council rarely wanders from its broad policy-making functions, leaving daily operations to the manager. The manager hires and fires all employees under his jurisdiction on a merit basis.

There are no patronage employees in River City; appointments by city council members are limited to nonpaying positions on the city's many citizen boards and commissions. These appointments, however, have assumed the air of patronage. Although council members often have difficulty filling some of the less prestigious positions, council members frequently award highly desired positions to persons who helped them at election time.

The proliferation of boards and commissions reflects River City's efforts to be responsive to the citizens and their diverse needs. In the years preceding this case, the city made adjustments in housing, health and social services, and neighborhood integration. The city adopted policies on civil rights, affirmative action, economic opportunity, fair housing, employment, gay rights, and open meetings. A citizen-participation organization was created: River City was divided into sixteen districts from which citizens were popularly elected to serve the city council in an advisory capacity. Numerous additional citizen boards and commissions were created, for example, commissions on women, handicapped people, aging, crime and corrections, alcohol and drug abuse, and human resources.

River City government clearly has been capable of responding to the long-term, but often fluctuating, values and political interests that make up the community. At the time of this case, however, the city is faced with a new challenge—perhaps its greatest challenge of the twentieth century.

Fiscal problems

Changes in federal policy, particularly the loss of federal revenue sharing combined with federal policies designed to shift more responsibility for social service programs to local governments, had severely stressed River City's ability to sustain its social policy initiatives. "Cutback management," "doing more with less," and "fiscal stress" had become parts of the daily River City vocabulary.

The changes in federal policy could not have come at a worse time. River City was experiencing economic downturns exacerbated by significant shortfalls in tax-generated revenues. Favorable cash balances had kept the city from actually running a deficit, but a revenue-expenditure gap of some $16 million was forecast for the next three years if past trends continued and there were no major policy changes.

A controversial one-cent sales tax had been adopted by referendum, but only after bitter public debate involving the community's many business, labor, and neighborhood groups. However, the tax offered little immediate relief from the city's financial difficulties, because one-half of the proceeds were pledged to road and bridge improvements and the other half to property-tax relief. None were earmarked for deficits in operating funds.

The twin spectres of an increase in the city's property tax and severe cuts in programs loomed large; they led to open controversy between the city manager, Herb Upton, and council member Roy Tanner. Their disagreement over the causes of and solutions to the city's budget crisis became almost daily copy for the news media. Upton, a professional manager, had served the city for nine years; Tanner, an investment counselor, was a veteran council member in the middle of his second term who had well-recognized ambitions for higher office. Upton, who operated on the principle of deference to the elected body, resigned to accept a manager position in another community.

Thus, newly appointed city manager Mike Christian arrived in River City with a crisis confronting him. A career manager, Christian had systematically and successfully come up through the ranks of progressively larger cities. Like many other managers, he hoped to continue on this track. He had a reputation as a tough, no-nonsense budget and finance man; he was known for his penchant for detail when it came to city expenditures.

The city council was not necessarily seeking a change agent when it appointed Christian after a national search, but it was looking for someone with the skills needed to prepare the city for the tough financial times ahead. Nor was the new manager brought in as a hired gun expected to make a quick entrance and exit after implementing tough decisions. But from Christian's career perspective, River City was an important step up the career ladder. The need to succeed, by solving the city's financial problems, was high on his personal and professional agendas.

Political change

One opportunity for change came sooner than expected. River City voters approved a proposal to change the way citizens would be elected to the council. Departing from the tradition of at-large elections, the voters adopted a modified district plan: In the primary, two candidates would be nominated from each of five districts, and in the subsequent general election, one from each district would be elected by the city's voters on an at-large basis. The enabling ordinance for the new district system provided for four-year, staggered terms; under the provisions for the first election, all five council seats were to be filled at one time. The three candidates with the highest vote totals would receive four-year terms, while the remaining two successful candidates would win two-year terms.

Two members of the outgoing council, Tanner and Hiram Foley, were reelected to four-year terms after tough battles against other incumbent council members who had ended up in their respective districts when the boundaries were drawn. Foley, a prominent businessman, had completed one term on the council and had served previously on the school board.

The third four-year term was won by Duane Baker, a political newcomer elected from a blue-collar neighborhood that previously had had little direct representation on the council.

Elected to serve two-year terms were Rebecca Nichols and Susan Lancaster. Newcomers to elected office, both had previously been involved with River City government through participating in interest groups and serving on citizen boards and commissions. Each had run second in her district primary but had defeated the front runner in the at-large general election by a small margin.

Lancaster's district contained the city's largest black population, and she had defeated a black candidate in the general election. Nichols had been able to win only with last-minute support from the chamber of commerce.

Growing public support for another referendum on election procedures raised the possibility that in the next election, candidates would be elected by district in both the primary and the general elections. It was also expected that, for the first time, the mayor would be elected directly by the people rather than chosen by the council members. It was more than speculation that each of the five council members would like to be the first elected mayor.

The case

When the new council convened for its first meeting, it faced a unique opportunity to effect economies through organizational change. In anticipation of the new district plan, the terms of all board and commission appointments had been scheduled to expire during the forthcoming year. The new council had to appoint people to all of the several hundred positions that made up the city's board and commission system. The council members could use the opportunity either to build political support for future campaigns or to reduce the number of boards and commissions, which would result in substantial cost savings. (Board and commission operations cost nearly $500,000 plus hundreds of hours of staff time annually.)

City Manager Christian recommended to the new council that it undertake a study of board and commission operations with the aim of streamlining the system and gaining economies. The council members were enthusiastic about the study even though the timing was earlier than they had anticipated, given the number of other questions on the public agenda. The council voted unanimously to ask the public-affairs center at the local university to undertake the study and report the findings and recommendations back to the council for action.

Christian and the university negotiated an agreement that the study be broad in scope and emphasize the need for (1) full, positive public participation in the city's policy-making process; (2) the best use of city revenue and staff resources; and (3) organizational arrangements that would allow the boards and commissions to operate effectively and to be fully accountable to the city and its voters. The council agreed to place a moratorium on all appointments to boards and commissions pending the findings and recommendations of the report, scheduled to be completed in late summer.

The study

The study staff obtained comprehensive information from each board and commission and interviewed the mayor and individual council members, the city manager and his assistants, department heads, and board staffs. In addition, the study group obtained testimony from about thirty board members at a public hearing. Finally, the study obtained, for comparison, information about boards from fourteen other cities comparable in size to River City.

The study staff identified for examination thirty-five boards and commissions, to which the council was to appoint 270 members. The boards and commissions were classified into six categories.

1. The five *administrative boards* generated the most interest and debate during the study. They were the most prestigious boards, and each of them had the authority to appoint a director and staff, set salaries, purchase materials, let contracts, and establish policies and procedures to implement their programs. The administrative boards identified for study were the Art Museum Board, the Board of Park Commissioners, the Library Board, the Metropolitan Transit Authority, and the River City Airport Authority.
2. *Quasi-administrative boards* had authority over contracts, grants, policies, programs, and receipt and expenditure of public funds. They were the Metropolitan Planning Commission, the Board of Housing Commissioners, the Board of Health, the Alcohol and Drug Abuse Advisory Board, the Historic Preservation Board, and the Public Building Commission.
3. *Advisory boards* advised the council on programs, policies, litigation, and expenditure of funds within their specified policy areas. They were the Alarm Regulation Advisory Board, the Bicycle Committee, the Citizen Rights and Services Board, the Community Corrections Advisory Board, the Convention and Tourism Committee, the Economic Development Commission, the Historic Landmark Preservation Committee, the Human Resources Board, the Sister

Cities Advisory Board, the Commission on the Status of Handicapped People, the Commission on the Status of Women, and the Traffic Commission.

4. *Regulatory boards* had a regulatory, examining, and licensing function related mostly to the building trades. They were the Board of Electrical Examiners; the Board of Building Code Examiners and Appeals; the Board of Examiners of Air Conditioning, Refrigeration, Warm Air Heating, and Boilers; the Board of Examiners of Plumbers and Gas Fitters; the Board of Housing Standards and Appeals; the Pest Control Regulating and Examining Board; and the River City Athletic Commission.

5. *Quasi-judicial boards:* Only one board fell into this category—the Board of Zoning Appeals.

6. *Internal administrative boards* developed, administered, and implemented policies related to River City personnel and personnel benefits. They were the Group Life Insurance Board of Trustees, the Personnel Advisory Board, the Police and Fire Retirement Board of Trustees, and the River City Employees' Retirement Board of Trustees.

In River City, as in other communities, the extensive use of boards and commissions originated after citizen involvement had become a requirement of many federal grant programs. Citizen advisory groups flourished in River City, even during the Reagan presidency when the federal role in local government affairs diminished.

Study results

Despite the city's intensive use of citizen boards, the university study found little evidence that the boards and commissions affected decisions made by the council. The study raised the question whether citizen boards made any real policy difference or were merely political symbols. The study found that the trend in River City toward decentralized policy making with strong citizen involvement contrasted sharply with the city's reform type of government, which espoused the values of economy, efficiency, professionalism, and a centralized, responsive, and accountable organizational structure.

The study presented thirty-five recommendations of two basic types.

The first set of fifteen recommendations addressed general policies and operating procedures for all of the city's boards and commissions. The main focus of these recommendations was to correct demographic imbalances on the boards and commissions through improved recruitment, appointment, communication, and training procedures. White males from the business, real estate, banking, and investment communities made up the largest category of those serving on citizen boards. Women and blacks tended to be appointed to the less prestigious boards, for example, those addressing the status of women, handicapped people, and citizen rights. Over two-thirds of the appointees came from the two districts that made up the east and northwest sections of River City. One district elsewhere in the city had only 4 percent of the appointments, and another had only 6 percent. Although turnover was high on some of the less visible boards, the average tenure of a board member was long; thus, the number of citizens who could serve was limited.

The second set of twenty recommendations focused on duplication and accountability. These recommendations dealt with reorganization and elimination of individual boards and commissions. Numerous overlapping functions were identified among the boards and commissions and, in some instances, between a particular body and the city council. Two of these recommendations became the most controversial and generated the most pressure on the council to ignore the report and retain the status quo.

The first controversial recommendation, which became known as number 16, was that the Airport Authority, the Art Museum Board, the Library Board, and the Metropolitan Transit Authority remain as administrative boards but that the directors of these boards be appointed by, and responsible to, the city manager. The purpose of the recommendation was to make administrative operations more accountable to the city manager. The existing procedure was that the city council made appointments to the boards, and each board in turn appointed its administrative director, without input from the council or the city manager. The director served at the pleasure of the board and served as its chief operating officer, responsible for the board's budget, personnel matters, and policy recommendation and implementation. The council and the manager, ultimately responsible for all city policies, revenues, and expenditures, often found it difficult to exercise their responsibility because of the organizational arrangement with the administrative boards.

The other controversial recommendation, number 17, also tried to increase the accountability of administrative operations to the city manager. The recommendation was twofold: (1) that the city's parks and recreation function become a city department, with the director appointed by the city manager, and (2) that the Board of Park Commissioners be re-created as an advisory rather than an administrative board.

The study also recommended the following actions:

Consolidate the Historic Preservation Board and the Historic Landmark Preservation Committee.

Expand the Alarm Regulation Advisory Board into a city-county board with a one-year sunset provision.

Eliminate the Bicycle Committee and place bicycling and bicycling safety under the director of parks and recreation.

Merge the Commission on the Status of Handicapped People and the Commission on the Status of Women with the Citizen Rights and Services Board, develop a mission for the new structure, and allocate resources to support its combined purposes.

Eliminate the Traffic Commission and assign its duties to the department of public works.

Reorganize into a less complex arrangement the six separate boards involved in licensing or regulating eighteen activities related to housing and building codes.

Eliminate the River City Athletic Commission and transfer its duties and responsibilities to the director of community facilities.

Eliminate the Personnel Advisory Board and replace it with a procedure for appointing an ad hoc citizens committee to review employee grievances as the need arises.

Merge the city's two employee retirement boards to reduce the cost of money management, increase the return on investments, and correspondingly reduce the city's retirement liability. Retain the two existing retirement funds as separate funds to be administered by the consolidated board.

Public reaction

The dialogue following the study's release was far more spirited—and antagonistic—than the council members had anticipated when they commissioned it. The first set of fifteen recommendations was received relatively calmly by the public and by affected groups, but all of the second set of recommendations met opposition from interest groups in the community or from segments of the city hall bureaucracy.

The report immediately became the most visible and controversial topic on the local public agenda. The major daily newspaper lauded the report and editorially endorsed the recommendations as well reasoned, well documented, and worthy of implementation. But there was little, if any, support from members of the boards and commissions or their constituent groups. In fact, the collective outcry of these groups far exceeded what even the closest political observers would have expected. Together, they constituted a formidable lobby group.

The first indication of opposition came before the report had been completed, when speculation about the recommendations on the administrative and retirement boards began to float through city hall and around the community. An informal, friendly, but organized telephone campaign was launched to convince the authors of the report that "if it ain't broke, don't fix it." Police and fire employees let it be known that they would oppose any recommendation consolidating their retirement system with that of the other city employees. A group known as Friends of the Library began their own effort to ensure that the library director would not become answerable to the city manager. One caller argued that supporters and library benefactors would no longer give to the libraries if the libraries became part of city government. Another, echoing the calls of many, pleaded that the authors "safeguard the intellectual freedom of the libraries, which might be threatened if libraries were subjected to the politics of the city manager and the city council."

After the report had been submitted, letters to the editor began to appear and phone calls—sometimes threatening withdrawal of reelection campaign support—were made to city hall and to council members' homes. Council members' calendars were filled with names of those wanting to plead their cases.

No council member wanted to reject the report in its entirety; and most numbers were supportive, at least in principle, of the need to "reorganize to economize." However, every member was opposed to one or more of the recommendations that affected his or her particular interest. The campaign against the recommendations reached its peak on August 25, when the council held a public hearing on the report.

The decision problem

The council chamber was packed with people waiting to testify in support of the status quo or otherwise to oppose the report; few, if any, were there to endorse the report. Included among the opposition speakers were two former mayors, one former city manager, and dozens of board and commission members. Most visible were the directors of the Art Museum Board and the Board of Park Commissioners. Both were openly leading and orchestrating the opposition to recommendations 16 and 17. Arnold Benjamin, the Art Museum Board director, threatened to resign if his position were placed under the manager's control. In open defiance of the council and the manager, he led the cheers each time a speaker criticized the report or expressed dissatisfaction with the council if it were to adopt recommendation 16.

Dozens of citizens paraded to the microphone, each underscoring how the interests of the board or commission he or she supported would be threatened by the recommendations; all implied that they were speaking for a broad segment of the community. Lost throughout the testimony was the driving force behind the study—savings of critical tax dollars through organizational change. Typical were the comments of these citizens:

Humphrey Bonner, member of the Art Museum Board: "The museum will lose its attributes and assets if the position of director is placed under the manager's control."

Richard Green, president of the River City Golf Association: "The growth of the golf courses is due to the autonomous nature of the Board of Park Commissioners."

Former mayor Ralph Wheeler: "The city manager should have a voice in the hiring of the park board director, but not the sole hiring and firing capability."

Former city manager Walter Woolf: "Cities with park boards have better parks than cities whose parks are under the city manager's jurisdiction."

Francis Carson, president of the River City Open Space Committee: "If the park board is eliminated, it will leave our committee dangling and unable to raise money for the botanical gardens and other civic needs."

Ronald Meeker, Metropolitan Transit Authority member: "Retain the transit authority, but appoint people with dedication and expertise."

Jane Lawrence, member of the Commission on the Status of Women: "Merger with other boards will dilute the strength of women's input in city government. We need continued commitment and more resources from the council."

The comments, sometimes respectful but often not, continued from representatives of most of the boards and commissions. All sounded the same theme: "Don't change our status; leave us alone to continue to operate as we have been operating."

In the aftermath of the public hearing, the city council members, particularly the newly elected members, were stunned by the force of the combined opposition to their attempt at effecting organizational change and cost savings. They pondered the position they were in; they wondered about the political perils of implementing any of the changes recommended in the report. They could not adjourn into executive session because of open meetings requirements. Nor would the open meetings law allow them to seek each other's counsel, one on one, regarding the complexities of the tough decision they were facing. The dilemma was clear: Reorganization was needed to trim costs in the operating budget and to streamline accountability, but adoption of the report would carry with it the threat of political opposition within the community.

The council side-stepped the decision, at least for a short cooling-off period. Immediately following the August 25 hearing, the council voted unanimously to direct the city manager to prepare a staff report on implementation of the study's recommendations, including which, if any, of the recommendations should be adopted. The manager's report was due in two weeks and was to be put on the agenda for discussion and final vote at the September 8 council meeting.

The council then adjourned its August 25 meeting. City Manager Christian laboriously gathered his papers and headed for the privacy and temporary comfort of his office, pondering the difficulty of his situation. He was having second thoughts about his endorsement of what had appeared initially to be a straightforward attempt at reorganizing city functions, an activity that usually received little or no public attention. His conclusion, as he arrived at his desk, was that "everyone likes progress, but no one likes change." How would he prepare a report that would balance the city's administrative needs against the council's political concerns?

Discussion questions

1. What political considerations will affect the council's decision? What degree of importance should be attached to each?

2. Is there a strategy that would build political support for a council decision to adopt all or most of the recommendations in the report? If so, what is it? Evaluate it.

3. Is there a "minimax strategy"—one that would maximize cost savings and minimize political opposition? If so, what is it? What are its advantages and disadvantages?

4. What alternatives should Christian consider as he decides on his course of action?

5. What should Christian recommend to the council?

6. Since the prerogatives of the manager's office are involved, and since the city's fiscal health is affected, Christian might use the prestige of his office to promote his recommendation publicly. Should he do so? Summarize the arguments for and against his becoming publicly involved.

7. What, if anything, can Christian do to "sell" his proposal to the individual members of the council? To the council as a whole? What should he do?

The aftermath

Fortunately for Christian, he was given a reprieve from his dilemma. The opposition to the report gained momentum during the week after the public hearing. To head off further opposition and to defuse the issue, the council decided, in its September 1 meeting, to vote on the report without waiting for the manager's recommendation. Council discussion for the most part applauded the merits of citizen participation in River City government. After very little debate, the council, by a 4-to-1 vote, yielded to the combined opposition on the tough reorganization recommendations. Only council member Baker voted in favor of the recommendations, including numbers 16 and 17. The council adopted the noncontroversial recommendations dealing with board and commission appointments, recruitment, and training but left the administrative and retirement boards unchanged and outside the control of the city manager. Only the Bicycle Committee, which the council had never formally created, was eliminated. The vote was clearly for the status quo.

In private conversations with the manager in the weeks that followed, the council members who had voted against the report said the vote was one of their biggest mistakes. Too late, they realized the long-term negative impact that their vote would have on attempts to bring about needed change in the city's organizational structure.

Final discussion questions

1. What are the manager's role and responsibility in dealing with matters affecting the political structure of the city? Does the ICMA Code of Ethics (see Appendix) provide any guidance?

2. When citizen campaigns to promote other kinds of change are in process, what role should the manager play? Specifically, how and to what extent should he or she provide leadership or give advice to such campaigns? How and to what extent should the manager advise members of the council, individually or as a group, during such

campaigns? Would the answer to any of the above be different if the initiative for the change came from a resolution passed by the council, such as a call for a referendum on a tax increase?

3. In retrospect, how did the political climate, reflected in the change to district primaries, affect the environment for promoting organizational change? What factors made it a good time for such changes? What factors made it a poor time?

4. How might Christian have managed the introduction of the proposed changes differently? What else, if anything, should he have done? What should he learn from this experience?

5. After the August 25 meeting, with pressures on the council still mounting, what, if anything, could or should the manager have done to protect the proposed changes?

6. Were the changes that were designed to increase the manager's authority over the city's administrative structure of sufficient importance to justify a major effort by the manager? Why or why not?

7. In the aftermath of this defeat, what strategy should Christian pursue to reestablish his standing with the council? With the community? With the agency directors he sought to bring under his jurisdiction?

8. Given the regrets of the council members over the way they voted, should Christian devise a strategy that might accomplish some of the defeated changes? If not, why not? If so, which changes? What should the strategy be? Would your answer be different if the council members did not have such regrets? Explain.

Politics, user fees, and Barracudas

John Doe

Editor's introduction

Politics is not a problem only for local administrators. It is equally a problem, and equally frustrating, for citizens. This case looks at local politics from the perspective of a citizen who, in his capacity as an officer of a local swim team, attempts to negotiate a fee agreement with the city that will enable the team to use a city swimming pool for its practice sessions.

The city's park and recreation administrators proceed to propose a fee structure, seeking to negotiate an agreement that will provide adequate city revenues and be fair to other groups that contract to use the city's pool. The swim team, on the other hand, clearly wants to keep its costs down and believes the city's proposed fee is too high.

The request quickly becomes political. If the swim team were negotiating with a privately owned swimming pool, it would be just another potential pool customer. In this case, however, the team members and leaders are also citizens and voters who can, and do, seek to gain their ends by appealing to the city council. Political pressure is added to economic pressure, and the problem only becomes more difficult and more intense for the administrator.

Adding to the complexity in this case are differences in perspective between the city manager's staff and the park and recreation department staff. Each seeks different goals; each has its own public interests to protect. At its climax, the case revolves around differences of opinion among the swim team, the manager's staff, and the park and recreation staff while the city council is demanding that the issue be resolved, and resolved immediately.

Still another dimension that complicates decision making is the way in which the conflict escalates as the case proceeds. What starts as a disagreement over fees becomes a disagreement over administrative methods as well. What starts as a problem in parks and recreation becomes a problem for the manager and, ultimately, for the city council.

Finally, the case provides an instructive look at government administration from the perspective of the citizen. The reasons for administrative actions are not always apparent to citizens, and in this case failure to communicate fully and adequately becomes an administrative mistake that only exacerbates the administrator's political problems.

Case 6
Politics, user fees, and Barracudas

Background

The Uptown Skating and Aquatic Center (USAC) in Western City was to be the first indoor ice rink in that part of the state. Both the Olympic-sized pool and the rink were to be the premier facilities of their types in the region. City voters had approved a quarter-cent sales tax to finance it; construction had run ahead of schedule; and the final preparations were being made for the grand opening a few months hence.

Administrators in the Western City Department of Recreation were simultaneously proud of and nervous about USAC. On the one hand, it would add luster to the department's award-winning facilities and programs. On the other hand, the Western City Council had become increasingly concerned about the department's operating budget; recreation administrators were anticipating considerable pressure from the council and from certain sectors of the community regarding recovery of USAC operating costs. However, operating costs and revenues were impossible to project with confidence; technological and design innovations had been incorporated into USAC, and no data were available from comparable facilities, because there were no comparable facilities. Moreover, user demand—particularly for the ice arena—also was an unknown.

Chuck Morgan, the newly hired manager of USAC, felt the pressure more intensely than anyone. Although young, Morgan had several years' experience as manager of a public ice arena in another state. That experience was invaluable, because no other administrator in the department of recreation had any first-hand knowledge of ice rink operations. Morgan's relative inexperience in pool management was not considered critical when he was hired, because the department had several experienced pool managers on its staff. Moreover, Morgan had hired an assistant manager whose background had been primarily in pool programming and management.

During his relatively brief time in Western City, Morgan had tried to identify the community groups that were likely to become regular users of USAC. Anticipating a February 1 opening for the new facility, Morgan spent a good deal of time during the preceding summer getting acquainted with the leaders of these organizations and with their plans and preferences for using USAC.

Morgan had met on several occasions with David Arnott and Grant Winger, president and vice-president, respectively, of the Western City Barracuda Swim Team, the only year-round competitive swim team for youngsters in Western City. The team relied almost exclusively on public pool facilities for its practice sessions and home meets. Although it was a private association, its membership was not exclusive, and it had developed a good working relationship with the existing aquatics staff in the department of recreation. As is typical of such volunteer youth organizations, the leadership was composed of a relatively small number of enthusiastic parents—in this case that number was especially small, because in recent years a series of problems had reduced the swim team's membership to approximately forty swimmers.

In their meetings with Morgan, Arnott and Winger repeatedly stressed their hope that the team would increase significantly in size in the near future. They emphasized that the availability of pool time at reasonable hours and at reasonable cost would be an important factor affecting their plans for growth. All three understood that a thriving swim team would help alleviate some of the performance pressures felt by Morgan. Morgan was careful in these conversations not to commit himself prematurely to any time or cost figures; however, he did let the team leaders know that he was sympathetic to their goals. On at least one occasion he indicated that charges at USAC would have to be somewhat higher than the $2.50 per lane-hour that the Barracudas had been paying to swim in the existing city pool. Arnott and Winger understood him to imply, however, that lane fees at USAC were unlikely to exceed $3.00 per hour.

As the summer waned, so did the interaction between Morgan and the Barracudas. Morgan's time was devoted increasingly to supervising the final details of constructing, equipping, and staffing USAC and of putting together the first year's operating budget, which the council was scheduled to adopt in October.

He did endeavor to keep Arnott informed of budgetary items of interest to the Barracudas, including the fact that lane charges were likely to exceed $3.00 per hour. Arnott did not share that information with Winger or the other members of the Barracuda Board.

The case

On October 9 the Barracuda Board was told of the USAC fee schedule. Invited by Arnott to attend the October meeting of the Barracuda Board, Morgan and his newly hired assistant manager, Jack Scott, announced that hourly lane charges were to increase 60 percent, from $2.50 to $4.00. Furthermore, the new fees were to be uniform at the existing Western City pool and USAC, so there would be no less-expensive alternative. Prepared to hear a worst-case charge of $3.00 per lane-hour, the board members expressed shock and outrage at the $4.00 figure. To make matters worse, Arnott's failure to inform the board earlier of the fee hike had permitted the figure to go unchallenged during critical stages of the city's budget process. Only two days before, the Western City Council had approved the $4.00 fee along with all other recreation department fees and charges.

Scott tried to calm the board members by offering to help them develop fund-raising ventures so that the club could pay the new fees without raising its membership dues excessively. The Barracuda Board showed no interest in Scott's offer. They feared that a fee increase would have a chilling effect on the growth of the club at precisely the time when other aspects of their membership drive were falling into place.

During the first week in November the Barracudas held their annual membership meeting and election of officers. Arnott had arranged with Morgan for the members to have an advance tour of the USAC complex and for Morgan and Scott to address the full group of Barracuda parents. Morgan and Scott hoped to gain acceptance of the fee increase by appealing directly to the membership.

Morgan and Scott explained the rate increase by citing projected operating costs of USAC and the need for users of city facilities to pay a higher percentage of operating costs. Scott also repeated the suggestion he had made earlier to the board that the club become more assertive in outside fund-raising activities. He also presented some figures showing that the new fees were in line with those paid by other swim clubs in the state and that the Barracudas had been subsidized by the city in the past and had an artificially low dues structure as a result. Despite this hard line, Morgan and Scott could tell from the questions and comments from the audience that they had not succeeded in winning acceptance for the new fees.

New leadership

Following the pool fee discussion, Winger was elected president of the Barracuda organization. During the month since he had first learned of the new fees, Winger had become convinced that in the short run, the only way the club could afford to pay the new rates would be to raise membership dues to levels that would discourage growth and confine membership to the relatively affluent. Such a prospect was unacceptable. He privately vowed that fighting the fee increase would be his top priority as president.

One of Winger's first acts after taking office was to schedule an appearance at the December meeting of the Western City Recreation Advisory Board (Rec Board), a panel of citizens appointed by the city council to review recreation department plans, programs, and policies and recommend appropriate action to the council. The purpose of Winger's appearance was to request a recommendation from the Rec Board to lower the proposed pool fees for the Barracudas.

Prior to the Rec Board meeting, Winger had the first of numerous sessions with Morgan to discuss fees, scheduling, and other aspects of Barracuda–Western City relations. At their initial meeting, Winger had two objectives. He wanted to make Morgan aware of the magnitude of the adverse effects that he believed the new fees would have on the swim club. Second, he wanted to explore alternative fee structures so that he could develop a sense of how flexible the recreation department might be.

Morgan and Scott (who sat in on this meeting) were willing to consider any formal alternative fee proposal that the Barracudas might offer. For their part, Morgan and Scott were under pressure to see that users of the new USAC facility paid a reasonable proportion of the costs of its services. They couldn't understand why the Barracudas had rejected their offer to help the club organize additional fund-raising efforts, since the youth hockey club, which they were helping to organize, had been successful in soliciting business sponsorship. Winger, however, was disappointed. He concluded that neither Morgan nor Scott understood the operations or financing of competitive swim teams and that they were less interested in providing youth sports programs than in generating revenue at USAC.

On the evening of December 10, Winger arrived at the Rec Board meeting accompanied by the Barracuda coach and one other member of the Barracuda Board of Directors. One of the nine Rec Board members was absent, but Winger noted that Elizabeth Conant, with whom he had a passing acquaintance, was present. He knew Elizabeth to be an open-minded person who would listen to the argument he had prepared and judge it on its merits. He did not know the other members but noted that several, including the board chairman, appeared to be highly deferential to Jake Willoughby, the long-time director of the Western City Department of Recreation.

When the time came to take up the Barracudas' request, Willoughby took control of the meeting. He introduced the Barracuda representatives and briefly outlined the issue, emphasizing the pressure on the department to generate revenue. He then called on Morgan to address the Barracudas' pool fees directly.

Morgan began his presentation by distributing a data sheet that compared projected USAC operating costs with projected revenues from the Barracudas and the youth hockey club. The figures indicated that, even with the fee increase, the swim team was being asked to pay a smaller percentage of its costs than was the hockey league. He pointed out that the pool fees paid by the Barracudas at the old pool had not increased in over two years and were artificially low as a result. It actually cost the city $5.20 to provide one lane to the team for one hour. Morgan concluded by noting that Barracuda membership fees were "the least expensive in our area" and that the club could and should do more outside fund-raising if it found itself in financial difficulty.

Throughout Morgan's presentation, Winger found himself growing increasingly angry at what he perceived to be factual distortions and unverified assertions. He felt that Willoughby and Morgan had prejudiced his case before he even had a chance to state it.

When Winger's turn came to speak, he began by pointing out the various ways in which the Barracudas contributed to the quality of life in the community and suggested that the club's social and economic contributions would be considerably greater if its plans for growth could be realized. He then described the negative impact the new fees would have if they were implemented in February as planned. He requested that the increase be delayed for six months to permit the club to grow to a size at which it could more easily absorb the additional costs. Winger concluded by questioning Morgan's claim that the club's membership dues and pool charges were low in comparison to those of other swim teams in the area. However, there was no way he could counter the comparison, because until that evening, he had never seen any of the figures that Morgan had cited.

From the questions and discussion that ensued, it was clear that the Rec Board was divided. Finally, Elizabeth Conant offered a compromise motion: that the Barracuda pool fees be set at $3.25 per lane-hour throughout the first year in the new facility, exactly halfway between the continuation of the current $2.50 charge requested by Winger and the staff's figure of $4.00. Although the compromise provided for a higher pool fee than Winger had requested, it had the advantage of extending the duration of the fee reduction to one full year. Winger and the other Barracuda representatives indicated that the compromise motion was acceptable to them.

An animated discussion followed, during which Willoughby and Morgan vigorously opposed the compromise. When the dust settled and the vote was taken, the compromise failed to carry by a vote of 4-4.

The search for alternatives

Winger and his colleagues were disappointed at the loss, but they took some comfort in the fact that the Barracudas had received enough support to permit them credibly to continue the fight. As Winger was preparing to leave the room, Willoughby approached him and congratulated him on his near success. He added that his opposition to the fee reduction did not reflect his personal preference but rather the cost recovery requirements imposed on the department by the city council. He also expressed the hope that the swim team and the recreation department would maintain the cooperative relationship they had developed over the past several years. Winger took this as a sign that Willoughby realized that he had only narrowly escaped defeat and that he would like to avoid further conflict with the swim team.

The Barracuda Board met the following evening. They concluded that their position was stronger than it had been before the Rec Board meeting. They clearly would have preferred a positive vote on Elizabeth Conant's motion, but even then the issue would not have been settled. They would still have had to carry the battle to the city council, where they could expect strong staff opposition. A Rec Board recommendation would have helped, but a tie vote was almost as good as a narrow victory.

Over the weekend, Barracuda Board members systematically contacted a number of swim teams in the state, including all of those that Scott had cited as having significantly higher dues and higher pool fees than the Barracudas. They gathered enough data to demonstrate that neither claim was warranted once adjustments were made for the greater amount of pool time the other clubs were utilizing. Armed with this information, Winger wrote a memo to Morgan in which he challenged the accuracy of Scott's research and the comparative cost data that Morgan had distributed at the Rec Board meeting. Winger's plan was to establish a written record that showed the Barracudas to be a responsible community organization that did its homework with care. He hoped to show by contrast that the data analyses produced by the rec department staff were haphazard and superficial. Such a record, he reasoned, would be valuable when the time came to appeal to city council for relief.

On Monday, before he had received Winger's memo, Morgan phoned Winger to tell him that Willoughby had been impressed with the support the Barracudas had received at the Rec Board meeting and that Willoughby was prepared to listen to any reasonable proposal the club might offer for an alternative fee structure. They agreed to meet on Thursday, December 18, to discuss the matter further.

The Barracuda Board met again on December 17 and discussed several alternative approaches for developing a pool fee proposal. They decided to propose that the Barracudas be charged on the basis of swimmer admissions rather than lane-hour rental. This approach had the virtue of placing the Barracuda youngsters on the same footing as other pool users so that their charges could be compared directly. No other community users of the city's pool facilities paid lane-hour charges; therefore, meaningful comparisons were difficult. The board authorized Winger to submit such a proposal if, after working out the details, it appeared to offer reasonable relief for the team.

Winger and Morgan met on December 18 as planned. Morgan had received Winger's earlier memo and responded orally to some of its inquiries. Winger had difficulty understanding the method by which Morgan calculated the costs attributed to the Barracudas, but he did not press the matter. He wanted to move on to discuss the admission-charge approach to pool fees. In the absence of a formal proposal, Morgan was unable to make any commitments, but he did not try to dissuade Winger from using swimmer admissions as the base of his proposal.

On January 2 Winger mailed a formal fee proposal to Morgan. It called for the club to pay on behalf of its swimmers the same pool admission per practice session that other youngsters paid for a recreational swimming session if they purchased a multiple-admission pass. Under reasonable expectations regarding membership growth and frequency of practices, Winger reasoned that the proposal would generate a considerable increase in revenues to the city while permitting the Barracudas to maintain a reasonable schedule of membership dues. Two additional financial sweeteners were built into the proposal: (1) a demonstration that the city would receive more than $4.00 per lane-hour whenever the team practiced in the full fifty-meter lanes at USAC, and (2) an offer to pay more than $4.00 per lane-hour to hold swim meets with other teams. The rental figure in such cases was to increase as the team's membership grew.

In January the Barracuda Board announced an increase in membership dues, to be effective February 1. The board reasoned that an increase would be necessary in any event and that the club did not have the luxury, financially, of waiting until the fee issue was settled. The increase was predicated on the optimistic assumption that the club's proposal or something similar would be accepted and, though more than some members wished, was less than would be required if the club ended up having to pay $4.00 per lane-hour.

When Morgan received Winger's proposal and calculated its probable impact on recreation department revenues, he knew that it would not be acceptable. On January 29 he met with Winger in his office. Barbara Matlock, one of Willoughby's chief assistants, was there to represent the department's administrative staff. Winger was told that the proposal had been rejected. Matlock added, however, that Willoughby was prepared to lower the Barracuda charges to $3.50 per lane-hour for the first year but that the fees would revert to $4.00 thereafter. Winger told them that he would relay Willoughby's response to his board at a meeting the following week and give Morgan a reply shortly thereafter.

The Barracuda Board received the news with indignation. Several of the members were in favor of taking their case immediately to the city council. Winger counseled against this course, because Willoughby would have the advantage in such a confrontation—particularly now that he was on record as having offered a reduction. To reject it out of hand and to go before the council prematurely would be to court disaster. Winger felt that when Willoughby had gone before the Rec Board, he had subtly portrayed the Barracuda parents as an ill-informed special-interest group seeking to indulge their children at public expense. He did not want the same scene replayed before the council. He had come to believe that a strong case could be made for the Barracudas but that time and considerable work were needed to do so. So long as Morgan's claim that it cost the city $5.20 to provide one lane of water to the team for one hour remained unchallenged, it was doubtful that the council could be persuaded that a lane charge of $3.50 was unfair. But to offer a credible challenge to Morgan's cost projections, the club would need more information. Winger succeeded in convincing the board to exercise patience.

Winger drafted a response and posted it to Morgan on February 8. He challenged the fairness of the $3.50 lane-hour charge and again questioned, for the record, the validity of Morgan's cost projections. However, he declared that the Barracudas would accept lane charges of $3.50 through May while monitoring the actual operating costs and revenues at USAC, and he indicated that a new pool fee proposal would be forthcoming from the swim club once actual cost data became available.

An accounting problem

During the next three months, Winger met periodically with Morgan, who shared USAC financial data with him. Morgan explained the cost-accounting system that he was using, which was based on the concept of a program-hour. Since the bulk of USAC operating costs could not be traced directly to specific programs, all the operating costs were apportioned to the various users in proportion to their shares of the total program-hours generated by all user programs. To arrive at a lane-hour cost for the swim team, Morgan simply divided one program-hour by ten, the number of lanes in the pool.

When Winger first encountered the program-hour concept, he understood it to mean the equivalent of one hour during which time the Barracudas rented the entire USAC pool—ten fifty-meter lanes. Thus, two clock-hours during which only five lanes were rented would amount to one program-hour, or so he thought. As Winger began to understand the concept and the role it played in Morgan's accounting, however, his suspicion increased that it was the cause of what he still believed was the attribution of excessively high costs to the Barracudas' pool use. At first his misgivings focused on the possibility that ice rink costs were being shifted to pool users. To document such an effect, however, would require that separate accounts be kept for each area. Since utilities, maintenance, and other accounts were not broken down by functional area, it was impossible for him to confirm this suspicion.

In the course of exploring this issue with Morgan, Winger unearthed two additional problems deriving from the program-hour concept. The first problem was that the overhead costs associated with several user locations in USAC were included in the aggregate cost figures, but no recreational programs conducted in those areas were assigned a share of those costs. Thus, the overhead costs were hidden in the operating costs charged to pool and rink users. The second problem stemmed from the fact that the USAC pool, which by this time was in use, had movable bulkheads so that it could be configured alternatively as a single pool having ten fifty-meter lanes or as three separate pools—a deep pool for diving at one end, a shallow pool at the opposite end, and a middle section containing ten twenty-five-yard lanes. The Barracudas most often practiced in the latter configuration, renting from three to seven of the twenty-five-yard lanes at a time.

Winger was troubled by the suspicion that Morgan's accounting system attributed costs to the Barracudas as if they were renting fifty-meter lanes even when they were swimming in the twenty-five-yard configuration. When he raised this concern, Morgan assured him that the accounting system was fair and that it conformed to accepted public cost-accounting principles. Nevertheless, Winger remained skeptical.

By June the Barracuda membership had grown fourfold to over 150 swimmers. Consequently, the club had become a heavier user of the city's aquatic facilities than anyone had predicted. Moreover, all types of user demand and revenues at USAC had exceeded even the most optimistic projections. Therefore, the Barracuda Board decided that the time had come to reopen fee negotiations.

Winger sent a second formal fee proposal to Morgan on June 14. He also proposed an alternative method of calculating the actual costs of providing practice lanes for the swim team. In contrast to the program-hour concept, Winger's method took account of the length of the lanes in which the Barracudas swam. His figures also differed from Morgan's earlier projected costs in that they were based on the actual costs of operating USAC during its first three months of operation. The new figures corresponded very closely to Morgan's projected costs as long as the team swam in fifty-meter lanes, but they were only about half that amount when twenty-five-yard lanes were used. According to Winger's calculations, the flat $3.50 lane-hour charge the Barracudas had been paying represented 67 percent cost recovery for long lanes and 134 percent cost recovery for short lanes. Both cost recovery percentages were higher than what he knew other youth sports groups paid for the use of public facilities. Nevertheless, he proposed a new fee structure that would yield approximately 90 percent cost recovery to the city on the basis of his cost calculations. The proposal called for rates of $4.75 per hour for fifty-meter lanes and $2.50 per hour for twenty-five-yard lanes.

Over a month passed before the city responded. On July 31 Morgan wrote to Winger and again rejected his proposal. Morgan explained that the city was placing a "greater emphasis on recovering a higher percentage of operating expenses" and noted that the proposed fees would reduce revenues "above and beyond the reduction in revenue the city is already absorbing from the adjustments of $4.00 per lane-hour to $3.50 per lane-hour." He affirmed the staff's intention to revert to the $4.00 figure in the second year.

Winger and the Barracuda Board were incensed. They had taken Willoughby's invitation to submit a proposal at face value and had submitted not one but two proposals. Each had been well reasoned, temperate, and offered in good faith. Now, each had been summarily rejected, leaving no apparent room for further discussion. They now questioned whether the original invitation had been genuine or merely a tactic by Willoughby and Morgan to buy time. They believed that the swim team was being victimized and agreed that the time had come to shift the battle to a more political arena. They decided that the best strategy would be to emphasize the flaws in the program-hour cost-accounting system and to frame their position as a request for a fair cost recovery rate applied to accurately determined costs.

Politics and the budget

The timing coincided with the city budget process, as the recreation department was to submit its proposed budget for the next fiscal year to the Recreation Advisory Board in August. The board, in turn, was to send its recommendation to the city council in September, and the council was to adopt the budget in October. Winger requested and was granted a slot on the Rec Board's agenda for its August meeting. Prior to the meeting he sent a letter to all members of the advisory board in which he reiterated his analysis of USAC operating costs, challenged the program-hour concept, and questioned the appropriateness of the cost recovery percentage that the Barracudas were being asked to pay. He also pointed out other aspects of administrative policy that the Barracudas believed were unfair. He requested that the board recommend lane fees of $2.50 and $4.75, the same figures that he had requested in the second proposal to Morgan and Willoughby.

Winger sent a copy of the letter to Blaine Perry, a member of the city council who he believed would be sympathetic to the Barracuda cause, and he enlisted several other Barracuda parents to lobby their council contacts on behalf of the Barracuda position.

The Recreation Advisory Board met on August 26. At the beginning of the meeting, Winger was given a copy of a three-page memo dated August 24 from Morgan to the board, which addressed several points made in Winger's letter. Winger read it hastily, and his first impression was that it contained incomplete information and appeared to discredit the Barracudas. The concluding paragraph contained an additional surprise. The department was requesting lane fees of $4.00 for twenty-five-yard lanes and $6.50 for fifty-meter lanes for the coming year. The principal justification offered for the increase was that the department needed additional revenue. After lengthy and at times heated discussion, the board deferred a decision until its September meeting and asked that the administration prepare an analysis of the implications of Winger's proposed cost-accounting methodology.

Morgan caught up with Winger after the meeting and apologized for the lack of warning about the proposed increase in fifty-meter lane fees. Morgan was embarrassed by the move and explained that it was a last-minute decision by his administrative superiors.

During the following week, Winger obtained additional USAC operating cost data from Morgan, covering the first six months of USAC operations. These data indicated somewhat higher operating costs than had the earlier figures. Winger revised his cost calculations, which now showed that it cost the city approximately $3.05 to provide one twenty-five-yard lane to the Barracudas for one hour and approximately $6.65 for a fifty-meter lane. Even so, he believed that the Barracudas' requested lane fees were reasonable, for they represented cost recovery rates of 82 percent and 71 percent, respectively. Both figures were above the 70 percent rate that was ostensibly the overall cost recovery goal of the recreation department.

On September 10 several Barracuda parents attended an informal community meeting conducted by the city council to hear citizen comments regarding the budget. They requested that the council issue clear and unambiguous guidelines to the recreation department regarding appropriate cost recovery rates. They were careful to avoid suggesting any particular percentage or to appear as special pleaders for the swim team. Instead, they tried to convey the idea that Willoughby's department was confused regarding the council's cost recovery expectations and, as a protective measure, had proposed excessive fee increases for many users of the city's recreation facilities.

At the September 23 Rec Board meeting, the recreation department administration once again produced an eleventh-hour memorandum that contained assertions and implications that the Barracudas found questionable. Winger tried to keep the discussion focused on the technical flaws in the program-hour accounting system, but Morgan told the board that he had used the same system elsewhere without criticism and that the Western City Office of Finance had approved it. The vote was 4-3 against a favorable recommendation of the Barracuda proposal; a divided Recreation Advisory Board once again failed to support a Barracuda request.

Over the next two days, Winger spoke to several experts in public finance and accounting. From each of them he received confirmation that his suspicions about Morgan's cost-accounting method were valid. Thus reassured, he scheduled a meeting with the Western City director of finance and Morgan for Tuesday, September 29. He invited one of the Rec Board members who had voted against the Barracudas to attend as an observer.

Over the weekend, Winger studied the complete recreation department budget proposal that was pending before the city council. He found several discrepancies between data reported in the budget document and figures the staff had cited on previous occasions to support its position. He summarized these inconsistencies and pointed out their implications for assessing pool charges and calculating cost recovery percentages in a three-page document that also outlined the club's objections to the program-hour accounting system. It was a technical document, but he believed it would demonstrate to the city's chief finance officer that the Barracudas had stumbled onto some potentially embarrassing information that cast serious doubt on the care with which the recreation department produced its financial and accounting figures. On Monday Winger made a courtesy call to Morgan to inform him of his findings and to offer him an advance copy of the document, which he planned to distribute at the meeting on Tuesday. Morgan said that he considered the program-hour accounting system to be a "non-issue" and that he was too busy to review any new material prior to the meeting. If Winger had harbored any reservations about embarrassing Morgan before his administrative superiors, they were dispelled with that phone call.

An appeal on accounting methods

The meeting on Tuesday, September 29, was held in the office of David Komives, the Western City finance director. Morgan and Barbara Matlock, assistant to the director of recreation, represented the recreation department. Winger opened the session by informing Komives that since the authority of his office had been cited to validate Morgan's cost calculations, the Barracudas had some questions that they hoped he could clarify regarding USAC budgeting and accounting procedures. Winger was careful to point out that he had already consulted several experts who had reinforced his misgivings. He declared that if Komives endorsed Morgan's accounting system after considering his queries, the Barracudas would press the issue no further. He then proceeded to work through the three-page list of questions he had prepared to illustrate the flaws in the USAC accounting system and budget data. Morgan had little to say until near the end of the meeting, when he offered a brief defense of the program-hour methodology and tried to show that Winger had an incomplete understanding of the concept. He pointed out that Winger had mistakenly assumed that a program-hour of pool costs represented ten lanehours of usage, whereas in fact a program-hour for the Barracudas was any clock-hour during which the team was swimming in any number of lanes.

Now the full implications of the program-hour concept became clear to Winger. The Barracudas had been upset when they believed that the system was attributing to them the costs of operating ten fifty-meter lanes when in fact they were using only ten twenty-five-yard lanes. Now Winger was being told that the Barracudas' hourly share of USAC operating expenses was the same regardless of whether they used the entire fifty-meter capacity of the pool or only two or three twenty-five-yard lanes while other users occupied the remainder. Winger pounced on this revelation and made certain that its implications were not lost on those in attendance.

Komives was attentive but noncommittal during the meeting; he said that he would need time to review the material Winger had presented and that he would get back to him. Winger hoped that the finance director would see that the administration had a potential problem on its hands and would counsel the city manager to avoid a public fight over such a minor issue.

October 6 was the date set for the Western City Council to adopt the recreation fee schedule for the coming year. Despite a follow-up phone call, Winger was unable to obtain a response from Komives prior to the council meeting. He hoped that Komives' silence indicated that he could not endorse Morgan's accounting system but was reluctant to admit it publicly. If that were the case, then Komives would likely alert the city manager to the potentially embarrassing situation that was developing.

Winger's optimism was well founded. As he sat in the audience at the October 6 council meeting, he heard Mayor Charles Franklin announce that consideration of the recreation fee schedule was being deferred until a subsequent meeting. The city manager had requested additional time to work out mutually acceptable fees with certain unnamed "affiliated groups." Franklin was looking directly at Winger as he spoke.

Winger was curious to learn what had transpired behind the scenes to produce this last-minute reprieve. He made an appointment to have coffee two days later with Blaine Perry, the council member with whom he had established the closest rapport. Perry was circumspect in responding to his inquiries; however, he left Winger with the distinct impression that at least some council members had become persuaded that Morgan's cost-accounting system was flawed and that the council had been more than a passive actor in the decision to defer consideration of the fees. Perry also suggested obliquely that the Barracudas give some thought to a fee schedule that would provide lower-cost pool fees for nonpeak demand hours, thereby signaling that the general principles of a compromise solution already had been discussed.

Moving toward a compromise

On October 15 Roger Young, the assistant city manager, called a meeting in his office. He invited Matlock and Morgan from the recreation department and Winger and Art Neighbors, the Barracuda vice-president, to represent the swim team. Young had been directed by the city manager to negotiate a speedy resolution to the pool fee controversy.

Like the city manager, Young was concerned that the question of pool fees had escalated into a public dispute, and he sympathized with the swim team's desire to keep membership fees affordable to families of modest means. At the same time, he felt that the Barracudas were being stubborn in the face of the increasing financial pressures on the city. The council had sent a clear message to the administrative staff that user fees were to be set high enough to cover a substantial share of the city's actual costs of providing recreation and other services.

Young also had mixed feelings about the substance of the dispute. He had personal questions about the program-hour concept that Morgan had used to establish the proposed fees, and he was annoyed that the methodology had been allowed to become the focus of a public controversy, for now he had to defend it. Even if the methodology was sound, he understood why it had the appearance of inequity to users of the pool. In short, he felt that the credibility and commitment of the city administration were under serious question by this vocal and assertive group of citizens.

Young set out to determine how much ground the Barracudas might be persuaded to yield in arriving at a compromise. Winger and Neighbors were steadfast in challenging USAC cost calculations and in supporting their alternative approach. While they reiterated the belief that their proposed lane charges of $2.50 and $4.75 were fair, they conceded that upward adjustments could be acceptable if they were supported by accurate operating cost data and an appropriate cost recovery formula. Young explained that the cost-accounting system could not be changed but asked the Barracudas if they would be receptive to the principle of reduced fees during low-demand hours of the day. They accepted, with the qualification that the baseline fees be determined on the basis of valid cost calculations. As the negotiating session ended, the participants agreed to continue their discussions one week later.

On October 22 Young convened the second and final meeting. He opened the meeting by restating their earlier agreement in principle to a two-tiered fee structure. He then tried one final time to dissuade the Barracudas from their explicit rejection of Morgan's cost-accounting system. Winger and Neighbors refused to yield. Young knew that the city could not accept an open rejection of the accounting system and therefore would be forced to concede on the issue of pool fees rather than back down on its costing methodology. He was relieved, therefore, when Winger suggested that they agree to disagree over accounting methodology for the time being and get on with the task of addressing the fees directly.

Young then asked Morgan how soon he could work up a new fee schedule based on some slight modifications of his cost calculations and incorporating an appropriate fee reduction for nonpeak hours. Morgan said he could have the figures in about one month. Young was livid. He had just won a major face-saving concession from the Barracudas, and a resolution to the controversy was at hand. He immediately called a five-minute recess and summoned Matlock to confer with him.

The decision problem

Now Young was faced with a problem. Both the city manager and the city council expected a settlement of the controversy by the next council meeting, which was only twelve days away. He had the pieces of a successful solution in hand but had just been undermined by one of the city's own players. Several options occurred to him.

1. He could accept Morgan's one-month delay and hope that he could convince the city manager and the council that the delay was warranted.
2. He could give Morgan one week to produce the requested figures.
3. He could reaffirm the recreation department's fees of $4.00 and $6.50 but provide a modest reduction during nonpeak hours.
4. He could accept the Barracudas' proposed fees of $2.50 and $4.75, thereby tacitly acknowledging the inappropriateness of Morgan's accounting system.
5. He could devise an alternative fee structure that would include the discount for nonpeak hours, would be acceptable to the Barracudas, and would produce more revenue for the city than option 3.

Discussion questions

1. How should Young deal with Morgan when the meeting reconvenes? How should he deal with him after the meeting? Should he have invited Morgan to join him and Matlock in the meeting during the recess?

2. How should the following considerations be ordered in terms of priority: increasing program revenues, protecting the recreation department from embarrassment, and settling the controversy? What steps should Young take to accomplish each one?

3. What other considerations should Young weigh?

4. To what degree should Young protect Morgan and his program-hour accounting system?

5. What would Young gain by postponing the negotiations for one month? What would he lose?

6. Should Young's personal views regarding the flexibility/inflexibility or the reasonableness/unreasonableness of the Barracudas' negotiators have any role in his decision making? If so, what role? If not, why not?

The aftermath

When the group reconvened after the recess, Young proposed that the Barracudas be charged base rates of $3.05 per twenty-five-yard lane-hour and $6.65 per fifty-meter lane-hour. These figures were exactly what Winger had calculated to be the actual lane-hour operating costs at USAC. Young went on to propose that the base rates be reduced to $2.65 and $5.80 respectively for nonpeak hours. He also suggested that the Barracudas receive an additional 10 percent discount in any month in which their practice sessions totaled sixty-five clock-hours or more. Winger and Neighbors quickly accepted the terms.

Since the enlarged swim team practiced more than sixty-five hours every month, the 10 percent discount was virtually ensured. Moreover, all fifty-meter practices were conducted during nonpeak hours, as were approximately 40 percent of the twenty-five-yard practices. Therefore, the effective rates under the terms of the agreement would average approximately $5.22 and $2.60 for long and short lanes, respectively. Annually, roughly 85 percent of the Barracuda practice sessions were in twenty-five-yard lanes; therefore, the annual average lane fee for the team would be approximately $3.00. This was a far cry from the $4.00 charge to which they had initially objected but which they had once been willing to accept provided they were given a six-month grace period.

The Western City Council adopted the negotiated fee schedule in November.

Final discussion questions

1. What strategic and tactical errors did Morgan, his assistant Scott, and Willoughby make in dealing with the Barracudas?

2. Should the city have employed and defended Morgan's program-hour cost-accounting scheme as long as it did? If so, why? If not, at what point should the city have modified or abandoned it?

3. Should Young have been more aggressive in defending recreation department interests during the final negotiations? What are the arguments for and against this strategy?

4. Could this controversy have been resolved before it expanded to involve the city finance director, the city manager's office, and the city council? If so, how? If not, why?

5. What is the city's responsibility for underwriting portions of the costs of programs such as the swim team? Is the answer different for a team that predominantly serves persons from disadvantaged or low-income backgrounds?

Part four: Intergovernmental relations

Introduction to part four: Intergovernmental relations

Local governments are the primary providers of the public services consumed by citizens on a daily basis, but they do not perform that function alone or in isolation. Local governments work with federal and state agencies in the delivery of a wide range of services. They also work with one another; perhaps a dozen or more different units of local government provide services to each local resident and each parcel of property.

To make the task of coordinating services among these many units of government still more difficult, most communities also house a number of not-for-profit agencies—publicly owned private corporations supported by government grants, private donations, and fees from those who can afford to pay for their services. These agencies share in the task of providing such human services as education, mental health assistance, family counseling, senior citizens' programs, and youth activities. Thus, any particular community may have several governments and any number of not-for-profit groups providing public services.

Because they are so visible and have the broadest grant of authority at the local level, county and city governments usually have the added responsibility for supplementing the funds available to not-for-profit organizations and for coordinating the activities of these diverse service providers. Since counties and cities almost never have the authority to require compliance from these other organizations, their coordinating role only adds to the size and political complexity of the jobs of their administrators.

It goes without saying, of course, that even organizations operated by people of good intentions, possessed of public service motivations, and acting rationally will sometimes find themselves locked in bitter conflict with one another. Such is the situation in the first case presented in this part. "A Jail in City Center" describes a major land use controversy between a city and a county, each of which has legitimate and reasonable plans for the development of a particular parcel, and each of which has the strong support of its citizens in the dispute. Conflicts between nations rarely reach impasse as severe as the stalemate confronting the city of Rollins and the county of St. Regis, and even the presence of the state government, which has jurisdiction over both local units, fails to ameliorate the conflict.

The next case, "Housing the Homeless in Willow County," explores a more common intergovernmental conflict, one involving the county, its major city, and a large not-for-profit agency active in the housing field. In this case, the agencies all agree generally on the goal of more and better housing for the indigent and on the methods for achieving the goal; the disagreements involve the specific strategies and especially the financial role of the county in the joint housing effort. As is often the case in government decision making, the ultimate problem for the county is not one of policy intent, but one of budgetary reality.

Problems involving intergovernmental relations at the local level have one thing in common with other local problems: Although they require the policy involvement of elected officials, it is the professional administrators of the affected agencies and governments who ultimately must undertake the negotiations, balance the political interests, and produce the solutions that keep services flowing to the public. The need to reconcile the interests of many different service providers, like the need to reconcile the interests of many different political groups, adds to the complexity of decision making and thus to the professional challenge of local government administration.

A jail in City Center

Bill R. Adams, Glen W. Sparrow, Ronald L. Ballard

Editor's introduction

Governor James R. Thompson of Illinois has been known to say that the hard part of government is that decisionmakers rarely get to choose between good ideas and bad ideas; instead, they have to choose between good ideas. Such is the situation in this case; a county and a city both have proposals for the development of a parcel of land in the center of the city. Both proposals make good sense, and both enjoy widespread public support from the governments' respective constituencies.

The case is described from the vantage point of the city, and the decision problem is posed as one that the city manager must resolve. His task is complicated by the structural differences between the city and county governments, by the different constituencies to which each responds, and by the presence of a court order forcing action by the elected county sheriff.

From an intergovernmental perspective, the central issue is the resolution of a conflict between two local governments, each legally independent of the other, but with overlapping jurisdiction. Each pursues its separate interests, but each is clearly also pursuing the public interest. What is best for the county and its residents is not what is best for the city and its residents. Which side should prevail? Which set of public interests should the professional local government administrator, with his commitment to democratic principles, pursue: the interests of the county, which represents more people, or the interests of the city, which employs him?

Questions of principle and ethics abound in this case. How should the manager act? What kind of authorization does he need from the city council? Should a lack of time to consult the council affect the manager's inclination to act in accordance with the council's clear mandate, even when the proposed action has not been specifically considered by the council? What is the extent of a manager's freedom to take action in the public interest?

The city's objective is to promote its economic development. The county's objective is to improve its public safety services. Does the difference in objective make a difference in the manager's freedom to act?

Also involved in the case are two other units of government: the state, which empowers both the city and the county, and a special district, which supplies water to the property in question. Their presence adds to the complexity of the problem and further challenges the resourcefulness of the public officials involved.

Case 7
A jail in City Center

Background

The residents of St. Regis County were whipped into a frenzy as news of jail overcrowding became public. The sheriff, Horace Farley, began beating the drums for a solution, claiming the jails were powder kegs about to blow. More jails were needed now, or prisoners would have to be unleashed onto the streets. Overcrowding was especially serious at the county's jail in the city of St. Regis.

The media, taking its cue from Farley, dutifully announced that, indeed, there was a jail crisis and, of course, something must be done about it. The citizens concurred: something should be done. And so, pressure was placed on the St. Regis County Board of Supervisors, the governing body charged with building jails for the entire county. The hysteria reached such a crescendo that the supervisors, who had neglected the issue for two decades, were compelled to declare the jail situation an emergency, and, in order to calm mounting public frustration, county officials searched frantically for a quick-fix solution.

During the flap, citizens of the city of Rollins went about business as usual, unperturbed by the hubbub over villains and jail overcrowding. And why not? The jail issue was of marginal interest to Rollins residents, who were rarely visited by crime in their outlying city of 50,000. However, interest rose precipitously when the county declared Rollins the ideal spot for a new, temporary, six-hundred-bed men's jail. This proposal seemed reasonable to most of the county, which perceived Rollins as an outback, representing cowboys, country and western music, and people who did not mind long commutes. Rollins, as might be expected, became quite agitated at the decision, swearing to pit itself against the county juggernaut. Undaunted, the county reiterated its resolve to build, accusing the city of undermining "law and order" and obstructing a necessary solution to the problem. Both governments prepared for conflict.

And, indeed, they did fight. Events that led to this clash had been festering for about two decades. Eventually, the jail overcrowding became so bad that the American Civil Liberties Union filed a class-action suit on behalf of jail inmates. The U.S. District Court ultimately ruled crowding in the county's city-of-St.-Regis jail to be "cruel and unusual punishment" and ordered the sheriff and the county board of supervisors to find a solution to it. The search for a solution became even more urgent when the court imposed a 750-inmate cap on the facility.

There was no denying that the problem had become a monster because of the inaction of former boards. Lack of money, competing crises, and public dissatisfaction with earlier proposed solutions had allowed the issue to be continually set aside. Finally, the county responded by declaring a jail emergency and launching attempts to erect a temporary men's facility in the middle of Rollins, adjacent to the existing, but unobtrusive, women's jail.

The proposed jail was to be placed on county-owned land within the redevelopment area known as City Center, a project envisioned as the city's future commercial hub. The Rollins master plan called for a multi-use project focusing on a vibrant commercial core, pedestrian paths and walkways, lush landscaping, open space, fountains, and ponds—a dramatic recreational, commercial, and residential mix along the St. Regis River. For the city, this project was a matter of pride as well as economic vitality. It was central to Rollins' attempt to show its sophistication, to overcome its "west-county cowboy" image, and to establish a solid commercial base that would carry it in relative economic comfort into the next century.

In contrast, the county was seeking a low-cost, low-conflict "fix," and, in the process, proposed a planner's nightmare: an open compound, warehousing six hundred inmates in ten barracks, featuring dual chain-link fencing capped with coils of razor wire, guard towers, and minimal landscaping. From a marketing perspective, the facility was hardly considered a draw for the 706-acre City Center redevelopment area.

The county's assurance that the facility would be temporary held no currency with the city. Aside from the county supervisors' refusal to give a definite termination date, there was little likelihood that, in the rapidly growing county, there would ever be enough empty beds to transfer six hundred or more inmates to other, yet to be built, facilities. Would the county give up an operating jail site knowing that it was getting progressively harder to find communities willing to tolerate new jails? To Rollins, the answer seemed clear.

The problem confronting the city was, What, if anything, could be done to derail the proposal? State law seemed to back the county's contention that it could erect anything without city approval if the land were used for public purposes. The irony was that a major reason for Rollins' incorporation years earlier had been to escape this type of external control. Legally, the county, owner of 371 acres in the northeastern sector of City Center, could destroy City Center by introducing all manner of unwanted public projects.

Rollins

It could be convincingly argued that Rollins, prior to its incorporation seven years earlier, had been a victim of benign neglect by the county of St. Regis, a neglect that had incited a revolt and sparked a home-rule movement in Rollins. The county's policy of approving strip zoning and high-density residential projects in Rollins had left a scar that became the major focus of city policy during Rollins' early postincorporation existence. Only time could heal much of the damage previously visited upon the community by unpopular county land use decisions, but a well-planned downtown could be built from scratch in a relatively short period.

At the beginning of the century, Rollins was a quiet, rural, farming and dairy community, remaining so through World War II. It had taken Rollins almost seventy-five years to reach its 1950 population of 2,000. However, the winds of change struck as Rollins entered the late 1950s. To the chagrin of some and the glee of others (particularly developers), water and sewer lines were extended to the area, inviting development. Two water districts were formed in the region and eventually merged to become an independent special district, the Indian Valley Dam Municipal Water District. Indian Valley Dam District provided both water and sewage-treatment services for much of the urbanized west county, including Rollins.

In the 1950s, when the urbanization of Rollins began, a nebulous community began to take on a form dictated by topography. Except to the south, where the growing city of Rock Hill was located, large rocky hills isolated the Rollins valley from neighboring communities, including the city of St. Regis to the east, most of the sprawling community of Riverfront on the west, and the rugged northern lands. Soaring land values quickly transformed the farming community into a suburb, albeit distant, of downtown St. Regis. Land had simply become too expensive to farm. New homes and small shops began sprouting around the community of Rollins—projects marked by high density and strip zoning. Eventually, runaway growth and questionable planning ignited Rollins' home-rule movement.

As Rollins had evolved from a rural to an urban community, its leaders, disturbed by county actions, began to wonder whether county policy was indeed a form of benign neglect or a device to turn Rollins into a receptacle for projects shunned by other communities.

Although the idea of incorporation continued to grow in popularity, Rollins voters rejected the proposition to incorporate in the elections of 1976. Undaunted, home-rule advocates continued the struggle for city status, redrawing boundaries and correcting other objections aired by voters. In 1980 the question again went before the voters. This time it passed; in December Rollins officially became one of sixteen municipalities in St. Regis County. Like all of the other cities, it adopted the council-manager form of government.

The creation of City Center

The center of Rollins was mostly vacant land surrounded by homes and small businesses. To Rollins' new city planners, it was almost too good to be true. Here was a chance to build a planned downtown—City Center—in a redevelopment area without first having to tear down existing structures. Adding to the lure was the St. Regis River, which bisected the property, making the land that much more attractive and valuable.

As one of its first major actions, the city council formed the Rollins Redevelopment Agency and became its policy board. Under state law, a city government, as a redevelopment agency, could issue bonds for revenue and use the proceeds to attract new development (through financial incentives) or otherwise improve a blighted or redevelopment area, hence increasing property values, quality of life, and the local tax base. The declaration of City Center as a redevelopment area would freeze property tax revenues from the area for all governments (including the county). The bonds would be repaid through property tax increments accruing from upgraded property values, with all of the increment, for the ensuing twenty years, going to the redevelopment agency. In the case of Rollins, the redevelopment agency acquired $6.4 million in debt to insure the success of City Center. If the project failed, the city would be responsible for the entire amount, plus interest.

With the redevelopment process defined, the Rollins Redevelopment Agency (the city council) went about the task of identifying the boundaries of City Center, which consisted of 706 contiguous acres of redevelopment land. This area included all of the property around two county facilities in the City Center area. One facility, Broadview, was the only county geriatric hospital and senior-citizens' home in St. Regis County. In 1966, across the street from Broadview, the county had opened Safe Haven, a "permanent" reform school for delinquent girls. The promise that it would remain a girls' reform school was breached a decade later when the structure was converted to a lockup for women—the first and only one in the county.

Several years later, the city began to tackle the tough questions concerning City Center land use. It took two hectic years for the city to approve a comprehensive land use package, called the City Center Specific Plan. During that period, the city council walked a thin line among groups of every political stripe: slow-growth advocates, free marketers, environmentalists, landowners, developers. "Get everyone involved from the start and negotiate a comprehensive, if compromise, master plan," was the city's strategy.

Complications

For the most part, the scheme worked. For two years, the city held open meetings, discussions, workshops, conferences, and public hearings on City Center. At the start of the process, the county and the city, in a written pact, agreed to plan City Center together.

Had it not been for structural differences between the city and the county, the cooperative planning venture for City Center might have worked. Both the city and the county had professional administrative leadership: the city with a city manager, Jerry Swanson, the county with a chief administrative officer, Jim Marshall. In theory, the resolution of differences between the city and the county should have been aided by negotiations between the city manager and the county administrator—professional peers.

The jurisdiction of the county administrator, however, was limited by the county's governmental structure, which provided for several elected administrative officers, including the county sheriff. The governmental responsibilities assigned to the elected officers fell outside the purview of the administrator; while the administrator could and did attempt to work with, and influence, the elected officials, his influence varied. On politically sensitive matters, the administrator frequently had limited influence with his elected colleagues.

The county jail was such a matter. Since the county's jails fell within the jurisdiction of the county sheriff, decisions regarding them were made either by the sheriff alone or by the sheriff in consultation with the board of supervisors. Pressured by the courts, the press, local law enforcement agencies, and his own staff on the problem of jail overcrowding, Sheriff Farley was not inclined to work with the county administrator. He needed a new jail; he needed it now; and he was not going to waste time with what he regarded as extraneous concerns as he worked to get a new jail. His ability to win reelection in a countywide race demanded that he resolve the jail crisis—and do it before the next election.

The case

As the planning for City Center trudged along and the plan began to take form, the county—City Center's largest single landholder—objected to two related proposals: the amount of park and open space proposed on county land and the resulting limits on the number of homes permitted on the remaining property. At first county officials protested quietly, but, angered that the city was holding fast, they went public, airing their differences openly and in the press.

Two months later, the county announced its plans to build the men's jail in City Center, contending that the project did not require city approval because it was a public facility and not a commercial venture. The city was offended at the county's failure to notify it of the decision before going public (as a courtesy, local agencies normally give advance notice when a policy decision will affect another's sphere of influence). Tensions heightened when the city procured pictures of the type of facility planned (barracks, chain-link fencing, razor wire, guard towers) and made them public. However, by year's end, the city had persuaded the county to build elsewhere. A new study was completed, identifying an isolated area along the county's southern border as the new jail site. From outward appearances, Rollins had won.

A second confrontation, increasing the bad feelings between the county and Rollins, occurred a year later in a dispute over one million dollars the county owed the city in unpaid tax monies. Being short of cash, the county had proposed a swap of some of its City Center real estate to settle the debt. The city, wanting control over as much City Center land as possible, agreed, and a memorandum of understanding was signed by both parties. Unfortunately, they could not agree on the property's worth, and negotiations subsequently collapsed. Apparently agitated by the impasse, the county made a unilateral decision to retain the land and repay the debt in cash. An equally irritated city took the county to court for breach of contract, but lost.

The jail issue resurfaces

Meanwhile, a storm was brewing in the city of St. Regis that would eventually affect Rollins. Because of jail overcrowding, the sheriff's department implemented a policy of book-and-release for misdemeanors, which included prostitution. Residents of neighborhoods with the greatest activity, however, complained to the city council that their streets were being overrun by prostitutes (and their potential customers) and that something had to be done. That sounded reasonable to the council, but what to do? Since all municipalities booked suspected criminals in the county jails, the city of St. Regis turned to the county. It decided to wave a carrot before the county supervisors: expand the women's detention facility at Safe Haven in Rollins so that more prostitutes could be locked up, and the city of St. Regis would cover half of the construction cost.

The county agreed. The Rollins City Council, attempting to smooth ruffled feathers, decided neither to oppose nor to support the expansion as long as it remained within the existing compound. The county agreed to Rollins' condition.

Nevertheless, fate dealt Rollins a double-cross when the board of supervisors, frustrated in its efforts to procure jail land in the proposed southern location, not only approved the expansion of the women's detention facility by almost two hundred beds but also ordered construction of the six-hundred-bed men's facility next door.

Rollins was stunned. Had this issue not been resolved less than a year earlier? The Rollins City Council, angered by the county's behavior, gave City Manager Swanson a free hand, financially and otherwise, to defend the city from the threat.

Publicly, the county reasoned that the men's temporary jail could be built quickly next to Safe Haven (and removed after permanent facilities were built elsewhere) because the infrastructure—roads, electricity, water and sewer capacity—was in place and the land already belonged to the county. Rumors that the jail was an excuse to punish Rollins for bucking the county on the City Center plan were denied.

The city argued the emotional issue of security: a male lockup located adjacent to homes, Broadview Hospital, and schools (Rollins Elementary School was only two blocks away) would present a real danger to the community and especially to the schoolchildren. The county waved off these concerns, saying people would actually be safer with more sheriff's deputies in the area.

Although the county's response to safety issues was anticipated, city officials were puzzled by the county's inability to grasp the economic issue. Both jurisdictions had much to lose financially if the jail were built. With population on the rise in Rollins, healthy commercial development in City Center was needed to expand the city's tax base, which in turn would be used to maintain city services.

The jail, it was feared, could undo all efforts to attract upscale business to Rollins, thereby sinking City Center and conceivably the city's future. City leaders wondered, Why would the county, which is always short of cash, squander its extremely valuable City Center property on a project guaranteed to scare off money-making ventures? The county answered that the land was not that valuable anymore, since a large segment of it had been zoned for park and open-space use. Furthermore, the county maintained, the jail would only be temporary and, after it was removed, land values would return to normal.

Crisis management

To respond to the threat, a jail task force, made up of City Manager Swanson, the city attorney, and staff members, formulated a four-pronged strategy—political, administrative, public relations, and legal—all salted with a hefty dose of publicity. The city hoped to sandbag the project with delays—a tactic of attrition.

Swanson was the focal point of Rollins' defense. It fell to him to provide the day-to-day management and coordination of the city's strategy. The city council took the lead on the political front, cajoling county officials and enlisting the aid of sympathetic politicians. The city staff undertook the task of managing the crisis administratively. This included doing technical work, tracking county actions, bird-dogging staff, attending meetings, studying jail-related documents, and publicizing, via the media, contrary city findings. A public information campaign involved the city's community services coordinator, city council members, and resident activists. It was decided that legal challenges would be used where and when necessary.

To assist in the preparation of its case, the city hired twelve consultants, experts in a range of fields including penal systems, criminology, ecosystems, flood control, fire regulations, socioeconomics, and public relations. The Rollins School Board also lashed out at the county for suggesting the placement of a men's lockup so near an elementary school attended by hundreds of children. The board members expressed concern over released and escaped prisoners, visitors, and increased traffic. The school district also hired a consultant to assist the city task force. Further, a Rollins citizens anti-jail organization regrouped and turned up the heat on the county with letters, telephone calls, rallies, and picketing.

The first legal volley was fired when the city filed in county court for a restraining order, arguing that the county was preparing plans to build before completing an environmental-impact report (EIR) as required by state law. This, the city argued, put the cart before the horse; that is, the county should not take steps to build in Rollins until the EIR was completed and had identified the best location for a jail. The county claimed it was following proper procedure—a contention with which the court eventually concurred.

At the same time, Rollins' mayor contacted local legislators and requested state legislation putting an end to the type of unilateral action undertaken by the county. While legislators expressed sympathy, they introduced no legislation.

Another government gets involved

About the same time, Indian Valley Dam District gave the county a scare with news that the sewer trunk line serving the district might be near capacity. If true, this meant that the jail would have to be put on hold until the line was expanded, which could be years down the road. As it turned out, the line was near the limit but not close enough to halt the jail.

While the county went about the business of writing the EIR, the city opened negotiations with Indian Valley Dam District for control of sewer lines in City Center. Under existing rules, sewer lines could be reserved from Indian Valley Dam even if landowners had no intention of developing the land. Moreover, the agency sold sewer hookups on a first-come, first-served basis. Landowners merely had to prove ownership and possible future need for the sewer units requested. No city or county approval was necessary, as Indian Valley Dam was an independent special district. (Sewer units are based on the average service one household requires: one sewer unit equals one household. The jail would require 112 units.)

Once reserved under the Indian Valley Dam scheme, sewer lines were locked to a particular property in perpetuity. This meant that a developer using less than the allotted quota was forbidden to resell, trade, or give away the remaining units to anyone else, including the dam district.

Because of the rapidly dwindling number of available units, Indian Valley Dam's regulations could have wreaked havoc on City Center development, leaving certain parcels shy of units while others had a surfeit. Such a system had the potential of turning the City Center development into a game of chance, and Rollins had no intention of gambling with its future. Rollins proposed to the dam district that because of its overriding interest, the city be granted control of the allocation of sewer capacity in the City Center area.

Two events had prompted the city's concern about City Center sewer lines. The first occurred when almost half of the remaining sewer capacity (1,460 units) available to Rollins was purchased by a major developer who had become worried by published reports of diminishing sewer capacity. That action left Indian Valley Dam with only 833 units. The precipitous drop in available capacity alarmed Rollins officials, who saw the whole City Center project in double jeopardy. The second event was the county jail proposal: The city would obviously gain significant leverage over the jail location if the county had to go through the city for sewer service.

The city argued before the Indian Valley Dam directors that, jail or no jail, the city must have authority over sewers in order to ensure the integrity of the City Center project. Following the presentation of Rollins' case, the Indian Valley Dam Board chose to postpone a decision for two weeks. City officials, concerned that either private developers or the county would purchase the remaining sewer units, countered by requesting a moratorium on the sale of capacity for all locations until the next hearing. The city explained that it feared a "run" on the remaining hookups. Unconvinced, the board denied the request, leaving intact the first-come, first-served policy. County officials had noted in an earlier newspaper interview that they planned to reserve the 112 hookups necessary for the jail in a "day or two."

The decision problem

As he drove home from the meeting with the dam board, Swanson reviewed his handling of the crisis and concluded that time had run out. For two years the city had moved to keep the county from proceeding with a plan that would have seriously, and perhaps permanently, damaged Rollins' economic future. Plans had been created; support mobilized; research undertaken; legal, publicity, and political actions implemented; pleas made; proposals put forward. Swanson realized, however, that the next morning he would have to act. Further, since there was no opportunity to meet with his council, any action he took would have to be rapid and unilateral.

The problem was more complicated than just stopping the county from proceeding with its plans to place the jail in City Center. While Rollins public opinion strongly supported action to block the county, public opinion outside Rollins was running equally strongly in favor of the county's plan for the temporary jail location. Which public interest must be served—that of city residents or that of county residents? Although the manager served the city, the population of the county was many times larger than the population of the city.

Still more factors were operating against the city. Rollins had lost on legal grounds in the court test; state legislation had not been forthcoming; other cities in St. Regis County had remained relatively silent lest the jail end up in their backyards; the county had the EIR, ownership of the property, and a federal district court order all going for it; and now the Indian Valley Dam Board had chosen to vacillate rather than support the city.

The alternatives were limited; most avenues for relief were closed or rapidly closing. Reliance upon other entities, judicial remedies, and political processes seemed to have been exhausted. If the county reserved the remaining sewer hookups, the city's cause would appear to have been lost. Yet no money had been appropriated by the city to pay the $600,000 required to reserve the hookups.

Was there anything Swanson should do? Was there anything he could do?

Discussion questions

1. How should the manager define the public interest in this case? Which group of residents should take priority? Does the interest of the larger jurisdiction always take priority over that of the smaller jurisdiction? If so, why? If not, under what conditions should the smaller jurisdiction prevail?

2. What different governmental agencies are involved in this case? What are their interrelationships? In such a situation, what are the prerogatives of the city to protect the interests of its residents?

3. What principles should govern the behavior of the manager in this case? Which should take priority—his responsibility to his constituents, his commitment to democratic theory and representative government, or the laws of the city and the state? How should these be sorted out?

4. Does the issue under consideration affect the answer to the preceding questions—that is, when the public safety (retention in jail of those accused of crimes) conflicts with community control (the opportunity for economic and land use enhancement), which should take precedence and why?

5. What interpretation would you put on the council's direction that the manager act with "a free hand, financially and otherwise" to defend the city? Does such an authorization enable the manager to spend money without an appropriation? How far does it go in justifying unilateral action by the manager?

6. Given that he is unable to meet with the city council (and regardless of the answer to question 5), are there other efforts at consultation that Swanson ought to make before he acts? If so, what are they?

7. Do the time constraints faced in this situation produce "emergency" conditions? Do such conditions permit the manager to exceed his usual authority? If so, by how much? If not, how does a manager defend governmental inaction in the face of emergency situations?

8. Are there situations in which the urgent need for action justifies a government, or an administrator, ignoring accepted and "normal" procedures and engaging in "guerrilla warfare"? Does this situation, with its long-term economic implications, justify such behavior?

9. What tactical options are available to Swanson? What option should he choose? How can it be defended?

The aftermath

When the administrative offices of Indian Valley Dam District opened the morning after the board meeting, Swanson arrived and presented Indian Valley Dam with a check for $600,000 to purchase the remaining sewer units. The scheme caught everyone by surprise, including the dam district, which had no option, under its first-come, first-served policy, but to sell the units to the city. The city had seized the offensive and won.

The county was stunned when it learned of the city's action. The city now controlled the sewer hookups. It had won the battle; the jail development was certainly stalled and perhaps stopped.

At a subsequent Rollins City Council meeting, the council voted quickly and unanimously to approve the expenditure of $600,000 for 833 sewer units for City Center.

By a 3–2 vote, the Indian Valley Dam Municipal Water District subsequently agreed to sign the accord granting the Rollins Redevelopment Agency the authority over sewer lines, which accompanies the sewer hookup purchase. The county of St. Regis and Rollins quickly became entangled in a mass of lawsuits and countersuits. One suit brought by the county accused both the city and the dam district of conspiring to withhold sewer service from the jail. In another suit, the city challenged the adequacy of the county's EIR.

Even while the lawsuits were being pursued, however, a strange quirk of fate handed victory to the county. By chance, the county operated a sanitary district some fifteen miles from Rollins, and the sewer trunk transporting sewage from the district to the treatment plant ran one-half mile from the proposed prison site. The county tapped into its own sewer main to provide a hookup for the jail and then proceeded to build the jail. Within eighteen months of the city's apparent victory, the county was moving prisoners into its new lockup in Rollins' City Center.

Rollins, meanwhile, continued to pursue a state appeals court ruling on the adequacy of the county EIR and to seek state legislation to ensure that the county would keep its promise to evacuate the "temporary" prison after seven years.

Final discussion questions

1. What issues of intergovernmental relations are posed by the case? List them in order of importance and explain your reasons.

2. Were there other actions that Rollins should have taken earlier in the controversy to keep the issue from reaching an impasse between the city and the county? Did Swanson effectively involve other governments in the decision process? What else might have been done?

3. How would an advocate of public choice theory respond to the conclusion that it was the presence of so many governments that produced the problem in this case? If that argument is true, what can or should the manager do in the face of such a situation?

4. How might this situation have been different if the difference in governmental structure (i.e., the presence of an elected county sheriff) between the city and the county had not existed?

5. Given the differences in structure, is there any action the county administrator might have taken or should have taken?

6. Did Swanson overstep his authority? Was his action legal? Was it ethical? Did the appropriation of the council "after the fact" justify the manager's action?

7. What can be expected to happen to a manager if he or she makes a bold move to protect the interest of the city? Is it any different if the manager is unsuccessful? Is success or failure a legitimate basis for distinguishing between "right" and "wrong" behavior?

8. Is the manager's action justified (or even analogous to) Thomas Jefferson's decision to make the Louisiana Purchase? Explain.

Housing the homeless in Willow County

Jacqueline Byrd, Terry Schutten, Steven A. Sherlock, Susan Von Mosch, Jon A. Walsh, Mary Theresa Karcz

Editor's introduction

Provision of human services is often a focal point for intergovernmental relations. Not only do human services tend to be highly complex, but the number of players—governments and notfor-profit agencies delivering these services—is much greater.

Typically, each not-for-profit agency has been organized to respond to a particular public service need. Each serves a specific constituency, and each has a core of devoted supporters, who usually include capable and influential residents of the local community. Consequently, while each provides a valuable public service, it does so in response to its supporters' perceptions of service needs. Organizational jealousies are common, and the agencies sometimes fail to coordinate their efforts with one another and with governments serving the same constituencies.

Thus, in most communities, the human services area poses major problems of service integration or coordination, a job that usually falls to the city or county government. From the perspective of the city or county, these agencies help get needed jobs done, but at a cost of complicated bureaucratic interaction in an intergovernmental setting.

In this case, Willow County must coordinate county, city, and private agency efforts to provide housing for the homeless. As is so often the case, the need is evident, but the resources to do the job are limited. The county administrator and his staff must coordinate an intergovernmental effort to increase the availability of housing for the homeless without exceeding the county's budgetary resources. They must achieve this goal in a way that simultaneously satisfies the other agencies and the county board. Complicating the problem is a well-meaning and influential member of the board who goes beyond his authority in making commitments to the other agencies involved. Thus administrator-board relations as well as administrator-community relations are additional factors challenging the administrative staff in Willow County.

Case 8
Housing the homeless in Willow County

Background

Willow County is a completely urbanized county with a five-member elected board of commissioners and an appointed administrator. The county seat is Saul, a large city with more than half of the county's population.

The membership of the county board has been very stable. At the time this case begins, four of the five members had served for more than ten years. The board has had a strong commitment to preserving its formal structure and acting as a group. Good, professional government combined with fiscal conservatism are the values of the Willow County Board.

The board uses a committee structure to conduct its business; information affecting potential decisions and requests for action are presented to the relevant committee or committees for review before going to the board for final action. The committees include finance, policy, and human services. A presentation to a committee is formal, with minutes and permanent records. As a result, discussion tends to be limited.

When more extensive discussion is needed on an issue, the county administrator calls an "administrative update," an open, public meeting led by the county board chair. This meeting is less formal than a presentation to a committee and encourages communication between staff and elected officials. Administrative updates are used infrequently and usually for major policy projects.

To support the county's policymakers, the county maintains the Policy Analysis Division, which analyzes issues for the board's consideration and recommendation. Options for action are presented by the staff. The division consists of a director and four analysts; it reports directly to the county administrator (see Figure 1).

Like many county governments, Willow County has a major responsibility for social services. Consequently, it has been addressing the problem of homelessness for a number of years. Historically, both the county and the private sector have provided food and shelter services for the homeless, and public-

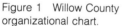

Figure 1 Willow County organizational chart.

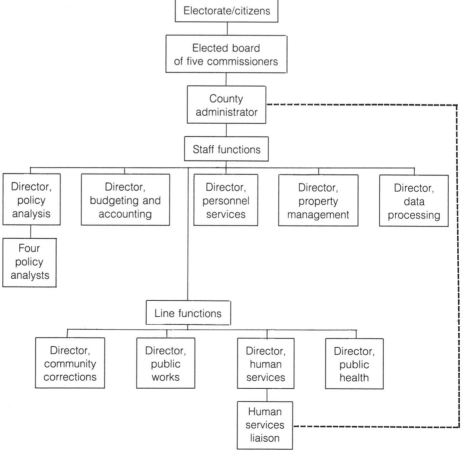

private cooperation has been strong. On the public side, for example, in one year Willow County financed $1.04 million in prevention programs that provided support for people in immediate danger of becoming homeless, including emergency assistance, emergency social services, and health service programs. The county also funded emergency housing, contributing $1.3 million to the WXYZ Association, Adult Shelter Services, several battered-women's shelters, and other emergency housing programs that provide immediate shelter to people who have no other housing. The emergency housing is usually short term (one to thirty days), and people are often required to leave the premises during the day. The county does not provide any transitional housing programs that offer shelter for extended periods.

Complementing the county's activity, the private sector finances or provides advocacy and legal services to prevent homelessness, as well as emergency shelter and transitional housing programs that help homeless people get jobs and training.

The case

In the early 1980s, a number of events affected Willow County's services and policies. National economic conditions, severe inflation, high unemployment, and emerging federal policies generally restricted the federal government's role in funding housing and human services.

In response, the Willow County Board of Commissioners appointed the Gold Medal Commission to examine the county's urgent human service needs and to develop recommendations. Represented on the commission were local government; trades and labor; the business, religious, and minority communities; and foundations and private nonprofit organizations. Three county commissioners also served as members, including Commissioner George Goodfellow, chair of the human services committee of the county board.

Commissioner Goodfellow was a powerful, long-time county commissioner with a special interest in addressing human problems, including homelessness. He believed in direct contact with the public and made decisions on that basis. He understood the political process of government and used the system effectively to translate his priorities into action.

The Gold Medal Commission's report made the following recommendations and findings:

Government has an obligation to address the basic needs of the population.

The private sector will address the increased need for basic services, such as shelter, only for a maximum of three years, after which government should assume the responsibility.

Cooperation between the public and private sectors should be increased.

The Willow County Board of Commissioners accepted the Gold Medal Commission's report. Goodfellow, because of his role in developing the commission's recommendations, had particularly strong feelings of ownership toward them.

In response to the report, a local foundation established the Priority Care Fund, whose purpose was to meet the community's critical need for emergency shelter in the short term by funding local shelter providers, such as the Salvation Army. Local governments, including Willow County, and private organizations supported the fund's development and contributed to it.

The next year, the Helping Hand Foundation assumed responsibility for operating the Priority Care Fund but agreed to do so only if its use was restricted to emergency situations.

Two years later, in July, the foundation initiated the Human Development Action Coalition (HuDAC) to study homelessness in the greater Saul metropolitan area and to suggest responsibilities for the ongoing funding of services for the homeless. HuDAC was a committee composed of community, foundation, business, and government representatives. Participants included Goodfellow and one other Willow County commissioner, planning staff from the county's human services department, the vice-president of the Helping Hand Foundation, and the chair of the Shelter Board.

HuDAC was composed of diverse groups trying to decide who should do what in the area of emergency services. HuDAC was intended to function as a proactive, forward-looking catalyst to move social policy toward an emphasis on human development and to address basic needs of society. The coalition's primary objective was to develop strategies for both the public and the private sectors.

About a year after its creation, the coalition published the *HuDAC Report,* recommending that

The Priority Care Fund be phased out

The county assume responsibility for funding the emergency services that were currently being provided by the Priority Care Fund, such as shelters and food shelves

The Helping Hand Foundation and the private sector assume responsibility for transitional programs, such as counseling.

The Willow County Board of Commissioners did not formally review, accept, or reject the HuDAC recommendations.

In the months following the *HuDAC Report,* the Helping Hand Foundation announced plans to discontinue the Priority Care Fund at the end of the following year. The rationale for the suggested change was not that the Priority Care Fund dollars were no longer needed but that emergency care needs had ceased to be a temporary crisis. They were an ongoing need and, therefore, a public-sector responsibility.

Willow County, particularly the human services department, came under increasing community pressure to expand county financial support for emergency housing and related services. For instance, the WXYZ Association, which operated a housing program for homeless women and children, requested that the county appropriate $400,000 in new funds. The WXYZ Association also requested that the county appropriate about $70,000 in additional funds above the county administrator's proposed budget of $31,200 for emergency shelter services in the forthcoming year, the last year of the Priority Care Fund.

The director of human services, Janet Hamilton, was becoming extremely concerned about the number of requests from private service-delivery groups for both increased and new funding of programs and services. In addition, the human services staff was feeling a lack of direction and the need for a comprehensive, countywide policy document for planning and funding emergency services. Hamilton asked the county administrator, Frank Gardner, for a policy recommendation regarding the county's role in providing services to the homeless, particularly in the area of increased funding for emergency services.

During this time, advocates started lobbying county commissioners with phone calls and visits. One of these advocates was the WXYZ Association, which applied pressure when the county's human services department did not immediately agree to fill the gap left by the withdrawal of private-sector funds, including the Priority Care Fund. The local press picked up on WXYZ's concerns and published a series of articles discussing the frustrations of social agencies in dealing with the county.

Organizing for analysis

In response to Hamilton's request, and to pressure from the community, Gardner appointed a work group to develop policy options for planning and funding emergency housing and related services. The group was composed of staff from the county administrator's office, including the Policy Analysis Division; the Community Development Block Grant program; the human services department; the public health department; the county attorney's office; and the city health department.

The group was directed to

Define the nature and scope of the need for services

Research additional funding and program options available to the county board and determine potential costs

Draft a policy report on the provision of emergency housing and related services for the county board's consideration

Develop funding recommendations, based on policy options, for the next year's budget, and develop recommendations for the possible use of available but undesignated contingency funds in the current budget.

Gardner sent a letter to the commissioners recommending that, pending release of the policy report and the development of a county policy, they not make commitments to community programs for new or additional funding.

Coincidental with the formation of the policy work group, the Helping Hand Foundation sent a letter to the Priority Care Fund agencies informing them that the Helping Hand Foundation was phasing out the fund as of December 31 of the following year. The memo went on to state that "the county has agreed, in principle, to assume at that time the role of funder of emergency services currently funded by the Priority Care Fund." The letter was not sent to county commissioners or staff.

The letter frustrated the policy staff. Where did the foundation get the idea that the county had agreed to take over the Priority Care Fund? Craig Beckwith, the director of the Policy Analysis Division, questioned Gardner about the validity of efforts to develop rational policy options if policy decisions were being made before the report was completed.

In response, Gardner sent a letter to Molly Parsons, head of the Helping Hand Foundation, with copies to the commissioners, stating that "Willow County has not committed itself to any action pending the completion of the policy report and recommendations of the board."

Beckwith had first convened the work group in October. The group developed four key questions for analyzing the existing situation as well as the implications of a series of county options for housing-related services. The four questions were as follows:

1. The legal question: What is the legal responsibility of the county and other levels of government (e.g., federal, state, and city) regarding homelessness? Is the county meeting its legal responsibilities?
2. The financial question: How much in resources does the county want to direct toward the problem of homelessness?
3. The philosophical question: What are the nature and extent of the problem of homelessness? What is the appropriate role for the county? Other levels of government? The private sector? Public-private efforts?
4. The administrative question: How should the county's response to homelessness be structured and administered?

While the work group included staff from a variety of divisions, the policy staff had primary responsibility for coordinating and completing the project. The approach to the study, as well as the report and the options that emerged, were consistent with previous studies from the Policy Analysis Division. However, not all commissioners recognized or endorsed the value of the approach normally taken by policy staff in analyzing an issue.

The controversy builds

In December, a year before the scheduled termination of the Priority Care Fund, Larry Canfield, director of the Shelter Board, convened a meeting of staff from agencies receiving or interested in receiving funds from the McKinney Act, federal legislation that provides funding for services for the homeless.

Canfield appeared at the meeting as a general advocate for the homeless rather than as an advocate for a specific agency or unit of government. His primary concern was that a lack of local, centralized coordination and administration of McKinney funds would result in duplicated or inefficiently delivered services or in loss of potential funding because no local organization had applied for it.

The meeting was attended by staff from the county's Policy Analysis Division, the city, the state, the Helping Hand Foundation, and private agencies. During the meeting, several participants suggested that the county assume responsibility for calling future meetings of the group and for coordinating McKinney funds and services. County staff could not commit the county to a coordination role, however, in the absence of an approved policy concerning the county's role.

Several days after the meeting, despite the absence of a board directive or policy, Goodfellow, as chair of the county board's human services committee, informed County Administrator Gardner that he wanted the county to take a lead in coordinating the McKinney funds. Gardner maintained that the matter should not be finalized until the board had considered the work group's report on homelessness and defined county policy.

Gardner and Goodfellow had intense exchanges over the establishment of a staff position to coordinate services for the homeless as well as oversee the McKinney money. When the discussion ended, the issue of the coordinator position was unresolved and remained a point of contention.

Shelter Board Director Canfield's concern about coordination and the role of local government in providing services to the homeless resurfaced in January. In order to advance the discussion, he exerted pressure to have the mayor of Saul, County Board Chair Nancy Able, and a local U.S. congressman call a press conference to announce the award of McKinney funding and a cooperative city-county effort to address the issue of homelessness.

Able, Gardner, and Beckwith were uncomfortable with the idea of a press conference. Again, the issue was the absence of a formal board statement concerning the county's role. How could the chair publicly discuss the county's role when the board had not defined it?

The press conference became a moot point when it became clear that the other participants—the mayor and the congressman—were not going to attend.

Meanwhile, during February and early March, the county work group prepared several drafts of the *Homeless Report*. A variety of issues arose during reviews and revisions by the work group and other key county staff.

As the report neared completion, several vendors and agencies providing services to the homeless inquired about it, afraid that the report might adversely affect services for the homeless. They thought the report would spell out who would receive funds and who wouldn't. Furthermore, all of the private organizations then providing emergency services and funded by the Priority Care

Fund were anxious for the county to acknowledge that it would be assuming responsibility for this fund.

The policy staff met with several noncounty agencies to explain the content of the report. The report presented five options:

Option 1a: Continuation of Willow County's existing preventive and emergency services.

Option 1b: Continuation of Willow County's existing preventive and emergency services, with increases in the level of support for emergency services to equal the level of funding provided through the Priority Care Fund.

Option 2: Continuation of existing preventive and emergency services and addition of intervention services without continued funding of the agencies currently receiving Priority Care funding. (Intervention services, such as assessment and case management, are provided to individuals who are homeless or at risk of becoming homeless and are not receiving services through the Community Social Services Act.)

Option 3: Continuation of preventive and emergency services and addition of intervention and transitional services without continued funding of the agencies currently receiving Priority Care funding.

Option 4: Continuation of existing preventive and emergency services and addition of intervention, transitional, and longterm housing services without continued funding of the agencies currently receiving Priority Care funding. (Long-term housing services provide housing on an ongoing basis. Single-room occupancy, or SRO, and public housing are examples of long-term housing programs. SRO residents often include deinstitutionalized mentally ill persons, chronic alcoholics, and low-income senior citizens.)

The information conveyed in the meetings appeared to dispel some of the concerns of the agencies, especially since none of the options detailed specific amounts of funding for their programs. Policy staff indicated that the report was really designed to deal with policy, not implementation. Before the agency representatives left, however, they pointed out that the *HuDAC Report* recommended that the county assume responsibility for emergency services (e.g., the Priority Care Fund); they said they would continue to worry about this issue.

In early March, shortly before the *Homeless Report* was to be mailed to the county board, Goodfellow requested that policy staff meet with a group, composed of staff from private agencies and the Helping Hand Foundation, that was concerned about homelessness and the current study. At the meeting, Beckwith and staff provided this group with the same information they had conveyed to staff from other agencies.

A major question from the group was whether or not a public hearing was to be scheduled. Policy staff responded by explaining that the report would be presented at an administrative update and that a public hearing was not normally part of that process. The private-sector participants were not satisfied, however, and expressed their concern to Goodfellow.

The day before the report was to be mailed in preparation for the administrative update, Goodfellow notified Gardner that because the issue was of such importance and urgency, it would come to his committee rather than to an administrative update.

Beckwith urged Gardner to try to persuade Goodfellow that the report should be presented at an administrative update. Gardner decided, however, that the issue was not worth fighting about.

Prior to the committee meeting on March 15, Gardner, human services liaison Betsy Markowicz, Beckwith, and policy staff met with Goodfellow to discuss the report. During that meeting, Goodfellow spoke very little of the report but expressed frustration and anger that time was passing and action had not been taken to coordinate the McKinney funds. As staff were working on the report, people were going homeless. "We need to assume responsibility for the Priority Care Fund," he said. "We need action!"

Goodfellow stated that he had made it clear in a previous conversation with Gardner that he wanted a coordinator designated. Gardner acknowledged that they had discussed the issue, but his understanding was that they had agreed to wait for the report and subsequent board action before moving ahead on coordination. The meeting ended without resolution of the issue, and Goodfellow told Gardner that he was not pleased.

The report

Beckwith presented the report to the county board's human services committee, which was meeting as a committee of the whole with Goodfellow as chair. Goodfellow directed the discussion to coordination of the McKinney funds and the need for a public hearing on the issue.

There was little discussion of and no action on the report. Concern was raised by members of the board about the roles and responsibilities of the other participants—the city and private organizations—in providing services to the homeless. Able, county board chair, made it clear that it was important to know what others were going to do before the county decided what it was going to do.

The outcome of the meeting was as follows:

Gardner was to see that staff was designated to coordinate the McKinney funds and programs for the homeless.

A public hearing on the report and the issue of homelessness was scheduled for May 3.

Goodfellow was directed to meet with officials from the city, the Helping Hand Foundation, and other organizations as appropriate, to discuss cooperative roles for addressing the problem of homelessness.

Goodfellow met with the mayor of Saul and other city officials, an executive from Helping Hand, and the author of the *HuDAC Report* in an effort to understand the roles of each. As a result of this meeting, Goodfellow circulated a memo explaining the agreement arising from the meeting to all of the commissioners and representatives who had been at the meeting. He asked for comment but received none.

The public hearing

The next step was the public hearing.

Before the hearing, Gardner, Beckwith, and human services liaison Markowicz met with Able to discuss the possible results of the public hearing. Able asked whether there was a staff recommendation. Gardner and staff said they were considering option 2 because adding intervention services rather than increasing emergency services was more likely to produce desired changes.

At the public hearing, many of the community's advocates and providers complimented Goodfellow for his support and efforts. Many of the people testifying recommended a combination of options 1b and 2—that the county assume the responsibility for existing preventive services, increased emergency services, and intervention services. Some even recommended that the county provide all services for the homeless.

An important issue was raised during the public hearing. Molly Parsons, executive director of the Helping Hand Foundation, stated that her organization expected the county to assume responsibility for funding not only emergency services, which included shelter and food, but also housing costs associated with transitional services. This surprised Goodfellow, who had assumed that if the county took over emergency services, Helping Hand, together with the city, would take over both the programs and the housing for transitional services. He said that he wanted county staff to meet with city and Helping Hand staff to clarify roles and responsibilities in the provision of transitional housing services. The board went along with his recommendation.

At the end of the two-and-one-half-hour public hearing, Goodfellow called for staff to cost out an option that he had discussed with the city and the private providers. This option was detailed in a memo indicating what responsibilities the private providers and the city and county might be willing to accept.

After the hearing, Beckwith and Markowicz met with Goodfellow to review his request. It became clear that the option Goodfellow wanted to be costed out was the same as option 1b in the *Homeless Report,* with the addition of a half-time coordinator position and a $33,000 rental assistance subsidy.

Within the month, a response to Goodfellow's request was prepared by county staff and sent to the human services committee of the whole for consideration. The committee reviewed the materials and asked staff to (1) meet with city and Helping Hand staff concerning roles in transitional service delivery and summarize the results, and (2) display, on one page, the costs associated with each option, including the items identified by Goodfellow.

The decision problem

Staff members from the county, the city, and the Helping Hand Foundation met to discuss the continuing matter of providing services to the homeless. During the meeting it became evident that the participants were operating under different assumptions. County staff assumed that the meeting was being held to clarify roles and understandings among the three agencies. City and Helping Hand staff thought all decisions about roles and responsibilities had been made at the meeting between Goodfellow, the mayor, and Helping Hand and that the current meeting was being held to prepare for program implementation. From Goodfellow's actions, the city and Helping Hand staff members had understood that the county would (1) assume the funding necessary to maintain the Priority Care Fund and (2) fund transitional housing. Helping Hand and city staff indicated that unless the county assumed these responsibilities, the city and Helping Hand would not take responsibility for the program portion of transitional services or for low-cost housing.

The county staff members were taken aback. Beckwith informed the city and Helping Hand staff that Goodfellow did not have authority to make decisions for the board. He pointed out that the board had directed Goodfellow to discuss respective agency roles but not to make decisions or commitments. All participants left the meeting feeling that they had missed the boat. What had gone wrong? Where should they go from here?

Beckwith and Markowicz met with County Administrator Gardner to explain the outcome of the meeting. Gardner then met with Goodfellow and Able to explain the situation and to recommend an administrative update to obtain board direction for further action.

The commissioners agreed to an administrative update, which was held on June 2. Beckwith and Markowicz presented the problem, summarizing the results of the May 27 meeting with staff from the city and the Helping Hand Foundation. Able indicated that she was not happy just to provide "band-aid" services; she wanted county programs that would help people in the long run, programs like option 2 with its intervention services. Some of the other commissioners agreed, arguing that intervention services could save money over time.

Goodfellow urged the board to take over the Priority Care Fund, as recommended by the *HuDAC Report* and the community. This would require the adoption of option 1b with Goodfellow's preferred modifications. He reminded the commissioners that at the public hearing, the community had urged the board to assume responsibility for the $200,000–$300,000 gap that would occur when the Priority Care Fund was phased out. He concluded by asking emphatically, "If the county doesn't take over the Priority Care Fund work, who will?"

Another commissioner emphasized that the county could not afford full funding for both options 1b and 2 but must decide which to fund.

Able moved that Gardner be directed to prepare a recommendation consistent with the commissioners' priorities and budgetary constraints and to work with the human services staff, the Helping Hand Foundation, and the city to develop an effective continuum of services. No mention was made of the role that Goodfellow was to play. The motion was approved.

Gardner was left with the task of finding a solution. He had to choose among the options, knowing full well that the influential Commissioner Goodfellow preferred a modified option 1b but that Able, the board chair, preferred option 2. In addition, he had to consider the preponderance of opinion expressed at the public hearing—that the county should pick up the slack from the termination of the Priority Care Fund. Finally, Goodfellow had clearly demanded that Gardner appoint a coordinator for McKinney fund activity. The expectations of city staff and the thinly veiled ultimatum from the Helping Hand Foundation could not be ignored. Finally, Gardner could not forget the board's admonition that the county could not afford to fund all of the options. He had to act, but how?

Discussion questions

1. What are the values held by the major participants in this case? Where do these values conflict?

2. How should Gardner structure his approach to the county board's directive?

3. Which administrative staff members should be involved in the development of and solution to the commissioners' directive?

4. What key factors would be involved in the development of Gardner's recommendations?

5. How should the objective policy analysis process be balanced against the political dynamics of the situation?

6. What should Gardner recommend to the county board?

The aftermath

Gardner worked together with the director of human services, Janet Hamilton, and the human services liaison, Betsy Markowicz, to develop the maximum dollar figure that could be authorized for services to the homeless. He then delegated to Beckwith and Markowicz the task of developing policy recommendations that reflected the dollar figure and addressed the points of view articulated by Goodfellow and Able. Together, the four developed the following strategy for resolving the policy issue:

Continue the existing level of support for preventive services.

Increase funding for emergency services sufficiently to compensate for the loss of the Priority Care Fund (essentially option 1b).

Increase support for intervention services (essentially option 2) by reallocating caseworker time in the department of human services.

Hire a half-time coordinator to oversee the county's activities and to work with the other agencies and the city to integrate services to the homeless.

With this strategy in hand, Beckwith and Markowicz met with management staff from the Helping Hand Foundation and from the city to negotiate roles and responsibilities in the continuum of services to the homeless. The county staff urged that the city and the foundation increase their funding for transitional programs and long-term housing. The county sought further to have the foundation assume the leadership in developing and expanding transitional housing services. These terms were accepted by all of the parties in the negotiations and became the basis of the recommendations made by Gardner to the county board.

The county board approved the recommendations unanimously.

Final discussion questions

1. Were budget concerns used appropriately to determine the level of services to the homeless?

2. To what degree should Gardner have considered the position of individual commissioners in developing recommendations?

3. What is the best way to consider the differences of opinion of adversary groups in policy decisions?

4. Were Gardner and the policy analysis staff too objective and insensitive to community advocates?

5. Could Gardner have done anything different to redirect the process? If so, when and how?

Part five:
Analysis and evaluation

Introduction to part five:
Analysis and evaluation

"Voters are rarely encumbered by concepts
of economic rationality."

This simple statement, uttered privately by the mayor in one of the cases that follow, cogently summarizes the overriding difficulty facing analysis and evaluation in local government. To the extent that management is a science, it is based on an empirical approach to problem solving and decision making. That approach, in turn, relies on such commonly held and widely articulated public values as the desire for efficiency, rationality, economy, and simple "good sense" in government. Yet, as the quotation suggests, the vagaries of a fickle political process result in expressed public preferences that do not always coincide with these values.

It is in these circumstances that the administrative analyst, and the administrative decisionmaker, find some of their most difficult challenges. As knowledge of organizational operations has expanded, and the technological capacity to process information has increased exponentially, the professional administrator has tended to rely increasingly on empirical analysis of policy and organizational problems as the key to effective decision making.

In so doing, the modern administrator is faithful to a long professional tradition in public management. Woodrow Wilson described the role of the nonpolitical administrator as knowing the best (most efficient) way of implementing policy; Frederick Taylor initiated the search for the "one best way" nearly a century ago; and modern behavioral scientists, such as Nobel Prize–winning economist Herbert A. Simon, have made empirical inquiry the hallmark of competent social science action.

Yet, as the cases presented here demonstrate, the job of organizational and policy management is not based solely on competent analytical work. In a community governed by democratic principles, the will of the voters is the ultimate decision-making criterion, and that will is not easy to fathom. Presumably the will of the voters is translated by elected officials, but a local government administrator will not spend many days in public office before learning that there are many public wills, usually at odds with each other and often at odds with generally acknowledged public values. Elected officials frequently take positions at odds with their own campaign rhetoric.

Politics not only makes strange bedfellows; it also poses strange anomalies for the analyst. Case 9 examines a clash between the "best solution" and an ongoing intergovernmental agreement between a city and a county, further complicated by human considerations. Case 11 poses similar problems as political considerations apply pressure to alter or ignore analytical findings in the decision-making process. Even in Case 10, in which the role of analysis is dominant, administrative staff cannot ignore the people who will be affected by any decision.

Throughout, the cases in this section describe the local government administrator at work "running the organization," putting into practice the precepts of organization theory, and applying decision-making technologies in such diverse activities as choosing a residential sanitation technology, planning the location of human service offices, and configuring staff computer services. Even in such purely "administrative" tasks, the reality of politics and political leadership is ever present. Even in these most technical of functions, the administrator must still be a politician.

Reconfiguring the computer center

Scott D. Lazenby and Jay Brent Covington

Editor's introduction

Never has the old saying "Nothing is certain but death and taxes" been more true than in the present era. The one certainty on which administrators can rely is that change will occur, and that it will occur with increasing speed and frequency.

This is a case about change. It is about the management of change caused by the rapid pace of technological progress and about the impact of that change on the organizational structure of a joint city-county computer center. In making her decision, the city manager must reconcile technological considerations—the rapidly changing field of computers and constant upgrades in hardware and software—with human, organizational, and intergovernmental factors.

Thus, this is also a case about administrative organization, about the linkage between the organization and the people involved in it, and about those people and their ties to the political system. Finally, since the existing, and perhaps obsolete, computer center is a joint city-county operation, the interests—and the politics—of two separate units of government are involved.

Governments frequently collaborate administratively, jointly building roads and bridges on their boundaries, sharing staff resources, contracting for the use of specialized equipment, undertaking joint studies, coordinating planning efforts, and even sharing administrative services. Such collaboration can and does produce significant benefits, even if it proceeds with little public awareness or recognition. Such collaboration, however, also presents its difficulties, some of which are encountered in the decision posed in this case.

The decision on reconfiguring the computer center could be made strictly on the basis of analytical findings. The fiscal impacts of the proposed alternatives can be examined and the payback periods can be calculated to identify a financially "best" alternative. But such empiricism does not account for political considerations, nor does it account for human factors. Yet these cannot be ignored; too much is at stake to risk disrupting such basic operations as accounting and utility billing. The reactions of the bureaucracy—of the computer center staff and of others utilizing computers—cannot be discounted.

The manager also needs to make a judgment about long-term probabilities. Computer technology will continue to evolve, and changes made today must be made with an eye on future developments and their impact on present and future needs.

In short, this is a case in which both the science and the art of decision making are challenged. The science requires the design, implementation, and use of good analysis; the art requires reconciliation of the analytical findings with human and political realities. With all of this involved, how can an administrator know what constitutes the "best" or even a "good" decision?

Case 9
Reconfiguring the computer center

Background

Acornvue is a northeastern city with a population of approximately 50,000. It has the council-manager form of government with a part-time mayor and six council members selected at large in nonpartisan elections. The city's charter provides that the council appoint the city manager, who in turn is responsibile for the day-to-day administration of the government.

Acornvue is the county seat and the largest city in Larch County, which has a population of 200,000. Larch County is governed by three full-time commissioners who are nominated by district and elected at large in a partisan general election. Many of the county's department heads, ranging from sheriff to coroner, are also chosen in partisan elections. Some members of the community have urged the adoption of a county charter that would provide for a professional county administrator, but not much progress has been made in instituting this change.

At the time of this case, the city political scene had been quiet for several years, and the residents of Acornvue generally supported the city government and the services it provided. They lived in blissful ignorance of the computer that took up most of a downtown building and that tracked their utility billings, calculated their property taxes, and had cost at least one public servant his job.

The majority of the residents of Larch County lived in the unincorporated urban area surrounding Acornvue; their water, sewer, and certain other services were provided by the city of Acornvue. Acornvue's interest in having the unincorporated urban area annexed to the city had been a sore point between the Acornvue City Council and the Larch County Board of Commissioners.

In spite of the annexation issue and other political differences that are inevitable between governments with overlapping jurisdictions, the Acornvue and Larch County governments had cooperated successfully in a number of service areas, including police and fire radio dispatching, animal control, public health, cable television administration, stormwater management, and computer services. In each of these areas, both governments had determined that the economy of scale inherent in combined service provision outweighed the loss of independent control over service levels or policies.

History of computerization in Acornvue

Fifteen years earlier, the governments of Acornvue and Larch County created, through a formal intergovernmental agreement, the City-County Computer Center. Existing data processing staffs of both agencies were combined in a single location, under a computer center director who reported to a board made up of one city council member, one county commissioner, and a third nonvoting member who was a private-sector computer professional appointed jointly by the city and county. The computer center agreement provided for periodic "sunset" reviews, and either party could end the arrangement with at least a year's notice.

The center acquired a large mainframe computer, which was used for about five years and was then replaced with the current mainframe computer from another company. The mainframe had been financed over five years, with the last payment still due at the time the case begins. It was large enough to accommodate many simultaneous users (the city alone had thirty-seven terminals and printers). Many "on-line" programs enabled users to view information ranging from property assessments to budget and expenditure trends, but the programs operated in "batch mode" rather than "real time." For example, the financial database was updated once each night rather than each time someone entered a financial transaction.

In spite of the batch orientation, the large mainframe computer had enabled the two governments to proceed with automation projects that probably wouldn't have been possible for individual governments of their size. Jointly developed software programs had also reduced the cost to each government. The city had developed programs for a "paperless" purchasing process, on-line budget preparation, and several other applications that were at the leading edge of automation in cities.

A fact of life for the big mainframe computer was the obsolesence of its operating system (the software that provided the ground rules for the interactions between other software programs and the computer's hardware system). Every few years, the manufacturer would release an updated operating system that substantially improved the productivity of programmers. The company helped create demand for the new operating system by withdrawing support for the old one—that is, the company would help debug the old operating system only for organizations that had an expensive maintenance contract, and new programs offered by the company would run only with the new operating system.

Consequently, the computer center had undertaken an operating system conversion some years earlier. Since every program had to be modified at that time, other programming improvements were set back more than a year. Aside from this nuisance, however, the computer company had provided superb customer support for its machines and programs and had carefully maintained good relations with its customers, ranging from the computer center's director to the elected officials.

Financing the computer center

Much of the cost of the center was fixed, including lease-purchase payments for the computer itself. In the early years of the computer center, annual costs (including fixed costs) were distributed on the basis of the estimated costs incurred by each government.

After several years of joint operation, the city suspected that the county was solving some of its budget problems by making midyear changes in its use of the computer center, primarily by slowing down development of new software systems. This action had the effect of shifting fixed costs to the city. As a result, the city proposed a key change in the computer financing agreement, and the change was adopted.

Under the new arrangement, each government started to budget for its share of annual computer center costs on the basis of historical patterns of computer use and planned software development. Payments to cover the costs of the center equaled the budgeted amounts for that year, regardless of the actual level of use; this prevented fixed costs from being shifted unexpectedly from one government to the other. Any fund balance remaining at year end was to be distributed back to the city and the county on the basis of the proportion of actual use. Thus, if one agency used more of the center's resources than had been anticipated in the budget, it not only avoided paying for this extra use but also got back a larger share of the fund balance than it had in fact paid for.

As a further complication, it was difficult to identify the proportionate shares of computer use. Some of the systems had few terminals but required a large amount of processing time (e.g., utility billing, tax assessment). Others placed large demands on the network of terminals but involved relatively little processing (e.g., the preparation of purchasing requisitions by departments). The computer center had initially estimated the computer use split as being 65 percent for the county and 35 percent for the city. In spite of changes over time in each government's use of the computer and growth in the county's unincorporated population relative to the city's, the cost allocation as reported by the computer center staff remained suspiciously at the 65-35 level.

The politics

Notwithstanding its technical orientation, the computer board appointment was sought out by city council members and county commissioners. It offered them an opportunity to build ties with their counterparts in the other government and to take credit for improving city-county relations.

Staff support to the city's representative was provided directly by the city manager's staff. Key policies for automation in the city were developed by the manager's top management team in response to the direction set by the full city council in workshop sessions. City programming priorities were based on a three-year plan that included a cost-benefit analysis of all major projects.

The dynamics worked differently for the county. The allocation of computer resources, like the budget, was one of the few areas where the commissioners held power over the independently elected "row officers" (e.g., the sheriff, the tax assessor, and the prosecuting attorney). The commissioners had attempted to remove automation decisions from the political arena by creating an advisory board made up of staff from each of the county agencies. Nonetheless, the commissioners clearly had final authority over who would get first priority in computer projects. With the exception of the financial system, all of the major county computer programs supported the operations of the row officers. In the case of some, such as the assessor and the treasurer, the computer was key to the success of their tenure in office.

The county did not formally conduct long-range planning for computerization. It made annual programming decisions on the basis of the political strength of the independently elected county department heads, not on the basis of a cost-benefit analysis.

This situation provided some advantages to the row officers themselves: If their performance was criticized, the computer and the commissioners' power over it were convenient scapegoats.

Within the computer board itself, the major point of friction had been the suspicion by each government that it was subsidizing the computerization of the other government. At times, the Acornvue representative had been frustrated because Larch County's budget process was on a later time schedule than the city's, and in order to balance the budget, the county often reduced its financial support to the center late in the planning process. This forced the city to decide to back off on some of its new computerization projects or be faced with picking up a larger percentage of the center's overhead costs.

Because of the nature of their governments, the city and county representatives sometimes viewed the role of the computer board differently. The county commissioner, holding both a policy-making and an administrative post, felt that the board should make decisions on technical matters such as program scheduling. The city council member, on the other hand, saw the board as setting the overall direction of the computer center and preferred to leave technical issues to the staff.

The people

Several years before the start of this case, the resignation of the computer center director (who had been with the center since its inception), had prompted a nationwide search for a new director. By that time the center had a budget that approached $2 million and a staff of twenty-six programmers, operators, and support personnel. The computer board looked for an individual who not only had good technical skills but also would be sensitive to the politics involved in the intergovernmental computer arrangement.

The new director found himself in the wrong place at the wrong time: he arrived in the midst of the conversion of the operating system, which was taking longer than originally promised. The programming manager, who had been acting director, quit, citing irreconcilable personality conflicts and incompetence on the part of the new director. The lack of progress in other areas, resulting from the conversion, caused city and county departments to put pressure on the center. The computer board, not convinced that the conversion was being managed properly, fired the director after a year.

His replacement, Peter Medana, was hired away from the city's largest school district. The operating system conversion was wrapped up before his "honeymoon" period was over, and he turned out to be skilled at managing the independent souls who made up the computer staff and at maintaining the trust of a wide variety of elected and appointed officials.

Medana had been highly recommended to the computer board by Barry Hogan, the owner of an Acornvue business that had been in the family for several generations. Medana and Hogan had been high school classmates and had worked together on school tax elections when Hogan was active in the chamber of commerce.

Hogan subsequently ran for and was elected to a vacant city council seat. At his request, the council appointed him to the computer board. The trust between the two old friends had clearly contributed to stability in the city's relationship with the center.

When Acornvue's incumbent mayor was relocated by his company, Hogan (who had previously been chosen by the council as vice-mayor) stepped up to fill the remainder of his term as mayor. Although (and perhaps because) he was not as articulate and commanding as his predecessor, and thanks also to his family's history in the community, Mayor Hogan was perceived as less threatening by the county commissioners. He had been able to build on this personal relationship with the commissioners to further the city's interests in a number of areas. In spite of the greater demands on his time, Hogan continued to serve on the computer board.

The county commissioners traditionally rotated their appointee to the board each year; the current member was Saul Bedford, a former fire district chief who had no strong interest in computers. Bedford and Hogan respected each other, but as computer board members, each advocated his jurisdiction's position, even if this meant an occasional disagreement.

Outside the computer center itself, a key player in the city's automation team was May Dazitrikor. She headed the city's word processing center, which used word processing and phone dictation equipment to prepare much of the city's written communication, including all city council agenda material. Under her capable management, the word processing center had expanded to include central filing, public works contract administration, and a city reference library.

Much of Dazitrikor's time had recently been spent fulfilling her duties as president of a major national professional association. She had told the city manager that she would soon retire to a cottage on Cape Cod, far from the pressures of weekly council agenda preparation.

The case

The city of Acornvue and the City-County Computer Center were facing a number of critical decisions. The manufacturer of the mainframe computer had announced another major change in operating systems. The center could avoid converting all of its programs to the new operating system only if it started to write its own software and abandoned hope of buying future software packages written for its machine. Board director Medana, well aware of the pitfalls of underestimating the effort involved in a major software conversion, had warned the board of the importance of this decision.

At the same time, many of the city's programs were over ten years old, well past the typical life expectancy of software. The software for the financial/accounting system had been patched so many times that the source code, when printed, stood several feet high. The utility billing system worked, but as one programmer put it, it was being "held together with bailing wire and spit." The constant firefighting needed to keep these systems running had taken its toll on employee morale: a programmer and an operator had recently left the center (these positions remained in the budget, but Medana was holding off on filling them).

"Off-the-shelf" software packages that performed the financial/accounting and utility billing functions were available for the mainframe computer. They were more flexible and powerful than anything that could be written in-house at a reasonable cost. These packages were not cheap, however. A financial package would cost between $120,000 and $200,000, which could be split 50-50 by the city and the county. Utility billing and payroll/personnel systems each would cost around $100,000. These packages didn't offer all of the advantages of custom-written in-house programs, but it appeared that they would be adequate if departments were willing to compromise. The computer center would probably have to custom write most of the specialized programs used by the city (building permits, budget preparation, and fleet management).

The cost effectiveness of the mainframe computer itself had come into question. It took a good deal of tending by operators and systems engineers. It did not seem to communicate well with the microcomputers that were quietly proliferating throughout the city. Other cities of Acornvue's size had reported success using minicomputers that cost less than mainframes, ran inexpensive software, and did not require a separate operating staff.

Knowing such decisions had to be made, and fully aware of their importance to the city in terms of both cost and operating effectiveness, Acornvue's city manager, Lucy Mattingly, appointed a staff committee to investigate options for the future of computers in the city. The committee reported the following findings:

1. A network of two or more minicomputers (e.g., one each for the city and the county) would require less staff support from the computer center, possibly eliminating the need for at least two positions in the computer center's budget.
2. A larger selection of "off-the-shelf" software was available for several of the minicomputer brands. The cost for these packages was lower, too: a financial package cost about $40,000. Like mainframe packages, these required more compromising on the part of user departments than would custom in-house programs.
3. A separate minicomputer could be added to the network to support the city's word processing center. This would provide a timely replacement for the aging equipment now used by the center and would allow departments to send documents to and from the center via the network.
4. Many of the minicomputers on the market claimed to offer simple interconnection with departmental microcomputers.
5. The city's one-time cost for converting to a minicomputer environment was estimated at about $382,000 (Figure 1).

Figure 1
Estimated one-
time cost of
conversion to a
minicomputer.

Buyout of existing equipment contracts	$ 58,252
Interim cost of running parallel systems	171,016
Miscellaneous (cables, etc.)	15,000
New applications software (city share)	64,200
In-house software conversion	65,055
Computer center training	3,255
City staff training	5,600
Sale value of mainframe	Negligible
Total	$382,378

6. The new equipment itself could be acquired through a five-year lease-purchase agreement. Once a new system was up and running, annual costs would be approximately $514,000 for the city (this included the lease-purchase payments as well as the city's share of staff and all other operating expenses for the computer center). The current city budget for the computer center was $610,000.

7. A total conversion of hardware and software would be enormously time-consuming and complicated. Some of the simpler COBOL programs could be modified to run on new hardware, but all of the more complex programs would have to be replaced or rewritten. The switchover to new machines would have to be complete within twelve months, since the computer center could not afford to own and operate two parallel systems any longer than this.

8. Separate minicomputers for the city and the county, connected through a network, could theoretically simplify computer center cost allocation, although allocation of overhead costs (e.g., operating staff) might still be difficult. Separate computers would also give the governments more flexibility in dissolving the center if the need ever arose.

Although county staff members did not participate in this analysis, the computer center staff advised Mattingly that the same principles would probably also apply to the county. It was not clear, however, whether the county would weigh decisions on computer investments in the same way as the city. Mattingly and her staff anticipated that the county's elected department heads might view a conversion as a threat to their ability to carry out campaign promises and might argue for continued investment in the existing system, regardless of the cost, since balancing the budget was the commissioners' problem.

Medana personally leaned toward conversion to a minicomputer network (he had run one at the school district), but he made it clear that he would support a decision on any of the possible courses of action.

The decision problem

Lucy Mattingly discussed the forthcoming decision with Mayor Hogan, who told her to make a thorough review of the options. "The council will want a recommendation from you. When the computer board meets, I'll argue whatever position the council takes on this one."

Both Mattingly and Hogan knew that the council had supported staff decisions in technical areas in the past. Both also realized that a bad decision either way would conjure up nightmares of failing financial programs or utility payments stacking up without being processed.

As she sat at her desk reviewing the problem, Mattingly jotted down several facts that might have a bearing on the computer decision:

The computer center occupied an entire building, which the city owned and leased to the center at a negotiated price.

City staff growth had caused some departments to overflow city hall, and they were now scattered in leased space in the downtown area.

The company that manufactured the mainframe computer was known to apply pressure on elected officials who considered buying a competing product.

The engineering department seemed to be building a clandestine network of microcomputers that was isolated from the rest of the city's computers but that apparently was functioning very well.

If the computer center converted to minicomputers, the majority of the center's costs could be tracked separately, providing more accurate data on actual levels of use of the center by each government.

As she considered the decision, Mattingly knew that she would have to address two separate issues in her report to the council:

The first issue was what to do about the existing computer. Should the center retain the mainframe, convert the operating system, and purchase or rewrite the major programs? Should it switch to a minicomputer network and rebuild its software assets from scratch? Or should it continue with the current equipment and operating system and wait for computer equipment to become more powerful and less expensive? Matttingly knew that to answer these questions she would have to do a simple cost-benefit analysis, using the estimates provided by her staff, to calculate the payback period for each of the three options.

The second issue involved the fate of the joint computer center in the event that the minicomputer option was adopted. Should it be dissolved? If so, how would the city proceed in forming its own data processing department? If not, how could the financing agreement be modified to ease intergovernmental friction? How should overhead expenses and year-end fund balances be handled?

Mattingly knew that the organizational and political aspects of this issue were as important as the financial aspects. Would a total conversion of hardware and software put too much stress on the computer center and on the user departments? The cost effectiveness of the minicomputer system might depend on a permanent reduction in computer center staff positions; if so, she knew she would have to advise the council on how these positions would be eliminated. She would also have to assess the nonquantifiable benefits and costs of each alternative.

From a purely technical viewpoint, Mattingly felt, the joint center should be dissolved if minicomputers were introduced. With minicomputers, there would no longer be an economy of scale in machinery. The advantage of sharing off-the-shelf software cost was slight for systems that would be amortized over five years. An independent city computer center could be more responsive to city users and would probably have lower overhead costs. With similar equipment, sharing of information between the city and the county could be continued under a simple agreement, without worrying about who was paying for whose computers. Furthermore, a city computer center would require less space than the joint center, and some of the city staff in outlying areas could be moved into the existing computer center building. (The loss of county lease payments would be more than offset by the elimination of payments on commercially leased space.)

Yet, Mattingly also knew that there were political reasons for not dissolving the center. One was the importance of retaining Medana and his management team. If Medana became the city's data processing director, he would find himself in a more stable political environment, but he would have a smaller staff and computer system and also would risk burning some bridges in the county. He might not be willing to make that trade, and the city certainly couldn't afford to fill the vacant programmer and operator positions. Mattingly could have offered to include the city's word processing department as part of a new data processing department on May Dazitrikor's retirement, but this would have denied a deserving city staffer a promotional opportunity.

To complicate the political issues still further, the council member and the commissioner on the computer board enjoyed their roles. The board offered a convenient source of bargaining chips for more serious intergovernmental negotiations. Mayor Hogan would not be enthusiastic about splitting up his friend Medana's computer operation. And both governments pointed with pride to the center as an example of city-county cooperation.

With a weary sigh, Mattingly gathered together the data and began to formulate her recommendation to the council.

Discussion questions

1. Which should Mattingly make a decision about first: the computer configuration or the continuation of the joint center? Which is more important and should have priority?

2. What methods and assumptions might be used to calculate the payback period for a new computer system? Explain which alternatives you chose and why.

3. Since advances in computer technology occur so rapidly and frequently, how does one know when to make an investment in new hardware? In new software? Is this a good time for Acornvue to make such investments? Why or why not?

4. The decision about the joint computer center appears to pit technological considerations against political ones. Which should take priority in principle? Which should take priority in this situation? Explain.

5. How can a value be assigned to the intergovernmental benefits provided by the joint center? How should those be weighed in the decision equation?

6. What, if any, influence should each of the following have upon the decision: (a) Commissioner Bedford's relative lack of familiarity with computers? (b) the attitude of the elected county department heads? (c) the past track record of the county in assuming its share of the computer center costs? (d) the opinions of May Dazitrikor of the word processing center and other city staff? (e) the personal relationship between Hogan and Medana? (f) the lack of any appreciable resale value for the computer center's existing mainframe? (g) the probability that the members of the city council and the county board will be lobbied intensively by the sales personnel from the company now servicing the mainframe?

7. What alternatives might be proposed to divide the costs of the computer center if the center is to be retained with the existing

mainframe? Evaluate each alternative and indicate which is your preference and why.

8. Should Mattingly initiate a series of staff conferences to explain the pending decision and its possible outcomes? Could she be accused of "playing politics" if she did so?

9. With whom, and for what reasons, should Mattingly consult as she makes her decision?

10. What should Mattingly recommend to the council?

The aftermath

Mattingly's cost-benefit analysis showed that a new minicomputer system would pay for itself in under four years, even leaving out of the calculations the cost of the new software that the city would have to make if it retained the existing mainframe. Thus, she recommended the purchase of the new minicomputer system.

Mattingly used the logic of "if it ain't broke, don't fix it" to recommend that the joint center be continued even though it had in fact outlived its technical usefulness. She also recommended that separate minicomputers be used for city and county business. Such a system would allow each government to budget and pay for only its share of the direct costs. She recommended that overhead, or nonidentifiable, costs be divided between the two governments in the same proportion as their direct cost allocations.

The city council accepted Mattingly's recommendations. In the ensuing computer board meeting, Hogan presented the city's position, Bedford indicated that the city proposal was consistent with the advice the county board had received from the county's computer users, and the computer board agreed to retain the computer center, modify the intergovernmental agreement, and purchase new minicomputers for the county and the city as well as for the city's word processing department.

Final discussion questions

1. For organizations, as for people, too much change can lead to stress. How should the conversion be managed to minimize the stress on the staffs of the city and the computer center? Should the manager's recommendation for change have been different if the city were facing other internal changes at the same time (for example, a shakeup of the financial management staff or a major budget crisis with staff layoffs)?

2. How would the situation and the decision have been different if the county had been managed by a professional administrator with a role similar to that of the city manager? How would this have changed the way the two governments worked out a mutually satisfactory solution?

3. How should Mattingly have changed the recommendation if she had known in advance that the the county would be unwilling to accept her proposal?

4. If the council had decided to terminate its participation in the computer center, what suggestions might Mattingly have offered to the council to make that decision more acceptable to the county and to protect the city from possible adverse public comment and reaction?

Contracting for trash

Scott D. Lazenby

Editor's introduction

This case poses an analytical problem that will face most if not all county and city governments in the next decade: how to find the best (that is, the most cost-efficient and effective) system for collecting residential trash. Solid waste is increasing in volume annually, landfills are nearing their capacity, the public continues to resist higher taxes and garbage collection fees, and recyclable materials must be sorted and collected separately. As a result, virtually every government providing residential sanitation services will be facing decisions nearly identical to the one posed here.

This case also examines a service delivery option that local governments are considering with increasing frequency: contracting with a private firm to provide a public service, in this case the collection of the city's residential trash.

Unlike many other cases, in which human and political factors are at least as important as analytical findings in the decision process, this case presents a problem in which the decision can rest primarily on the results of analysis. The human and political considerations, while present, are secondary to the need to find a collection method that minimizes both long- and short-term costs. Human factors enter into the problem as a secondary consideration: When a new collection system is ultimately selected, how can it be implemented so as to minimize adverse effects on employees?

Case 10
Contracting for trash

Background

The city of Newglade is located in a large metropolitan area and has a population of approximately 100,000. At the time the case unfolds, Newglade faced a problem with the collection of solid waste (garbage). Several different methods of collection were used by communities in the metropolitan area, and Newglade found itself forced to evaluate its present collection system and to consider alternatives.

The case has a cast of characters, as follows:

Charles Veracruz, city manager

Chris Smith, assistant city manager

Thomas H. Moses, Jr., director of public works

Alfred E. Newhouse, budget director

Pat Chamber, administrative assistant, public works

Kay Hernandez, administrative assistant, finance

The case unfolds through the communication among these officials. The memo that launched the development of this case problem summarizes critical elements of the background.

CITY OF NEWGLADE
MEMORANDUM

DATE: May 2
TO: Charles Veracruz, City Manager
FROM: Pat Chamber, Administrative Assistant II
SUBJECT: Status of Residential Sanitation Operations

Per your request, this report provides information on the status of the residential sanitation operation.

Roughly 80 percent of Newglade's population is served by curbside collection of an unlimited number of cans (the other 20 percent of the population lives in apartments or other forms of housing that are served by the city's commercial sanitation operation). Residential collection is twice a week, as mandated by the state—presumably to keep the fly population down. As you know, parks maintenance staff also collects uncontained waste or "loose trash" twice per month.

The city has taken steps to reduce its garbage collection costs. The three-person rear-loading trucks were replaced with two-person manual side-loading packers. These in turn have been gradually replaced with one-person manual side loaders (the operator gets out of the cab to dump the garbage cans into the packer). In spite of the city's average annual population growth of 10 percent, the sanitation staff has decreased from 43 (including supervisors) two years ago to 25 today (22 driver-loaders and 3 supervisors). No staff members were laid off; positions have been either vacated by normal attrition or transferred to other field operations.

The annual cost of operation is now approaching $1.5 million. Salaries and fringe benefit costs account for $956,000; vehicle maintenance and operation accounts for $241,000; landfill and waste disposal charges are $212,000; and lease-purchase payments on equipment are $44,000. These costs are covered in the general fund through taxes; residents are not billed separately for sanitation service, although separate billing is the practice in some of the other cities in the metro area.

While the reduction in personnel has definitely lowered operating costs, the manual operation is not very efficient. The time taken by the driver to jump out of the cab and load the garbage cans adds to the time taken to complete a route. Of equal concern, the manual operation takes a physical toll on the driver-loaders. Last year there were twenty-two industrial insurance accidents that cost the city $18,000.

Field operations staff has done some preliminary investigation of automating residential collection (i.e., using trucks with equipment that picks up trash cans and dumps them mechanically into the truck), and we have reached the conclusion that this option should be pursued. Perhaps the new public works director will have had some experience in this.

Please feel free to contact me if you desire further information.

The case

WHILE YOU WERE OUT

DATE: 5/3   TIME: 12:50
TO C. V.
Mr. Tractar
Of: City Council called
Message: Said he was contacted by owner of Valley Waste Collection, who was upset that city doesn't contract out residential san. and doesn't allow private companies to provide commercial san. service in city. Call him ASAP.

R. L.

FROM THE DESK OF CHARLES J. VERACRUZ

5/3

Tom, here's a project to help you get your feet wet here! Could you and the public works staff look into contracting out residential garbage collection? There's some interest on the part of council.

C. V.

FROM THE DESK OF CHARLES J. VERACRUZ

5/3

Al, please have your budget staff do some analysis on the pros and cons of billing residents directly for garbage collection. Who pays for it now? What would we have to charge? How would this affect residents?

C. V.

Clipping file, Los Diablos Times, 6/14

NEWGLADE LOOKS AT SOCKING RESIDENTS FOR TRASH

NEWGLADE—In a workshop session, the Newglade City Council on Tuesday considered charging residents as much as $10 per month for collection of garbage.

Citing legal limitations on property taxes and political barriers to raising the sales tax rate, city staff proposed a sanitation "user fee" that would make garbage collection self-supporting and free up $1.5 million in general taxes now dedicated to trash collection.

Budget Director Alfred E. Newhouse stated that reducing general fund support for the residential sanitation operation would allow additional resources to be dedicated to police, fire, streets, and other critical city services. The garbage fee would be phased in over a period of several years, according to a staff report from City Manager Charles Veracruz. Collection service would remain the same under the proposal.

Veracruz also noted that the final rate could be as low as $6.00 per month, depending on cost-saving methods now being investigated by the city. The council took no action but referred the matter to the council budget committee.

CITY OF NEWGLADE
MEMORANDUM

DATE: June 21
TO: Charles Veracruz, City Manager
FROM: Al Newhouse, Budget Director
SUBJECT: Follow-up on Workshop on Garbage Fee

Given the circumstances, the press treated our report on the garbage user fee fairly kindly. One thing we didn't highlight in the report is the shift in tax burden that might result from the user fee. Here's some background:

As you know, the city uses several tax sources to fund sanitation and other city services. The most significant local tax is the 1 percent sales tax. This provides $13 million, or 37 percent of general fund revenues. Staff estimates that less than half of this is paid by local residents through normal retail purchases; the majority is paid by builders through their purchases of home and office building materials and by car buyers, many of whom come from neighboring cities to buy from Newglade dealers.

City property tax revenue for operations (i.e., excluding taxes levied for repayment of principal and interest on bonds) amounts to $2.8 million, only 8 percent of general fund revenues. The tax rate for residential property is $0.60 per $1,000 of value (0.6 mills) for the operating levy (the bond levy rate is 0.5 mills). Commercial and industrial properties are taxed at 2.5 times this rate. State property tax limitations prevent the city from increasing the rate for the operating levy.

About 9 percent of revenue comes from development fees, utility franchise fees, and business licenses, and the remaining 46 percent comes from taxes that are collected by the state and distributed to cities on the basis of population.

While it certainly seems equitable to charge residents for service costs they incur, this does seem to shift the burden of funding from the commercial sector (and nonresidents) to the city residential sector. Further, the user fee can't be deducted for federal tax purposes, unlike some local taxes (notably the property tax).

According to economic theory, people make decisions based on how they would be affected financially. Therefore, the "economically rational" voter would oppose a fee that shifts costs away from businesses and would prefer a tax increase. Should we bring this up with the council?

On a related subject, our commercial sanitation operation more than pays for itself. The fund balance is at 50 percent of annual revenue, and the rates have been set lower than those of many of the surrounding cities in order to avoid building up an excessive balance. As a way of holding down the residential fee, we could combine the two operations into a single fund. Commercial sanitation could subsidize residential sanitation and still be competitive with rates charged by private companies for business garbage pickup.

---

* E L E C T R O N I C   M A I L *

INBOX FOR USERNAME NEWHOUSE
FROM USERNAME: VERACRUZ
POSTED: JUNE 25/8:11:01 AM

Al, thanks for the follow-up report—shared it with the mayor last night. He said that "voters are rarely encumbered by concepts of economic rationality"!

C. V.

REPORT ON CONTRACTING FOR SANITATION SERVICES
JULY 6
Thomas H. Moses, Jr., Director of Public Works
Pat Chamber, Administrative Assistant

At the direction of the city manager, the Public Works Department has completed an exhaustive and in-depth study of the merits and implications of contracting with the private sector for the provision of residential and commercial sanitation services. The background of this issue and staff recommendations are contained herein.

Commercial sanitation

Cities use several methods for providing commercial sanitation services. In some areas commercial sanitation is unregulated, and each business is free to choose which private company it will use to collect its refuse. Some cities franchise one or more private haulers. Other cities, including Newglade, provide commercial sanitation as a municipal service, following the same philosophy as for the provision of sanitary sewer service.

Notwithstanding the fact that some larger cities divide their service area into several sectors for contracting out commercial sanitation services, it is felt that in an operating area the size of Newglade's, commercial sanitation can be provided most efficiently by a single operator. Moreover, if municipal overhead costs are kept low, the city will be able to compete effectively with the private sector, which must maintain sufficient rates to provide an adequate profit.

To contract for a service, the city must conduct a number of activities. It must draft, review, and advertise specifications. It must devise a selection process that weighs service quality against cost. It must review bids and check references. Following the award of a bid by the city council, the city must develop a service contract that protects the city against inadequate performance of the service; the contract should also include renewal provisions. Finally, the city must administer the contract, including inspecting the quality of the work, resolving service complaints, and providing contract payments.

Contracting out a service previously provided by the municipality has an impact on existing equipment and staff resources. In the case of commercial sanitation, a portion of the staff could be absorbed by other field operations. The successful bidder could also be required to offer jobs to city staff affected by the transition (although salary and benefit levels could not be guaranteed). The equipment would have to be sold; even if the contractor purchased the equipment, it would be at a depreciated value, thus reducing the city's assets.

The city uses service contracts in custodial and parks maintenance services. At one point, the city had to cancel the custodial contract because of poor performance, at a cost to the city of $8,000 for a new contract. The higher administrative costs and potential loss of service quality are felt to be outweighed by the reduced labor cost inherent in the privately provided service.

Residential sanitation

Provision of residential waste collection follows the same patterns as for commercial sanitation, except that municipal provision is more common for residential than for commercial sanitation. Service quality is of potentially greater political concern because of the considerable interaction between the service providers and residents/voters. Prompt and courteous service, including such things as careful handling of waste containers, is a critical component of municipal residential sanitation service.

Recommendations

1. Seek bids for the provision of commercial sanitation service under contract, and compare the bid costs with city costs to determine whether the city should continue to deliver this service.
2. It is felt that current residential operations are competitive with comparable service provided by the private sector, particularly if collection is automated. Service reductions will not be tolerated by residents, especially if a user fee is created, and the Public Works Department does not recommend contracting for this service.

---

* E L E C T R O N I C   M A I L *

INBOX FOR USERNAME NEWHOUSE
FORWARDED BY USERNAME: VERACRUZ
POSTED: JULY 10/2:05:01 PM

FORWARDING COMMENT:
Al, Thought you might be interested in this message. . .

C. V.

FORWARDED MESSAGE:
TO USERNAME:VERACRUZ
FROM USERNAME: MOSES
POSTED: JULY 10/11:51:20 AM

It has come to my attention that the budget director has proposed combining residential sanitation financing with the commercial sanitation fund. This is totally unacceptable. These must be kept separate to allow separate tracking by the operating managers and to avoid cross subsidies between the services. Charles, you must understand that I will not tolerate this kind of interference in the functioning of the Public Works Department.

—Thomas H. Moses, Jr., Director of Public Works

The decision problem

CITY OF NEWGLADE
MEMORANDUM

DATE: July 24
TO: Chris Smith, Assistant City Manager
FROM: Charles Veracruz, City Manager
SUBJECT: The Case Problem

Chris, I need your help in evaluating the city's options in residential sanitation. I will give you my file on the subject; please see other staff as necessary to gather the information you need for your analysis.

Specifically, please analyze and give me your recommendations on the following:

1. Should the residential sanitation operation be automated? What would be the savings to the city in automating? Can you give me an idea of the payback period, net present value, or some other cost-benefit measure? If we do automate, should it be done at once, or phased in over time? How would we handle the reduced staff needs?

2. As an alternative to automating, should we seek bids for contracting out the provision of residential sanitation services? Again, how would we handle the human resource issues? How would we guard against a decline in service?

3. Under either scenario, how should residential sanitation be financed— i.e., should we continue using general funds or establish a user fee? If the latter, should it be phased in? If user fees are initiated, should the residential and commercial operations be combined in a single fund?

Please summarize your conclusions in a memo that I could share with the mayor.

MEETING NOTES

7/26

Meeting attendees: P. Chamber, K. Hernandez, C. Smith

Garbage Collection Assumptions:

Sixteen manual collection routes for the next two years (1 person per truck), with a route added every other year for population growth. Additional backup labor pool of 6 (to cover absences, training, etc.) for an initial total of 22 driver-collectors. 2.5 FTE supervisors (1 split with commercial san.). Automation would reduce initial routes to 13 and the backup labor pool to 5.

Assume inflation factor of 5 percent per year.

Labor costs (including overtime, uniforms, etc.) are $29,600 per driver and $32,000 per supervisor. Add 30 percent for fringe benefit costs.

Assume workers' comp (industrial accident) insurance at current $18,000, proportional to number of drivers and inflation. Figure workers' comp will be one-quarter of this amount under automated system and also reduced in proportion to the reduction in drivers.

Both manual and automated trucks cost $90,000 each. The acquisition schedule for the current fleet of trucks is to replace two in 1985, one in 1986, two in 1987, and so on at the rate of three trucks every two years. The current fleet could be sold for roughly $576,000 total (assumes trucks have depreciated 50 percent on a straight-line basis and that the city would face a 20 percent price reduction in the used truck market).

New containers for the automated routes would cost $60 each. Would need enough for 80,000 population, assuming 3.5 people per household.

Vehicle operation and maintenance costs are now $241,000 and are assumed to be proportional to the number of routes and inflation.

A new fleet of automated trucks could be financed through a lease-purchase contract. Assume a ten-year term and 10 percent interest rate (annual payment is 0.16 times purchase price).

For net present value calculation, use a discount rate of 10 percent.

Discussion questions

1. What should Assistant Manager Smith recommend to the city manager? (To assist him in his work, Smith prepared a worksheet summarizing the relevent data. That worksheet is presented on the next page as Table 1. The last several rows, containing the calculations on which the recommendation should be based, need to be completed.) Complete Table 1 and prepare Smith's recommendation in detail, including the reaction Smith should present to both automation and privatization, and include a justification for the recommendation in terms of both short- and long-term considerations.

2.   City staff in Newglade analyzed the questions of automation and privatization simultaneously. Was this the best way to proceed, or should these issues have been addressed separately? Give reasons for your answer.

3.   Was the mayor correct in his assessment that voters "are rarely encumbered by concepts of economic rationality" when considering tax and service fee questions? What role should these considerations play in the decision being made here?

Table 1

RESIDENTIAL SANITATION AUTOMATION WORKSHEET
Prepared by C. SMITH   Date: August 6

	Year 1	Year 2	Year 3	Year 4	Year 5
MANUAL SYSTEM					
Labor costs:					
Inflation factor	1.00	1.05	1.10	1.16	1.22
# Routes	16	16	17	17	18
# Drivers	22	22	23	23	24
# Supervisors	2.50	2.50	2.50	2.50	2.50
Labor cost	$950,560	$998,088	$1,090,417	$1,144,937	$1,248,957
Workers' comp.	$18,000	$18,900	$20,747	$21,784	$23,868
Equipment costs:					
# Trucks purchased	2	1	2	1	2
Cost (× inflator)	$180,000	$94,500	$198,450	$104,186	$218,791
Vehicle O&M	$241,000	$253,050	$282,309	$296,424	$329,554
Total oper. cost	$1,389,560	$1,364,538	$1,591,923	$1,567,332	$1,821,170
AUTOMATED SYSTEM					
Labor costs:					
# Routes	13	13	14	14	14
# Drivers	18	18	19	19	19
# Supervisors	2.50	2.50	2.50	2.50	2.50
Labor cost	$796,640	$836,472	$920,720	$966,756	$1,015,094
Workers' comp.	$3,682	$3,866	$4,285	$4,499	$4,724
Equipment costs:					
Vehicle O&M	$195,813	$205,603	$232,490	$244,114	$256,320
Subtotal, oper. cost	$996,134	$1,045,941	$1,157,494	$1,215,369	$1,276,137
New equipment costs:					
# Trucks purchased	16				
Cost, new trucks	$1,440,000				
Salvage, manual trks	($576,000)				
New containers	$1,371,429				
Net equipment cost	$2,235,429				
Lease/purchase cost	$363,806	$363,806	$363,806	$363,806	$363,806

Annual savings, automated system, before new equipment investment
Annual savings $_____ $_____ $_____ $_____ $_____

Cum. payback period   _____   _____   _____   _____   _____
Simple payback period: _____years

Net annual savings, including lease/purchase cost of new equipment
Net annual savings $_____ $_____ $_____ $_____ $_____
Discount factor   _____   _____   _____   _____   _____
Discounted savings $_____ $_____ $_____ $_____ $_____
Net present value over 5 years: $_____

4. As the city manager, how would you have responded to the memo of July 10 in which the public works director opposed consideration of a merger of commercial and residential sanitation services? Would you include a combined system in your policy recommendation?

5. Under what circumstances would it be desirable to implement an automated collection system immediately? If such a change should be made, should the entire system be automated at once or gradually over time? Upon what considerations would you make such a decision?

6. Questions of privatization involve both ideological preferences and objective, analytical considerations. List the ideological and analytical considerations. Under what circumstances should ideological considerations weigh more heavily than dispassionate analysis in making such decisions? What factors should weigh most heavily in this decision, and why?

7. How should long-run and short-run cost and savings considerations be weighted in this decision? Are elected officials and professional administrators likely to agree on the answer to this question? If not, how should administrators handle differences in perspective?

The aftermath

Jean More, Mayor   *Chris Smith, City Manager*

CITY OF NEW GLADE
"Commerce, Residents, and Prosperity"

July 5 [five years later]
Mr. Jay Sellick
Assistant City Manager
City of Acornvue

Dear Jay:

It was good hearing from you. I've enclosed some of the material you asked for on the automation of our residential garbage collection operation. As the analysis summarized in the spreadsheet shows, the investment has been marginally cost effective. Strangely enough, the initial material presented to the city council by the public works staff assumed a productivity increase of only 15 percent, and the automation decision didn't appear to make financial sense, at least within the first five years (this fact was buried in an appendix to the staff report). The most surprising cost turned out to be for the roll-out containers that had to be bought for all households; it was far greater than the cost of the new trucks.

Nevertheless, it seemed to make intuitive sense to automate, and we have in fact seen a 25- to 30-percent increase in the productivity of the drivers. Lease-purchase costs are now reaching $700,000 per year (we ended up using a five-year term), and a manual operation would still be cheaper, but once those containers are paid off, we should start saving money.

Public works phased in the automated system over four years in order to get more use from some of the newer manual trucks and to make it easier to absorb the extra drivers (and partly to disguise the high start-up cost of the conversion). The residents seem to like the larger containers; and, as important as real cost savings, the automated system does seem more efficient to the voters.

One thing the citizens haven't been crazy about is the rate increases—they've been phased in over the past four years to the current rate of $7.50. This is supposedly the self-sufficient level, but in fact the operation doesn't pay its full share of city overhead costs (e.g., accounting, personnel), so it's still partly tax supported. The fee is included in the water bill and comes on top of water/sewer rates that have been creeping up. The net effect is a voter backlash that is preventing the council from doing anything with general tax revenues. To compound the problem, larger than expected operating deficits in the sanitation operation have drawn down general fund reserves. Maybe Veracruz had the right idea when he moved on after starting all these user fees!

The public works director, Moses, got his way in most aspects of the sanitation policy issues. The city never attempted to contract for residential sanitation service. The bids for commercial sanitation were rejected on the assumption that city costs were comparable. The analysis done by public works underestimated the cost of city overhead support and ignored taxes or franchise fees that a private hauler would pay.

Ironically, the state now prohibits cities from having an exclusive franchise for commercial sanitation. In his eagerness to run his operations like "businesses," Moses is pushing to compete with the national solid waste firms. The operation will probably have to rely on some tax support (if indirectly through understated overhead payments) to undercut the private commercial sanitation rates. In an interesting reversal, public works is now proposing to combine the residential and commercial sanitation funds in order to protect the lucrative apartment collection operation from competition.

It's sometimes easy for the entrepreneurial city to lose sight of the fact that its primary mission isn't to be a business but to serve its citizens.

Hope this is helpful. Look forward to seeing you at the ICMA conference this fall!

Sincerely,

Chris Smith
City Manager

Final discussion questions

1. Why would a city council or county board want to continue to deliver residential garbage service (assuming a private contractor is available) when citizens seem reluctant to pay either the taxes or the user fees necessary to support it?

2. Suppose you were the mayor or manager of a city or county that operated a nonexclusive commercial sanitation service, and a major national company priced its service so low that the city could not compete. Would you recommend contracting for its services? Would your course of action be different if you had reason to believe that the national company was underpricing its service in order to establish a monopoly so it could later drive prices up?

3. Some government agencies offset tax revenues by engaging in entrepreneurial activities such as golf pro shops, library gift shops, or restaurants in historic buildings. Is such competition with businesses, especially local taxpaying businesses, in the best interest of voters? Can a government make a profit in areas where private businesses do not operate? What are some examples?

Moving the multiservice center

Jack Manahan

Editor's introduction

The first case in this section posed a question in which the findings of analysis were subordinated to political and behavioral considerations; the second case dealt with a problem in which analytical findings were the primary basis for decision making. This third case is a synthesis; the question of where the county should relocate one of its multiservice centers pits political considerations against analytical (empirical) ones and, in the process, poses the ultimate ethical dilemma for an analyst.

Simply put, this case explores the appropriate role of the analyst in the decision-making process. The focal point is a conflict between the solution desired by local politicians and the solution found to be most cost-effective by competent analysis. Caught in the middle are the county administrator and an analyst from the county's management and budget office. Furthermore, the analyst does not agree with the strategy favored by her boss.

The result is a decision problem of substantial complexity. In addition to the relationship between the administrator and the county board, and between the administrator and the analyst, the case also focuses on the intergovernmental relationship between the county, which must relocate its multiservice center, and the city in which the center is currently located. Also involved is a concern that the center be located conveniently for the county residents who will be served by it, particularly the poor, who need easy access to the human service offices located there.

Most important, however, the case probes a contemporary question of democratic theory: How should the results of empirical policy analysis, fashioned to maximize public values regarding cost and service effectiveness in the long term, be reconciled with the policy preferences of elected officials who, although their vision may be focused on short-run political considerations, still have ultimate responsibility for policy decisions? Similarly, the case questions the role of the analyst as a participant in the politics of policy making.

Case 11
Moving the multiservice center

Background

Madison County is an urban/rural county of over 300,000 in a major metropolitan area of the country. About 80 percent of the population lives in two dozen incorporated cities, mostly in the southwest part of the county. The remaining citizens reside in rural areas to the east and the north. At the time of this case, the county had enjoyed excellent growth for several years, and the local economy had been a bright spot in an otherwise depressed state economy. Population growth had been explosive, and the county was rapidly becoming more urbanized. In addition to the courthouse in the county seat and a smaller satellite office building in the urbanized southwest part of the county, the government operated several "multiservice centers" designed to bring county services to citizens in various parts of the county.

At these multiservice centers, citizens could pay taxes, register vehicles, borrow a book from the county's excellent library system, and access various human services programs provided by county offices. Two multiservice centers in the more populated areas of the county provided office space for some staff of the county department of human services and aging, other state and local agencies, and nonprofit organizations involved in the delivery of human services.

The first multiservice center was opened ten years earlier in the city of Oakridge, one of the oldest cities in the southwest part of the county. The center, which was known as the Southwest center, contained offices for the county's housing authority and housing counseling programs as well as a remote office for the state's welfare department and offices of three local social service agencies. The state welfare department and the social service agencies sublet from the county. The Southwest center was located in a light-industry and warehouse area near the junction of an interstate highway and a major state highway. The rent the county paid was very low, about $2.50 per square foot annually, owing in part to the fact that the county had paid the cost of initial interior construction and finishing. Newer space in a better location would cost four to five times the current rental expense.

Although the space was more than adequate when the center opened, it had now been badly overcrowded for several years. Moreover, the location was difficult for visitors and clients to find, and flooding and water damage often occurred when the nearby creek overflowed during periods of heavy rain. County staff had hoped for some time not to renew the lease, scheduled to expire at the end of the current year. After a tour by the county commission in the spring, the staff was directed to begin looking for a new location for the Southwest center.

A second multiservice center had been opened in the city of Clearview, about four miles west of Oakridge. Many citizens who previously might have visited the Southwest center had begun to use the Clearview center instead. The Clearview center is in an elementary school building that had been purchased and renovated by the city of Clearview. Despite the nearness of the two centers, the city had persuaded the county commission to cooperate in the Clearview center's management and operation in a spirit of "intergovernmental cooperation."

The case

Sally Adams was the analyst in the county's management and budget office who was assigned to work with the Department of Human Services and Aging on finding a new location for the Southwest multiservice center. Before a request for proposal (RFP) for rental space could be issued, a key decision had to be made regarding the general location of the new center.

The staff did not want to move the Southwest center any closer to the Clearview center, because this could result in underutilization of both centers. Because the county's population growth seemed to be occurring to the east and the north, it made some sense to move the Southwest center farther east. However, upon learning that the county might move its center from Oakridge, the city's Republican mayor accused the Oakridge district's Democratic county commissioner of wanting to move the center because the mayor happened to be supporting the commissioner's Republican opponent in the upcoming election. Regardless of whether or not this was true, the incumbent county commissioner could not afford the perception that he was failing to represent his district and the cities in it by endorsing the removal of county services. The commissioner called Gerald Davis, the county administrator, who then called Adams. Against her better judgment, Adams decided that it would be best to try to relocate the center within the city limits of Oakridge.

While Adams was drafting the RFP for rental space, Davis stopped by her office and related a telephone conversation he had just had with Harry Sheppler, the Oakridge city administrator. Sheppler had called concerning a potential location only two blocks from the Southwest multiservice center's current location. The building he proposed was a three-story native-stone elementary school building. It had been built in the 1920s, and an addition was constructed shortly after World War II. The school district had abandoned the building twenty years earlier. Since then, it had been the home of a trade school, a community college, a preschool, and, most recently, a Christian private school.

Sheppler told Davis that the city council wanted to purchase the building and propose that the county lease the building from the city for use as the new location for the Southwest multiservice center. The council was most anxious to ensure the continued presence of a multiservice center in the city. Davis told Adams that he was aware that the mayor of Oakridge had contacted the chairman of the county commission about the idea.

Davis asked Adams to analyze the proposal to see if the idea was feasible. Her analysis (Table 1) showed that renovation would be costly and that in order for Oakridge to purchase and renovate the school building, the city would have to charge the county about $3.00 per square foot more than the going rate for first-class commercial space in the area. In addition, the building was not energy efficient, and operating costs would be high. After reviewing Adams' analysis, Davis asked her to run another set of numbers, this time assuming that the county would pay 50 percent of the cost of renovation and all of the costs of making the building accessible to the handicapped, including installation of an elevator. If the county contributed funds for some of the renovation costs, Oakridge could charge the county less. Davis said that it might be possible to use the county's Community Development Block Grant funds for some of the renovation costs, but he was not certain. Adams challenged the county administrator's assumptions: In her opinion, the county had no business subsidizing a project such as this. Either the project was feasible or it was not—strictly on the basis of the numbers. She told Davis that she believed he was trying to aid the county commission in justifying a course of action that was not in the best interests of the county.

Davis was taken aback by Adams' reaction to his suggestion. He attempted to explain to her that both of them worked for the county commission, that the commissioners were anxious to work with the city in this matter, and that every opportunity to advance the goals of their elected superiors should be explored. He noted that objective analysis of data was certainly an important part of policy making, but he reminded her that all analysis is designed to serve the needs of elected policymakers and that those policymakers were certainly entitled to set the values or assumptions on which the analysis was based.

Davis concluded the discussion by suggesting that Adams rethink her reaction and get back to him.

The decision problem

Adams felt strongly about her position. Like all local governments, the county worked on a tight budget, and spending more money than necessary on an office lease simply to satisfy the city's political leaders seemed to her both unnecessary and unwise. Besides, she reasoned, the county had already made a gesture of goodwill to the city by examining the school site and doing a cost analysis.

Table 1   Original cost
analysis of alternative
sites.

Option 1. City purchases and renovates school building for lease to county. Building is 65 years old, 15,000 sq. ft., three stories. Exterior is native stone; interior is lath/plaster with oak flooring. Heating is provided by a natural-gas, gravity-flow furnace. No central air conditioning; some rooms have window units.

Cost of building		$350,000	
Estimated renovation costs			
Architecture & engineering	$35,000		
Interior walls & ceilings	70,000		
Floor coverings	30,000		
Electrical	10,000		
Plumbing	10,000		
Heating & ventilation	30,000		
Parking, exterior	40,000		
Handicap accessibility	125,000		
Total		350,000	
Total to be financed by city		700,000	
First-year debt payment to be amortized in lease (level principal payments, 10-year bonds at 8.5% interest)		129,500	($8.63/sq.ft.)
Operating costs			
Utilities @ $4.00/sq.ft.	60,000		
Janitorial service @ $720/mo.	8,640		
Maintenance @ $1.50/sq.ft.	22,500		
Total		91,140	
Total annual costs to county		$220,640	($14.71/sq.ft.)

Option 2. County leases other commercial space. Under a typical commercial lease, the landlord provides building maintenance, but the tenant provides janitorial service. Any renovation required is negotiable, but the landlord will usually provide moderate finish-out to meet tenant needs.

Estimated cost of leasing 15,000 sq.ft. of retail space in the area @ $9.75 per sq.ft.		$146,250	
Operating costs			
Janitorial service @ $720/mo.	$8,640		
Utilities @ $1.50/sq.ft.	22,500		
Total		31,140	($11.83/sq.ft.)
Total annual costs to county		$177,390	

Adams also felt that, with population growth in the county occurring in the north and the east, any decision to keep the multiservice center in Oakridge was already a questionable accommodation to local politics. She believed that an optimum site for the center's relocation would be farther north and east of the city, farther from the Clearview center and closer to the new residential areas.

In short, Adams felt that, for reasons of both cost and service accessibility, the proposed school location was not in the best interest of the county or its residents.

On the other hand, Adams also recognized the validity of the point that Davis was trying to make. She understood the political nature of the county government; she recognized that the members of the county commission were elected by the voters and thus felt a responsibility for determining what would be in the best interest of the county. She also recognized that it was reasonable for county officials to desire to cooperate with Oakridge in this project. The proposed building was old, but an adaptive reuse of an old building with unique architecture could benefit the city in many ways.

Adams reminded herself that analysts and administrators function in a representative political environment and that, as a result, they frequently must deal with what *is* rather than what, in their opinion, *should be*. She knew that it is neither unusual nor always bad for governing bodies to pursue goals that the staff does not find important.

Adams also believed that governing bodies tend to emphasize short-range considerations in their decision making and that it is the responsibility of staff to inject a long-term perspective into policy deliberations. In this case, she felt sure, the long-term needs of the county dictated that the multiservice center be located farther north and east than the city of Oakridge.

It was the cost of the project that Adams found most difficult to justify. Why should the county pay a rental cost for the renovated school building that would be as much as 16 percent higher than the cost of regular commercial space— particularly if such space could be found in a location that would better serve the long-term needs of the county? If the city felt that the building, with its architecture, was valuable, the city should subsidize the project and not expect a subsidy from the county. The idea of a county subsidy for the renovation made absolutely no sense to her at all.

Adams thought of Davis' problem. She knew that the county administrator was charged with carrying out the will of the county commission. Should he then feel obligated to justify what the commission wanted to do, even with an analysis that might be based on limited information? Did he have a responsibility to justify the commissioners' preferred course of action, or should his goal be to assist them in determining the best course of action in this situation? Was an ethical question involved if the county administrator was supporting a decision that would benefit the city at the expense of the county?

Adams also had to think about her own situation. What was the proper relationship between an analyst and the county administrator? Was the question of ethics a problem only for the administrator, or was it a problem for her, too? Did her responsibility end when she expressed her views to him, or did she have a responsibility to pursue the issue further? These questions had personal repercussions as well. Her refusal to do what Davis had requested could result in disciplinary action.

For Adams, the situation appeared to be lose-lose. If she did not produce the new analysis, she would be insubordinate. If she produced a new analysis that showed the new option to be still too expensive, Davis might view her as uncooperative at best, or, worse, as a part of the problem itself.

At a minimum, Adams decided, she should do the analysis that Davis requested. It would be easy to do, and it just might produce results that would surprise her and support what the commissioners wanted. Still, there was a risk. If her new cost figures were an improvement over the old ones, Davis and the county commissioners would undoubtedly be even less inclined to listen to her objections to the proposal.

When she finished the analysis of Davis' proposal (Table 2), she knew her

Table 2   Revised cost analysis of school building site.

Option 3: Option 1 with county participation in financing renovation. Assumptions:
1. The county would sign a five-year lease for the building with a five-year option.
2. The county would pay 50 percent of the cost of renovation and all of the costs of making the building accessible to the handicapped, including installation of an elevator.

Cost of building		$350,000
Estimated renovation costs		
Architecture & engineering	$ 35,000	
Interior walls & ceilings	70,000	
Floor coverings	30,000	
Electrical	10,000	
Plumbing	10,000	
Heating & ventilation	30,000	
Parking, exterior	40,000	
Handicap accessibility	125,000	
Total		350,000
Total project costs		700,000
Less costs paid directly by county		
Handicap accessibility	125,000	
50% of all other renovation	112,500	
Total		237,500
Total to be financed by city		462,500
First-year debt payment to be amortized in lease (level principal payments, 10-year bonds at 8.5% interest)		84,312 ($5.62/sq.ft.)
Operating costs		
Utilities @ $4.00/sq.ft.	60,000	
Janitorial @ $720/mo.	8,640	
Maintenance @ $1.50/sq.ft.	22,500	
Total		91,140
Total annual cost to county		$175,452 ($11.70/sq.ft.)

Note: In addition, the county would incur $220,000 of one-time costs for renovation of the building. These costs would have to be taken from the county's contingency funds.

worst fears had been realized. The annual cost to the county would be just under the cost of commercial space, but the county would still have to provide $220,000 up front in renovation costs—it would still have to pay a premium to rent space in a sixty-year-old building. The county would still be subsidizing the city under this option but at figures that might be attractive to the commissioners. Adams felt that the $220,000 this option required could be better spent in other ways that would enhance human services or community development in the community.

As a professional dedicated to the public interest, she felt she had a moral obligation to try to sell her position, and her first set of numbers (Table 1), to Davis. She asked herself whether her obligation extended beyond that. Sally Adams had to chart a course of action for herself.

Discussion questions

1. If you were Adams, would you have objected to Davis' suggestion that the county contribute to the renovation costs? How would your response have varied, if at all, from hers? Why?

2. During the course of making her decision, Adams asked herself some basic questions about the role of the analyst. Did her responsibility end when she reported her findings to Davis, or did she have a responsibility to the public to see that her data were used to support sound public policies? Is there an ethical question involved? Explain your view.

3. Would your answer to question 2 have been different if the marginal difference in cost between option 2 (bottom of Table 1) and option 3 (Table 2) had been $5 million rather than $220,000? What dollar figure would justify a different response?

4. How, if at all, should Davis' and Adams' actions be affected by the fact that two different constituencies and two different groups of elected officials—the city and the county—are involved in this decision? Does "promoting the public interest" mean that Davis and Adams should be concerned for the interest of the city, or just for the interest of the county? How does the fact that the city's residents are also county residents affect your answer? Explain your reasoning.

5. To what extent does the county government have a responsibility to promote the well-being of the city? How should this responsibility affect the way in which Davis responds to the county commissioners?

6. In her reasoning, Adams gave no consideration to the quality of either the long- or the short-term relationship between the city and the county. To what extent should this consideration be relevant? How should Adams factor this consideration into her decision?

7. If you were Adams, how would you resolve your questions? What course of action would you take on the matter?

The aftermath

To encourage the county to leave the Southwest multiservice center in Oakridge, the city council did try to purchase the school building.

Adams decided that she should first "go by the book" and attempt to influence Davis' thinking about the alternatives. She was successful in persuading him to show both sets of figures to the county commission. A discussion followed in which the commissioners attempted to determine which set of figures to use, and thus what kind of commitment the county should make to the use of the building. From the discussion it became evident that, although the idea of renovating the school building was attractive for a variety of reasons, the costs outweighed the benefits to the county. When the Oakridge City Council understood that the costs would be considered excessive by the county, it was willing to settle for a county promise to search only within the city limits for alternative sites.

The RFP process turned up several potential locations in Oakridge. A convenient location in a shopping center, on a bus line, was selected. The new site had more than the amount of space needed by the county, but the additional space was quickly leased to other human service agencies. As a result, the net increased cost to the county was less than anticipated.

Final discussion questions

1. In retrospect, did Adams overestimate the seriousness of the situation facing her? If so, should she have anticipated this? How? If not, why not?

2. In a similar situation, what arguments would you have presented to Davis to persuade him to support your position, or at least to submit both sets of figures?

3. If Davis had not agreed to present both sets of figures to the county commissioners, what should Adams have done at that point?

4. If you were Davis, caught between the desires of the commissioners and a strong stand taken by a valued subordinate, how would you have handled the matter? When, if ever, is it appropriate to discipline a subordinate who is acting on a perceived matter of principle?

5. If the county commission had decided to go ahead with the school building renovation and lease, would Adams have been justified in "leaking" information about the decision to the press? Why or why not? If she had done so, what, if any, response should Davis have made to such a "leak"?

6. Under what circumstances, if any, would one government (e.g., a county) be justified in pursuing a higher-cost alternative in order to accommodate the needs or interests of another government (e.g., a city)? Explain the rationale behind your answer.

7. Did Davis act appropriately in carrying out the wishes of the county commission even in the face of contrary analytical data? How should an administrator act when there is a conflict between such data and the preferences of elected officials?

8. Under what circumstances is it appropriate for a government to proceed with a course of action even if that action is not the lowest-cost alternative for achieving a particular goal?

Part six:
Personnel
and labor
relations

Introduction to part six: Personnel and labor relations

Management theorists are fond of proclaiming that administration and management are generic functions, that they are the same in any kind of organization. Nothing could be further from the truth. While technologies might be similar—computer programs for keeping personnel records might work equally well in corporate and government agencies, for example—and while human behavior patterns tend to be the same from organization to organization within in a given culture, the context in which administration occurs is not the same everywhere. The difference is particularly marked when public-sector administration is compared with private-sector administration.

A good example is the field of personnel administration and labor relations. Human nature in public and private sectors might be the same; both need rules and regulations to govern personnel practices; and both must work with employee organizations as well as with individual employees. But public accountability requires that rules must be applied much more stringently in the public sector; many public-sector personnel matters, such as salary schedules, must be made public; public-sector labor relations must be conducted in an atmosphere charged with political as well as economic consequences; and public employees hold a political trump card—the ability to vote their bosses out of office—that has no private-sector counterpart.

Part Six demonstrates these unique characteristics of public-sector personnel management even as it provides a flavor of the kinds of personnel decisions that confront the local government manager. The first case, for example, poses two common challenges: fulfilling a commitment to affirmative action and designing a better fit between an employee's capabilities and the organization's needs. In trying to accomplish these goals, a local administrator finds herself faced with the need to deal with personality conflicts as well as stereotypes and prejudices. But the case has political overtones as well: The employee in question has connections that limit the supervisor's effective discretion in decision making.

The second case focuses on problems commonly found in the administration of a union contract. In this case, the task is to decide how the contract applies to an employee whose job involves elements of both management and labor. Even a decision on that question does not settle the matter, however, for still to be resolved are questions concerning just compensation and the managerial component of the job. While these issues are pending, the focus of concern transfers to questions of job classification. The case, in short, is full of the kinds of issues that fill a personnel officer's life with challenges and headaches.

But if that case is tough, the next is even tougher. It involves questions of sexual preference in a police department, the line between personal and official behavior, and whether an employee can do too good a job. In particular, it raises the question of how a local manager should reconcile these questions as they apply to one individual. Here, too, the unique nature of the local public service comes into play: All of these questions have to be resolved under the glare of public scrutiny. Privacy rights are easy to overlook when allegations of misconduct are made publicly. Citizens may demand a course of action that poses a real conflict for the local manager, who may have to choose between fairness to the employee and responsiveness to legislative concern and public opinion.

But the goldfish bowl of public personnel administration is most clearly demonstrated in the last case, in which the manager must act against the backdrop of an intense, angry, and occasionally violent labor confrontation between local management and the city's police officers and firefighters. This case affords an excellent demonstration of the fact that life is not always either fair or reasonable in public management. The employee demands come just after, not just before, the adoption of the new budget and the approval of a new tax levy. The public opposes higher taxes, but the firefighters are able to win significant public sympathy for their demands for higher wages. Caught in the middle, the public managers must try to resolve an untimely dispute, find new moneys in an already tight budget, avoid mistakes that would cost them council support, and hold true to the council's desire not to enter into negotiations with employee groups. Not surprisingly, their first choice of a solution, contracting with the private sector for fire protection services, sparks political opposition. Their second choice raises problems within their own administrative leadership corps.

Whoever said that the life of a public manager would be easy?

12 Affirmatively managing Helen

Mary Timney Bailey

Editor's introduction

Affirmative action is often equated with the recruitment of women and minorities into professional positions in an organization, but, as this case points out, there is much more to it than that. An equally important part of affirmative action, and indeed of any good personnel system, is to utilize individual employees to the maximum advantage of both the employee and the organization.

That is the challenge in this case—the challenge to administrative leadership to secure maximum benefit from a nonproductive but competent employee who has the potential to make important contributions to her department. The task is made more difficult both by the employee's lack of finesse in her dealings with other people and by constraints against her dismissal. Since those constraints are political, the case also explores the nature of administrative leadership in a political setting.

The fact that the employee in question is a woman should be incidental to the larger question of personnel management. In a society emphasizing affirmative action principles in its movement toward equality in the workplace, however, that fact cannot be ignored. Thus the case also involves the problem of fitting a professional woman into an agency that has traditionally employed only men and in which male prejudices and stereotypes still abound.

The management challenge in the case, then, involves more than just managing affirmative action efforts; it involves educating other employees—in this case, men—who must learn to work with the woman and abandon sexist patterns of behavior.

The case thus involves a multiplicity of issues in organization theory and human resource management.

Case 12
Affirmatively managing Helen

Background

Rusty City is an aging industrial city with a population of about half a million and a strong-mayor form of government. Since the 1930s, it has been dominated politically by the Democratic party. Today, only remnants of the once-powerful machine remain. In recent years, the party bosses have been embarrassed by members of their own party running successful independent campaigns against the party's endorsed candidates. This not only has created stress throughout the party organization but also has diminished government effectiveness. Successful candidates have found themselves constantly battling potential opponents in their own party, thus reducing their ability to perform effectively in their elected offices.

The city has a modern personnel system, but pockets of patronage remain. All department heads and assistant administrators are appointed by and serve at the pleasure of the mayor. Special positions can be created by the mayor with the consent of the city council. Certain departments, particularly those with a large component of laborers, also tend to have a substantial number of ward chairpersons and party workers. Several of the supervisors of these departments were hired as a result of political patronage. The mayor's office and the city council have been controlled exclusively by Democrats for more than fifty years.

The case

Mayor Sam Hartman, a lifelong Democrat, came to office after running an independent campaign against the party's candidate. Once in office, he set out to rebuild bridges with the party faithful. He was approached shortly after the election by a powerful ward chairperson who asked him to create a position for her daughter, Helen Miller, a mechanical engineer with a graduate degree in energy management. Miller herself had never been interested in politics, but she was having a hard time finding a job in the city and didn't want to leave her family. Mayor Hartman saw the opportunity to achieve several objectives at the same time: soothe some ruffled feathers in the party, demonstrate his concern for energy conservation, and employ a qualified woman at a mid-level position. It seemed to be a golden opportunity, and Hartman happily grabbed it.

The city's engineers were scattered throughout various departments in the organization. There were no other female engineers at the time, although there had been some female student interns in earlier years. Miller was initially placed in the public works department. No one knew exactly what an energy engineer should do, but the mayor was sure that the department could identify an appropriate role for her. Still, the men in the office were more than a little uncertain about how to interact with what they perceived as a diminutive, fashionably dressed, rather attractive young woman.

Given little direction, Miller tried to define her job. She began to develop a library of energy books and energy management journals. There were many good ideas in these publications, and Miller tried to share them with the other engineers. But these were new ideas that didn't fit the practiced ways of doing things in the department. Nobody seemed to care very much about energy management. They just left her to do her little projects.

Month after month, Miller waited for recognition that never came. Her frustration mounted during budget-preparation time, when she failed to get approval for pet projects. Even though she had calculations that could prove that the projects would pay for themselves, she could never convince her superiors that the projects should be given priority. On top of this, she was very uncomfortable in the office. There were no private offices in the department, only cubicles. Her cubicle was located near the director's, and he was a cigar smoker. Finally, unable to stand it any longer, Miller sued the director for polluting her air space.

Miller's next assignment was in the parks department, which managed and maintained about half of the city's buildings. The engineers there were primarily civil engineers, who, along with a few architects, were responsible for designing recreation centers and swimming pools. They didn't really know what an energy engineer should do, but it seemed a good idea to have her expertise available for consultation, at least.

Now that she was in a department with responsibility for specific buildings, Miller assumed that her job was to identify ways that the city could save money on energy use. She set out to devise conservation strategies for the recreation centers. Although she did find some big problems, like antiquated heating systems, most often she found that the buildings were poorly maintained and needed simple things like caulking and weatherstripping. She also found several cracked windows. When she tried to get these conditions corrected, she encountered stiff resistance and even hostility from the maintenance staff. These men had been doing their jobs for years. They were doing the best they could with the resources given to them. Who did this lady think she was, to come around and tell them what to do!

The superintendent of maintenance was an old hand who worked closely with the top administrators of the department. Although the administrators thought that energy conservation was a fine idea, they were not inclined to take sides against the maintenance crew just because this woman, who had been forced on the department, couldn't get along. After several clashes with the superintendent of maintenance, Miller expressed her frustration to the mayor loud and clear, as did the department administrators.

Miller was rapidly developing a reputation for being hard to get along with, although it was easy for the mayor to see how a bright woman could ruffle the feathers of the maintenance crew. The mayor felt that she just needed more supervision and perhaps a position where she could influence policy decisions. So she was reassigned to the mayor's office, where she was given the responsibility of developing a strategy to carry out the emergency energy conservation guidelines of the Carter administration.

At last, Miller thought, she had a position where she could accomplish something. She was determined to conserve energy even if she had to turn out everyone's lights herself. Before long, she had alienated a significant number of managers throughout the city government, almost coming to blows with one when she attempted to remove a desk lamp. She finally managed to humiliate the mayor's staff by writing a minority report to the U.S. Department of Energy, accusing the mayor's staff of covering up their lack of commitment to energy policy. Everyone waited for the ax to fall.

The mayor maintained his commitment to keep Miller employed. While he was a good-hearted soul, he was also a pragmatic politician. At that time he was involved in his reelection campaign and did not want to risk the potential fallout from firing Miller, from either the party leaders or the feminist and affirmative action groups in the city. So Miller was assigned to the building management department, which had responsibility for the other half of the city's buildings.

The department had a new director, Roger Newton, a civil engineer who had been lured from the private sector and had a reputation for being firm but fair. Newton had management skills honed in business and was confident that he could manage this recalcitrant employee. She had expertise and Newton welcomed the challenge to put it to good use. Initially they got along well, and for the first time in her career with the city, Miller seemed happy. Newton was not exactly sure what an energy engineer could do, but Miller seemed to have a clear idea of the parameters of the position. He encouraged her to develop ideas and projects for all of the city's buildings and implied that he would provide budgetary support for implementing her projects.

Miller set up visits to all police and fire stations. She discovered that there was no comprehensive set of data on energy use, so she decided to develop basic data on electricity and natural gas use for all city-owned buildings. This was a monumental undertaking, since the data had to be obtained from individual gas and electric bills for two hundred buildings.

Miller spent most of her time gathering the data, and a good bit of secretarial time was devoted to typing the reports. Miller felt very proud each month when she delivered reports that showed, along with the dollar costs, electricity usage in kilowatt hours and natural gas usage in cubic feet. She also calculated the usage in BTUs per degree day to show changes in energy use from year to year. Several copies of these massive lists were made and circulated to the mayor's office and to all department heads, including the police and fire chiefs. Despite her extensive work, recipients of the reports found them almost unreadable. They did not want to take the time to examine all the numbers, and some of the jargon was incomprehensible to them. Newton seemed to appreciate her efforts, although he did not have time to read the reports either.

Miller also spent time in the buildings, identifying potential energy conservation projects. She got along well with the firefighters, who always seemed to appreciate a visit from the "lady engineer." They had lots of ideas on how to save energy and were supportive of her efforts to improve their buildings. This good relationship did not exist with the police. In addition to finding her visits a nuisance, police officers remembered the troubles that one precinct had had with a modern building that was supposed to be energy efficient. The building had a fixed thermostat, set by "some dizzy engineer" (not Miller), and the heating and cooling system never worked right. The cops in the station froze in the winter and boiled in the summer. They never could get anyone to fix it right until one officer, in a rage, shot the darn thermostat with his service revolver.

Miller also had clashes with the maintenance staff in the building management department. These hostilities were mollified somewhat by Newton, who was able to establish a truce between Miller and the maintenance superintendent that permitted the two to work together even though they did not like each other. During this time, Miller identified several projects that could pay for themselves and save the city several thousand dollars each year; she submitted them to Newton for inclusion in the department's capital budget request. But Newton was faced with a budget crunch, and, although he thought she had some good ideas, he felt he could not justify approving these projects if it meant he would not be able to obtain funding for more critical projects.

The honeymoon in the department ended when the energy projects were not included in Newton's recommendations for capital spending in the next budget. Miller's frustration finally boiled over. She raged publicly at Newton at a staff meeting. He was furious. It seemed that Miller's days were numbered at last.

Once again, the mayor's staff found themselves dealing with the problem of Helen Miller. The mayor was not pleased by this turn of events, but he still did not want to offend his political friend. He insisted that his staff find another place for Miller and a director who would supervise her more closely.

Shortly after the most recent incident, several departments were reorganized. The building management department was eliminated, and many of its functions were placed in the new Department of General Administration. The engineering function was centralized in another new department to streamline operations and coordinate all capital and construction projects. The new director was a highly respected engineer who had been the assistant director of public works. He had heard about Miller and, as part of his agreement with the mayor's office on the reorganization, one engineer—Miller—was excluded from the new arrangement.

Miller was assigned instead to the Department of General Administration, which had been given many of the functions of her former department. The new director, Gloria Asbury, had been assistant director of the budget and finance office. She was known to be a tough administrator who wasn't afraid to fire people. The mayor's staff was convinced that Asbury would be able to handle Miller. Perhaps, after all, Miller just couldn't get along very well with men.

The decision problem

As Asbury began the task of establishing administrative norms and procedures for the new department, she faced the problem of Miller. How could she develop a good working relationship with this person who had alienated everyone with whom she had worked up to now? Was there a way to have peace in the department and make Miller a productive employee? How could she, Gloria Asbury, be any more successful with Miller than all of her predecessors had been? How much control did she really have in light of the mayor's continuing refusal to remove this troublesome employee?

Asbury considered also the needs of the department and the skills that Miller could offer her. As a former budget analyst, Asbury knew how much the city spent for energy each year. Her department budget included $2 million for heating and lighting bills as well as $1.75 million for automotive fuels for the city's vehicles. Miller's expertise, if properly harnessed, could be a way to control the growth of these budgets or even to reduce them. Just a 10 percent difference, which energy experts claim can be obtained with no-cost or low-cost efforts, would mean a decrease of $200,000 in the utility budget. If Miller could find ways to save more than that, it would certainly make Asbury's job easier.

Miller had developed several proposals over the years, but they had never gained budgetary approval. Asbury recognized that part of the problem had been the way Miller had presented her ideas at budget time. As an engineer, she tended to believe that the numbers spoke for themselves; she didn't seem to understand the politics of the budget process. Asbury felt that the presentation of the data could be improved in ways that would make it more understandable. Further, the support of a director who was a budget insider would make it possible for Miller to be more successful at budget time.

But the primary question remained: How would it be possible to get Miller's cooperation? She had a reputation for being very hard to get along with. She didn't really have any friends in the city organization. As a female engineer, she didn't have the opportunity to interact very much with other professional women, and she clearly did not get along with the men.

Within the department, the maintenance superintendent considered Miller a domineering female. His cooperation would be necessary to carry out any energy maintenance projects, but he resented any suggestion from Miller that smacked of trampling on his territory. In the old building management department, they had had some legendary arguments, and the truce between them was uneasy. Yet Asbury knew him also to be a team player, an old hand who would carry out requests from his director even if he didn't like them. The trick, then, was to establish some ground rules for both of them

In thinking through how to deal with Miller's outbursts, Asbury had to consider how she would be viewed as a manager—both by Miller and by the rest of the department. She was sensitive to the stereotypes of women as being too emotional to be trusted in management positions, but she was also concerned about being labeled as too hard or rigid, another part of the stereotype of women managers. She would have to walk a fine line, but she had to make it clear to Miller and the rest of the department that her tolerance of certain behaviors was limited. Moreover, she had to do it in such a way that she would be taken seriously but would also be seen as a fair-minded manager.

Finally, there was the problem of the mayor's loyalty to Miller. Others in the city might have fired her long ago, but Asbury knew that it was not unusual for an organization to retain a difficult employee. There was always the possibility of a lawsuit by a disgruntled employee, and it seemed to be cheaper to transfer than to fire. Asbury knew in her heart, then, that it was not likely that Miller would ever be fired. It was far more in Asbury's best interest to find a way to manage Miller so that Miller could exercise her expertise and Asbury could benefit from it.

In considering these factors, Asbury realized that she had few options. If she simply laid down the law to Miller about her behavior, it was not likely to bring about a change in Miller's relationships within the department. Moreover, Asbury would have little recourse if the behavior did not improve. Given no power to fire Miller, Asbury might ultimately be seen as an ineffectual manager and might find her authority with the rest of the staff undermined. Clearly, she had to find a managerial solution that would give Miller a sense of professional accomplishment and bring about cooperation between her and her fellow workers. But what kind of strategy could accomplish those ends after so many past failures?

Discussion questions

1. If you were in Asbury's position, what additional information would you need to make a decision?

2. One of Asbury's options might be to seek an interview with the mayor to see if she could change his mind about retaining Miller. What are the possible outcomes of that strategy?

3. Another of Asbury's options might be to arrange training for staff in communications skills and/or team-building techniques. How would this be likely to work in her department?

4. What contribution could an affirmative action program or an affirmative action officer make to the solution of Asbury's problem?

5. Upon what management tools or skills could Asbury draw in searching for a strategy to solve the problem of Miller?

6. Is there any way Asbury could solve or reduce the problem by making adjustments in the organizational format of her department or in Miller's organizational assignment? What could she do?

7. Are there behavioral interventions (e.g., getting the affected persons to sit down together with Asbury or with a counselor) that might be attempted? What are the possible outcomes of this strategy?

The aftermath

Asbury's best strategy, it seemed to her, was first to develop a clear definition of the roles of, and the relationships among, all personnel involved in the management of the city's buildings and then to work to obtain the employees' cooperation.

Asbury developed a mission statement for the energy management function in the department. The mission statement defined the roles of, and the relationships among, personnel responsible for energy management and included a job description for Miller. In all Miller's interdepartmental travels, her supervisors never had a clear sense of what her job should entail. She was able to define each job herself, but her expectations were unrealistic in terms of what city administrators could or would implement, and she had little understanding of the budgeting and management processes of city government. Her supervisors, in turn, had little understanding of what her duties could or should be; they accepted her as a "gift" from the mayor's office. Miller was always viewed as a political reality, not as a serious employee. Thus, neither she nor her ideas were ever taken seriously. Consequently, when the going got tough, Miller got going— and became the mayor's problem once again.

Part of Miller's frustration was related to her lack of authority to make sure that maintenance tasks were carried out. When the maintenance superintendent refused to do the jobs she requested, she would simply explode. Having no clearly defined position in the organization, she had no power to sanction line personnel even though she was a part of the professional staff. She also had no support from her supervisors, all of whom were men, with the exception of

Asbury. When the maintenance men would complain to the directors, the directors tended to treat Miller as a problem employee rather than as an employee with a problem.

The mission statement laid out clearly the purpose of the energy management function in the department. It described the general goals and the specific elements of the function. The role of the maintenance superintendent in achieving energy savings was defined. In this way, energy management was identified as a specific part of the superintendent's job, and the statement also established the organizational relationships between this job and that of the energy engineer.

A major portion of the mission statement was devoted to a comprehensive description of the job of the energy engineer. The description clearly defined the tasks and responsibilities of the position, including reporting requirements, and it identified the relationships between the energy engineer and other professionals in the department and in the budget office. By focusing on the coordination of the jobs, the mission statement minimized the importance of the personalities involved.

Asbury had developed the mission statement with the assistance of the mayor's staff and an outside consultant who was knowledgeable about both energy management and public organizations. She met separately with Miller and the maintenance superintendent to explain the statement to them and to make certain that each of them understood her expectations. She also explained that their cooperation in making this program work would improve both of their jobs and would make the department operate more effectively.

Now that a clear-cut job description and a regular reporting procedure had been established, Miller felt for the first time that someone was listening. Gradually, she began to trust her supervisors, and she became a much more productive employee. Her relations with the maintenance superintendent became more effective, since they were now working toward the same goals. The superintendent learned what the firefighters had discovered earlier, that Miller had a sense of humor when she wasn't feeling threatened and that she had some very good ideas for the buildings. The two of them learned that they could do a much better job working as a team than as adversaries.

Final discussion questions

1. Part of the problem in this case was that because she was a woman, Miller was different from the other engineers. She was unable by herself to break down the environmental barriers that exist for women and also for minorities in established organizations. How can managers develop mechanisms to mentor such employees and to encourage other employees to work with them?

2. Asbury ultimately decided that Miller's behavior was related to the powerlessness of her position in the organization. What lessons about the responsibilities of management can be drawn from this observation?

3. All city governments exist in a political environment, and many employ some people for political reasons. What can management do to encourage patronage workers to be productive? What effect does merit hiring have on the problem? Would merit hiring have made a difference in this case?

4. Although many in the city thought that Miller should have been fired, she was not. What factors does a manager consider in deciding to fire or to retain an employee? Do organizations fire employees frequently? Why or why not?

13

Unionizing the office manager

Nina Naffziger Nissen

Editor's introduction

Should all employees be treated equally in accordance with a standard set of rules, especially rules that the employees have helped to make through collective bargaining, or should employees be treated in accordance with their individual circumstances?

This is not an easy question to answer. On the one hand, strict adherence to rules is criticized as "bureaucratic" and inhumane; on the other hand, rules help assure fair treatment of all employees, and those established through collective bargaining have been sanctioned by the employees themselves. Even the collective bargaining process, however, can offer no guarantee that general rules will apply equally well to each individual situation. Yet, ironically, these rules are often harder to waive in individual circumstances than the rules ordained solely by legislative or executive action.

Although hard to answer, this question arises with increasing frequency as unionization becomes more commonplace in local government. It is a particular trait of small organizations, and thus of most local government organizations, that their employees perform a broad mix of duties. This breadth, in turn, makes the organization's jobs harder to categorize, especially for purposes of unionization. This is precisely the problem in this case: An office manager in a small county agency functions as both a clerical worker and a member of management. When county workers are unionized, the office manager finds herself enjoying neither the salary level of management nor the fringe benefits of clerical workers. Which should she be?

Caught up in the case are two other important questions. The first is compliance with the contract under which the office manager is adjudged to be a member of the union. The second is the equally vexing question of how to retain the services of a valuable and valued employee. Management wants to retain the employee, and the employee wants to stay on the job; but the guidelines in the county's compensation plan combined with the rules in the collective bargaining contract create barriers to reaching these goals.

Fundamentally, then, this case presents classic problems of bureaucratic operation within the boundaries of a collective bargaining agreement.

Case 13
Unionizing the office manager

Background

According to the most recent Census figures, Crowsville County has a population of approximately 200,000. Since the Census, however, the population has declined as a result of substantial layoffs by several of the county's major industrial employers. Crowsville County includes the city of Centerville, with a population of 120,000; several colleges and universities; and three hospitals with a regional reputation for quality of care. This case involves a woman who was laid off by an industrial employer and subsequently hired by Crowsville County—at a 20 percent reduction in salary.

Approximately 800 full- and part-time county employees (supplemented by temporary help) work in 20 departments that range in size from 5 to 215 workers. Nine departments are headed by elected officials. The county manager is appointed by and reports directly to the county board, the governing body. The personnel administrator, an appointed department head, reports directly to the county manager.

The county manager directly supervises the county departments that are headed by appointed officials, such as the County Home, data processing, highways, assessments, and zoning. In addition, the manager is responsible for making annual budget recommendations for all departments, including departments headed by elected officials (e.g., the sheriff, the county clerk); departments responsible to the judiciary (e.g., clerks of the court, adult probation); and departments that report to a separate board or commission (e.g., public health, veterans' affairs). Although the manager is expected to administer a consistent personnel policy and pay plan for all departments, the reality is that elected officials and separate boards and commissions have autonomy, subject to budgetary guidelines, in managing their own staffs. As a result, some of these departments have adopted personnel policies that conflict with the standard policies proposed by the manager and adopted by the county board. Thus, the county has variations in personnel policies and practices among its departments.

In recent years, approximately 75 percent of all county employees have become unionized, partly as a result of a recently passed state law that permits public-sector collective bargaining. Thus, labor relations activities are still fairly new to this county, and not all bargaining units have successfully completed negotiating their first contracts.

Shortly after the collective bargaining law was passed, the U.S. Supreme Court ruled, in *Garcia* v. *San Antonio Transit Authority*, that all local governmental units were covered by the overtime provisions of the Fair Labor Standards Act (FLSA). In a previous case, the U.S. Supreme Court had ruled that the Constitution prevented the application of the FLSA minimum wage and overtime provisions to state and local governments. The court had stated that matters relating to "traditional" state and local governmental functions could not be dictated by the federal government. However, in *Garcia*, the Supreme Court held that state and local governments *are* covered by the FLSA. The court found that the "traditional government function" test was unwieldy and in contradiction to federalist principles in the Constitution. The *Garcia* decision effectively voided years of lower-court decisions. It also put new pressure on local governments to examine positions in terms of eligibility for overtime pay.

The Assessment Appeal Office of Crowsville County is housed in the court-house. Responsible for hearing complaints regarding property assessments and for submitting tentative and final lists of assessments to the state each year, the office is an integral part of the county's property tax system. It is permanently staffed by three assessment appeal officers, an office manager, and the office manager's assistant.

The assessment appeal officers, all of whom are appointed officials, hear taxpayer complaints about, and make determinations regarding, the assessed valuations of residential, commercial, and agricultural properties, regardless of whether those valuations have been determined by county or by township assessors. Citizens who remain dissatisfied with assessments or with the decisions of the assessment appeal officers may file formal appeals with the state Department of Revenue and Taxation or may file lawsuits. The office manager bears heavy responsibility for answering citizens' questions, during both regular and overtime hours, especially when the assessment appeal officers are not available.

During the peak of the assessment appeal season, the office manager hires temporary workers, and the office manager's assistant works long hours of overtime. The office manager supervises the temporary workers and shares the burden of overtime work.

At the time this case begins, the office manager's job in the Assessment Appeal Office had been partly managerial and partly clerical in nature. Historically, the office manager had been considered a supervisor and member of management by co-workers, the personnel department, superiors, and the citizenry. Consequently, the incumbent of this position, Coralee Reid, had not been eligible for overtime pay.

The case

At about the time of the *Garcia* case, the State Labor Board had ruled that the position of office manager in the county's Assessment Appeal Office was a bargaining unit position. Reid's bargaining unit was among those for which contract negotiations had not been completed. While the negotiations dragged on, salaries were frozen, and Reid became impatient for a change in the status quo. Moreover, she began to question why she had ever been included in the bargaining unit when everyone at the county viewed her as a member of management.

When a visibly agitated Reid appeared in the office of Nancy Brown, the county personnel administrator, Brown already had two questions about Reid's position demanding her immediate attention. First, she was formulating a recommendation on whether the office manager's position qualified for an administrative exemption from overtime pay under the FLSA. Second, she was considering a suggestion from the assessment appeal officers, Reid's supervisors, that Reid's position be upgraded from salary grade 7 to grade 8. The appeal officers, aware of Reid's heavy workload and mounting frustration, felt that this was the only way to retain this indispensable employee.

When Reid, who had a long-standing friendship with Brown, came into Brown's office, she confronted Brown with yet a third issue: She asked for an official determination of whether she was "union" or "management." Surprised by her friend's vehemence, Brown invited Reid to sit down and say what was on her mind.

Evidently, Reid had attended her first union meeting the previous week, where she had heard that contract talks with management were stalled; this meant further delays in raises for bargaining unit members. A policy decision by the county board had *already* delayed raises for Reid's unit for almost two years: The county board had prohibited unilateral raises—such as across-the-board general increases or merit increases—until all bargaining was completed. Raises as well as conditions of employment had to be negotiated at the bargaining table with the authorized bargaining agent (the union); otherwise, the action could be construed as an unfair labor practice. At the meeting, Reid had also been upset by a comment she overheard: A clerk in a lower classification had snubbed her and whispered to Reid's subordinate, "Why is *she* here? She's a supervisor!"

The Labor Board's decision

As Brown well knew, the county did indeed consider Reid a supervisor. After the state had passed its public-sector collective bargaining law, union representation petitions were filed before the Labor Board to include the office manager's position in the bargaining unit. Although the union and the county agreed that the office manager's full-time subordinate be included in the bargaining unit—

and that the assessment appeal officers be excluded on the basis of being managerial employees—the county maintained in testimony at the Labor Board hearing that the office manager's position should be excluded from the bargaining unit under the law that exempted "supervisory," "managerial," or "confidential" employees (see Exhibit 1).

In the view of county representatives, Reid should have been classified as a supervisor because she directed and assigned work, prepared performance evaluations, made recommendations regarding salary increases and bonuses, maintained personnel files, trained new employees, and had the power to discipline employees. On the basis of the office manager's testimony, however, the Labor Board hearing officer issued an opinion, based on his finding of facts (see Exhibit 2), that placed the office manager in the bargaining unit. After the Labor Board had accepted the hearing officer's opinion, the county reiterated its position in post hearing arguments, but the final decision of the Labor Board upheld the earlier finding of the hearing officer.

Evaluating the salary upgrade

Trying to calm Reid, Brown reviewed for her the process by which her placement in the bargaining unit had been decided. Although Brown expressed sympathy with Reid's position, she told her that there was little use in appealing again to the Labor Board unless Reid's duties had substantially changed, to the point where she was spending more than 50 percent of her time supervising subordinates. Brown then took the opportunity to ask Reid to meet with her on another matter concerning her status: In order to evaluate the appeal officers' proposal to upgrade the job, Brown would need to update Reid's job description. Reid agreed to return later that afternoon.

Any doubts that Brown had about the validity of the request for an upgrade were only confirmed by her subsequent meeting with Reid. Although the appeal officers had based their request for an upgrade on increased responsibility, it became clear that the increase was in the amount—rather than in the nature—of the work. The number of appeals to be processed had indeed gone up, but

---

Exhibit 1   Definitions of supervisory, managerial, and confidential status under the state public-sector collective bargaining law:

A *supervisor* is an employee whose principal work is substantially different from that of his or her subordinates and who has authority, in the interest of the employer, to hire, transfer, suspend, lay off, promote, discharge, direct, reward, or discipline employees, or to adjust their grievances or effectively recommend same, if the exercise of such authority is not of a merely routine or clerical nature but requires the consistent use of independent judgment. A preponderance of employment time must be spent in exercising this authority in order for the employee to be so categorized.

A *managerial* employee is an individual who is engaged predominantly in executive and management functions and is charged with the responsibility of directing the effectuation of management policies and practices.

A *confidential* employee is an employee who, in the regular course of his or her duties, assists and acts in a confidential capacity to persons who formulate, determine, and effectuate management policies with regard to labor relations or who, in the regular course of his or her duties, has been given authorized access to information relating to the effectuation or review of the employer's collective bargaining policies.

Exhibit 2   State Labor Board hearing officer's opinion:

Finding of facts

The Assessment Appeal Office has the duty to ensure that all property in Crowsville County is assessed at one-third of its fair market value. The Assessment Appeal Office consists of three (3) officers, an office manager, and a deputy clerk, who assists the office manager. The officers work only part time. They do not have private offices but share a conference table in the Assessment Appeal Office. They generally work two to four hours a day, three to five times a week.

The office manager spends 40 to 50 percent of her time processing assessment complaints filed by Crowsville County citizens. This includes assisting the public in filing procedures, scheduling hearing dates, notifying complainants of hearings, and notifying complainants of new assessments. About 20 percent of her time is spent in processing home improvement exemptions and renewals of property exemptions and in sending reports to the treasurer. She also types correspondence and personnel records and opens and distributes the office mail. Approximately 50 to 75 percent of her work is the same as that of her full-time assistant and the part-time, temporary workers she hires during the peak season.

The office manager maintains attendance records, establishes vacation schedules, approves sick leave, evaluates her subordinates, assigns work, and hires part-time employees. She makes recommendations to the board regarding hiring, salary increases, and discipline. She has issued a written reprimand without first asking the board's permission. She prepares a draft budget for the chief officer, who reviews it and makes any necessary changes. She and the board chair meet with the county manager's office and county board committee concerning the budget; she supplies any requested substantiation. It is her responsibility to ensure that the office is operated in a timely and efficient manner. The officers do not get involved in the processing of complaints; they hold hearings and make decisions. She can implement new office procedures without their prior approval, but she needs board approval to make most purchases of over fifty dollars.

Decision

Although the office manager performs certain supervisory functions, a preponderance of her time is not spent doing so. She spends about 50 percent of her time processing assessment complaints. Since this duty, and not the supervisory functions, constitutes the most significant allocation of her time, I find that she is not a supervisor under the act. Neither is she a managerial employee: Although she assists in budget preparation and implements certain office procedures, I find that she is not predominantly engaged in such managerial and executive functions. The evidence does not indicate that the office manager's supervisors, the appeal officers, currently have or expect to have any role in management's labor relations policies. There is also no evidence that the office manager has access to any information concerning organizational campaign strategies, collective bargaining proposals, or matters concerning contract administration. Therefore, I find that the office manager is not a confidential employee under either prong of the statutory test.

a significant part of the job continued to be clerical. Moreover, the appeal officers relied on Reid's accuracy and attention to detail and preferred that she remain involved in actual clerical tasks. Brown feared that what had prompted the appeal officers to request an upgrade was a desire to pacify Reid by circumventing the bargaining process and obtaining a raise for her. Although she recognized that Reid's responsibilities were substantial, she was uneasy about placing the job in

Exhibit 3 Excerpts from the office manager's job description:

The incumbent in this position is accountable for supervising and maintaining all the clerical duties of the Assessment Appeal Office, which include processing tax complaints and various tax exemptions. . . . This position includes secretarial functions such as taking letters, preparing expense records, and typing. The incumbent works at a CRT to enter and extract data or for posting. The incumbent is responsible for notifying complaining parties of new assessments and for changing appropriate records. . . . Little day-to-day supervision of employees is required. This position requires a high school diploma or equivalent and possibly several related college courses. The incumbent should have several years' experience in secretarial/clerical office operations, and any supervisory experience would be an asset. This position requires an ability to deal with members of the public, who at times can be irate over their property assessments.

---

grade 8 when no other job in grade 7 *or* 8 had a clerical component of any kind. A portion of Reid's job description is presented in Exhibit 3.

A new strategy

Reid sensed Brown's doubts about the upgrade making it through the evalution committee, and she knew that Brown was an influential member of that committee. That evening she reviewed her situation and decided that the strategy of fighting her unionized status and emphasizing the managerial aspects of her duties was getting her nowhere. She was desperately frustrated, felt in her heart that she deserved a raise, and decided to bring new information to Brown's attention the following day. She knew that what she was about to say would cause concern and appear to contradict what the appeal officers were saying in trying to get her an upgrade, but she had come to a breaking point.

When Brown reported to work the next day, she found an urgent message from Reid taped to the door of the personnel department. Appearing in Brown's office before Brown had had a chance to call her, Reid presented her case: First, Reid noted that she had worked many more than forty hours per week for an extended period of time. Since her subordinate was paid for this overtime, Reid questioned why, as a union member, she couldn't receive overtime pay herself. The Labor Board had admitted that she and her subordinate were doing similar work (even though she was also reviewing the work of her subordinate when working overtime). Next, Reid produced statistics from the annual budget demonstrating the substantial increase in workload. Three years earlier, for example, there had been two thousand assessment complaints to process; two years ago there had been twice as many.

To Brown's amazement, Reid then produced a log she had kept on her word processor substantiating her overtime work. These records indicated that in each of the previous two years, she had averaged forty-eight hours of overtime per month for six consecutive months. Although Brown was puzzled that Reid had kept this log when she knew she wasn't considered eligible for overtime, she believed in Reid's integrity and knew she would not have falsified such records. Brown had also seen Reid working on many Saturdays when she herself came in to catch up on work.

Applying the FLSA

Reid's new approach to her situation meant that Brown would have to tackle the problem from yet another perspective. Before coverage under FLSA, county policy had stated that all positions in the six lowest salary grades were eligible for overtime, whereas those above this level were not. (The only exceptions were shift positions, such as registered nurse and deputy sheriff.) Brown suspected that the evaluation committee *knew* how many hours Reid worked—and that was why the job had initially been awarded a grade 7.

Since all county job descriptions predated both the collective bargaining law and the decision that placed counties under the overtime provisions of the FLSA, Brown had the task of reviewing each job description and gathering the additional information needed to determine whether the county was in compliance. Now Reid was pressing for an immediate decision, and Brown wondered just how narrowly county officials expected her to interpret the law.

Under the FLSA, positions fitting into any of six categories could, by definition, be exempt or excluded from overtime: elected officials and their personal staffs, independent contractors, certain volunteers, executives, administrative employees, and professional employees. In reviewing Reid's case, Brown reasoned that the position might qualify for exemption from overtime pay under either an executive or an administrative classification (see Exhibit 4).

It was a time of fiscal constraint, and Brown knew that management was particularly irritated by the FLSA requirements. Coming as they did on the heels of the collective bargaining law, the requirements had provided the union

---

Exhibit 4   FLSA definitions of an executive and an administrative employee:

Requirements to meet the definition of an executive employee:

Performs duties consisting primarily of managing the enterprise in which he or she is employed or of managing a department or subdivision customarily recognized as being part of that enterprise.

Customarily and regularly directs the work of two or more employees.

Possesses the power to hire or fire employees; alternatively, his or her suggestions and recommendations on hiring, firing, and promotion of employees are given particular weight.

Customarily and regularly exercises discretionary powers.

Does not devote more than 20 percent of work time to activities not directly or closely related to performance of executive duties.

Receives a salary of not less than $155 per week exclusive of board, lodging, or other facilities.

Requirements to meet the definition of an administrative employee:

Performs duties consisting primarily of either (1) nonmanual or office work directly related to management policies or general operations, or (2) administrative functions in an educational establishment in work related to academic instruction or training.

Customarily and regularly exercises discretion and independent judgment.

Regularly and directly assists a person employed in an executive or administrative capacity; performs, under only general supervision, work requiring special training, experience, or knowledge; and executes special assignments and tasks under only general supervision.

Does not devote more than 20 percent of work time to activities not directly or closely related to performance of administrative work.

Receives a salary of not less than $155 per week exclusive of board, lodging, or other facilities.

with yet another means of obtaining more money. Increasing overtime line items might leave less money available for raises. Brown was uncertain how committed department heads would be to the letter of the FLSA if it meant they had to reduce other line items in their budgets.

The decision problem

Brown knew that Reid's "about face"—from declaring herself a member of management to declaring her rights as a union member and public employee subject to the FLSA—would shock both the county manager and the assessment appeal officers, who had always encouraged Reid to view herself as a member of management. Brown feared that her own superior would view Reid's "catch 22" situation as a legitimate reason to deny both overtime eligibility and a job upgrade. Brown also believed that without movement on one of these fronts, the county was sure to lose this indispensable office manager to the private sector, because Reid's job put her in contact with a number of influential business owners and investors. Reid's contributions to the Assessment Appeal Office were of critical importance, and a way had to be found to address her concerns and ensure her continued productivity.

Brown had to make a recommendation to the county manager. Unfortunately, there did not appear to be any clearcut answers.

One possibility would be to add clerical staff to the Assessment Appeal Office to reduce the amount of time the office manager devoted to clerical work, thus strengthening the case to exempt the position from the bargaining unit. This option posed two problems. First, the Assessment Appeal Office was funded out of the county's general fund, and the cap on that fund had just been lowered 20 percent by a citizens' referendum. Since the county manager was already looking for ways to reduce the county's base budget, he would probably be unreceptive to suggestions for new clerical positions. Second, the assessment appeal officers had made it clear in their request for an upgrade that they opposed any reduction in the office manager's clerical duties, because they had come to rely on her attention to accuracy and detail.

Another possibility would be to reduce the office manager's decision-making and supervisory duties, thereby definitely locating the position in the bargaining unit. Although this option would require a reclassification of the position to a lower grade, it would clearly entitle the incumbent to substantial overtime pay. However, this approach also posed problems. First, it would amount to a demotion for Reid. Second, while it would pay her overtime, it might have little effect on her overall annual income, as her salary might be reduced. Finally, it was not feasible to shift the office manager's decision-making and supervisory duties to the assessment appeal officers, because they were involved in other business ventures and lacked the time to deal with those functions.

In short, as the personnel officer, Brown had to formulate a recommendation for the county manager that would both satisfy Reid and keep the position as it was currently defined—with its mixture of managerial, technical, supervisory, and clerical duties.

Discussion questions

1. If you were in Brown's position, what factors would you consider in making a decision? How would you weigh each one?

2. One of Brown's options is to recommend that the county make yet another appeal to the Labor Board to exempt the office manager from the bargaining unit. What grounds would she have for this

recommendation? How would you evaluate the advantages and disadvantages of this strategy?

3.   Brown has received two very conflicting sets of requests from Reid. Clearly, there are some emotional as well as economic considerations affecting Reid. To what extent, and how, should Brown address these personal considerations?

4.   To what extent should Brown seek the counsel of Reid's supervisors— the assessment officers—in resolving her problem? Is it more important to uphold the autonomy and integrity of her office or to attempt to pursue the course of action preferred by the assessment officers (e.g., to upgrade the position to an 8)? Why?

5.   How legitimate is it for supervisors to want to keep a competent employee in lower-level work because the employee is "good at it"? How should Brown respond to this dimension of the problem?

6.   Would Brown be better advised to attempt to resolve this problem on her own initiative, thereby assuring greater conformity with countywide personnel policies and asserting the role of the personnel office? Explain your rationale in responding to this question.

7.   If you were Brown, what would you recommend to the county manager? Why?

The aftermath

After thorough investigation, Brown updated the job description to reflect the job as a mixture of 35 percent managerial/technical duties, 15 percent supervisory duties, and 50 percent clerical/secretarial duties (of a complex nature and requiring technical background). She made no recommendation to appeal for exemption of the position from the bargaining unit or to add an additional clerical position. She reasoned that such an appeal was unwarranted, since (1) no more than 50 percent of the office manager's time was spent in supervising or managing, and (2) the appeal officers would resist any recommendation that would reduce the office manager's involvement in clerical work.

Brown did recommend that the office manager position not be considered for an administrative exemption from the FLSA, that the position be classified as eligible to receive overtime pay, and that Reid receive back pay for overtime worked during the previous twenty-four months. Unsure how this would be accepted, Brown winced as she recommended back pay. Brown's ultimate recommendations were based on the updated job description and on her determination that the duties performed by the office manager during overtime hours were a mixture of clerical and supervisory/managerial tasks, with supervisory/managerial duties accounting for no more than 50 percent of those hours.

After consulting with the staff of the county attorney's office, the county manager readily accepted Brown's recommendations, even for retroactive pay. A revised position description was adopted, the office manager position was left in the bargaining unit and made eligible for future overtime pay, and Reid received a sizable check for retroactive overtime pay.

The following week, the assessement appeal officers took the revised job description to the job evaluation committee. Although the description clearly outlined the extent to which the job contained a clerical component, the officers' verbal testimony emphasized Reid's managerial duties. The committee, on a 5–2 vote, upgraded the office manager's position to a grade 8 on the basis of "added responsibilities." In Brown's view, the decision was ironic, considering that Reid's demand for overtime pay was based on the similarity of her work to that of her subordinates.

Reid's pay increase and overtime eligibility fulfilled their purpose of sustaining her motivation to continue working in the office manager's position. One year later, the union contract still had not been finalized, and county employees continued in everyday interactions to treat the office manager as a member of management.

Final discussion questions

1. Under what circumstances should short-term financial considerations be allowed to dictate solutions that have major, long-term, personnel implications?

2. To what extent should a personnel officer seek to change or modify personnel regulations to retain the services of a valued employee? Explain your reasoning.

3. The "letter of the law" does not always produce the most workable day-to-day rules and procedures. When conflicts of this nature exist, how should they be resolved? Under what circumstances can the "letter of the law" be set aside? Under what circumstances, if any, should it be set aside?

4. The dilemma in this case—an employee who is classified as a union member, but treated as a member of management by both management and union members—will become increasingly common as unionization expands among public-sector employees. What, in general, are the principles that management should follow when such situations occur?

5. How should grievance procedures be developed to cover situations in which immediate supervisors are in bargaining units along with their subordinates?

14 Is the good cop a bad cop?

Ralph Jacob

Editor's introduction

Problems are inevitable whenever questions of sexual behavior come into the workplace. When sexual misconduct is suspected in the police department, and when the behavior in question is homosexual, the stage is set for a potential explosion. Those are the messy circumstances that evolve in this case.

A small community employs a dedicated police officer who enforces the law in a stringent and unyielding fashion. The officer endears himself to the mayor and council by writing tickets in such numbers that substantial revenues are generated for the municipal treasury. When the officer takes a personal interest in counseling young men who are having problems with the law, his work is applauded.

The good cop becomes a bad cop, however, when allegations of homosexuality, and use of his authority to gain homosexual favors, start to circulate in the community. The case poses a range of problems. What is the appropriate reaction to the suspicion that a person in the sensitive area of law enforcement is homosexual? What are the legal limitations on dealing with such an employee and encouraging him to seek help? Can an officer removed from patrol duty for medical reasons be reinstated to help cover a shortage of available police officers? What is the role of administrative leadership in dealing with a subordinate who is the target of such charges? What is the obligation—legal and moral—of the government employer to help an employee with a personal problem?

Overall, then, the case poses some of the most difficult problems in the field of personnel administration. Perhaps none is more difficult than the problem of simultaneously protecting the rights of an employee, guarding the community against the possibility of misbehavior, and dealing with the reaction of an insensitive public to rumors of scandal in public office. That, ultimately, is the administrative challenge posed by this case.

Case 14
Is the good cop a bad cop?

Background

The village of Porterville hired Henry Ritter as a police officer to serve on a traffic-enforcement task force. The chief of police at the time, Clem Harvey, had started the task force as a way to add two officers and a squad car to an existing eight-person department. Ninety percent of the cost of the addition was paid by a federal grant established with the goal of tightening traffic law enforcement.

Ritter and his partner in the program, Gerald Kleinstein, were hired through the usual procedures. Candidate applications were submitted directly to Chief Harvey, who selected the finalists best fitting his criteria for the position. Next, Harvey interviewed the top five candidates and directed an investigator to check their personal backgrounds. The final selection was made by the village council after receiving Chief Harvey's recommendations, subject to candidates' passing successfully the required physical examinations.

Ritter was finishing his second year as a patrolman in Homer, a smaller community forty miles west of Portervillle. The investigator found that Ritter had been disciplined twice for leaving Homer while on duty to assist friends with auto repairs. The first such offense had been considered minor, but the second was deemed a violation of a direct order and drew a three-day suspension. Nevertheless, because Ritter was already trained and could be put immediately on the street without waiting for state certification, he was considered an ideal candidate and was hired.

The 24-year-old Ritter was placed directly into the traffic-enforcement program. He and Kleinstein were limited to working on traffic enforcement, except for emergency situations. They took extensive training in federal, state, and local regulations. Porterville established a monthly quota and an extensive reporting system to document compliance with federal requirements. The officers were ordered and encouraged to make traffic stops, to give verbal warnings, and to issue citations for the slightest violation. Separate tallies were kept for the number of tickets given for cracked tail lights, bald tires, and loud mufflers, as well as for the more common violations of speeding, driving under the influence, and reckless driving.

The federal grant under which the two new officers were hired was designed to last three years, with the federal funds being reduced each year. To afford the new officers, then, Porterville had to generate new revenues to cover their salaries and expenses. Thus, Ritter and his partner were given to understand that their continued employment would depend on the new village revenues that would be generated by the fines paid as a result of the tickets they issued. Failure to write a sufficient number of tickets would jeopardize the federal grant program and their employment. The ticket writing would hardly be popular with local citizens, but, for Ritter and Kleinstein, the alternative was unemployment. Therefore, Ritter and Kleinstein wrote many tickets.

The new officers were rewarded for their strict enforcement of the rules. One of the areas of police work that can be easily quantified is traffic enforcement. Working full time in that area gave Ritter and Kleinstein an advantage in personnel evaluation sessions over the other officers, who were spending less time on enforcement and more time on community work, youth programs, and other aspects of police work that do not generate the same kind of productivity statistics. The new officers were praised by the chief, who held up their aggressive ticket-writing success as an example for the more senior officers to follow.

The task force was effective in bringing in added revenues and in slowing down traffic in the village. The village's elected officials appreciated the increased revenue and generally supported the new task force, but the officials did prefer that most fines be levied against nonresident travelers going through town.

The work of Ritter and Kleinstein had adverse side effects as well. Since the two new men were restricted to traffic enforcement, they were not cross-trained to substitute for regular officers. This limited their career potential; worse, it separated them socially from the rest of the department.

Furthermore, Porterville developed a reputation as a speed trap. Respect for the department was on the decline, and its officers were viewed locally as "cowboys." The wide-brimmed hats and leather boots sported by many only worsened the image. Conflicts between task force members and the public became more frequent. Complaints against all officers increased. Rumors of departmental excesses spread throughout the area. Porterville's police officers closed ranks and developed an "us against the world" mentality in which rules were to be enforced and authority respected.

The case

Ritter soon became frustrated in his assigned role. The repetition of tasks, the separation from other members of the department, and the working conditions themselves were leaving their mark. His contact with the public was limited primarily to traffic stops. Since the task force had become notorious in the community, Ritter was often confronted and subjected to verbal abuse, citizen accusations, and questions about his integrity. To combat such hostility, he needed the acceptance of his superiors and peers. To this end, he gradually developed a narrowly legalistic approach to personal complaints. He studied the laws carefully, memorizing the strictest interpretations. He provided long, detailed reports outlining how he had followed the letter of the law. These reports gave his superiors the impression that he was a model law enforcement officer, crossing every "t" and dotting every "i." He showed respect for authority and was rewarded with a promotion to sergeant.

As sergeant, too, Ritter continued his strict enforcement of regulations. Within a paramilitary organization, such behavior was acceptable. His tough-guy approach would soften, occasionally, when others came asking for his help. He even served as a father figure to some who seemed to need an authority figure or model. If a teenage boy was in trouble and asked for his help, he would do his best to assist. Ritter met with parents, counseled kids on how to stay out of trouble, and asked other officers to give certain kids a break. He acted the role of tough cop with a heart of gold. He demanded respect from the young teenage offenders. At times he bullied them and wielded his authority. Still, Ritter received letters of thanks from parents for "straightening out" their sons.

The federal traffic grant was phased out in Porterville, but the new enforcement revenues still played an important part in balancing the budget. The police supervisors supported enforcement efforts, which brought in dollars that relieved pressure on their tight budgets.

With the appointment of a new police chief, Harry Anderson, the officers closed ranks even further in regard to complaints. Suggestions that officers were often curt, abrasive, or abusive were shrugged off with excuses or with the suggestion that the complainant was looking for a way to avoid paying a fine.

Problems relating to complaints about police officers were handled by the new chief, who reported directly to the part-time mayor and council. Questions regarding ethics or activities unbecoming to an officer were decided by the chief. The new man Anderson was very supportive of his employees, so discipline was a private matter to be handled one on one. The elected officials, the public, and the department members did not hear of the complaints, much less the corrective actions taken by the chief. The authority of the chief and his command staff grew. Citizens became distrustful of the department. Any questions about the police that came to elected officials were submitted to the chief. Soon the citizens gave up, and the number of complaints declined.

Thus, Ritter worked in an atmosphere of strong authority and control. He was finally supported by fellow officers, because he stuck up for them when citizens called with complaints. They returned such favors. Moreover, Ritter enjoyed demonstrating his expertise in law enforcement. He volunteered to speak at the local high school's civic and health classes, and he lectured about the problems of drinking and driving, drug abuse, and traffic violations.

Ritter was single and spent a lot of time serving as a big brother or working overtime as needed. He was always available to help, and he gave numerous high schoolers his home phone number in case they had problems and wanted to talk them out with someone.

These endeavors with teens, his counseling beyond normal expectations, and his single marital status eventually gave rise to rumors that he was homosexual. There were suggestions that Ritter used his position to force youths to come to him to get out of trouble. His hard-line approach to law enforcement had made many enemies within the community, and, as rumors spread, some parents told their teens to avoid contact with Porterville police officers. Rumors that Ritter's counseling sessions included more than conversation ran through the local high school, yet letters from parents grateful for his help continued to arrive.

Complaints

The first complaint Chief Anderson received about Ritter was from Carol Boggs. Boggs' 19-year-old son, Bobby, had been arrested for hitchhiking by Ritter, who warned the youth of the dangers of hitchhiking and accused him of selling drugs. Boggs denied that he had any drugs. Ritter ordered him to strip to check his clothing. Mrs. Boggs felt that a strip-search was inappropriate for a hitchhiking arrest. The department did not have a clear-cut policy regarding search procedures, and, as no state laws had been violated, Chief Anderson told Mrs. Boggs that the inspection was justified. Rumors continued about possible homosexual activity by Ritter, but nothing outside the law was reported. No formal action was taken.

In the second complaint, Mr. and Mrs. Fred Selchow contacted Dan Rowe, Porterville's city attorney, regarding improprieties alleged to have been committed by Ritter when the Selchows' 19-year-old son, Larry, was arrested. The Selchows wanted the city to be aware of illegal activities by the sergeant, but they also wanted to spare their son the embarrassment of a public hearing or trial. They said that Larry would talk to the municipal officials only if the village would guarantee that he would not be forced to testify in any criminal or disciplinary hearings.

Attorney Rowe presented the Selchows' proposal to the mayor and council. They determined that staff should obtain the information from Larry Selchow. The waivers were signed and a deposition was taken with the guarantee that the information would serve only as background to assist the department in finding out whether there was a pattern of illegal or inappropriate actions committed by an employee.

In the deposition, Larry Selchow stated that six months before, he had been arrested with a friend for underage drinking. While waiting to be picked up at the station, he was sitting in a room and saw Ritter's jacket next to him, hanging over a chair. Selchow said that he thought it would be a great joke to play on the sergeant if he removed the officer's badge: "I took the badge with me, and Ritter didn't notice it was missing."

As it turned out, several days later Ritter did notice that the badge was gone. He was frantic, for the loss of a badge could have major consequences. It could be misused in criminal activities. Ritter, always a stickler for rules, had chided subordinates for far less serious violations. He contacted Detective Reggie Tambo and asked for his help.

Tambo was an expert investigator whose reputation as an effective interrogator was well known among the community's youth. He had a wide range of contacts who could be pressed for information, people such as small-time drug users, dealers, snitches, and thieves. Tambo was a team player and would help Ritter get the badge back without the chief's ever knowing it was lost. Indeed, Ritter could face disciplinary action or worse if the badge was discovered to be missing.

As Selchow reported in the deposition, Tambo discovered that Selchow had the badge and had him drop it off. Tambo explained to Ritter how and when it was taken. Ritter then contacted Selchow himself and told him that to avoid prosecution, Selchow would need to receive counseling from him. Ritter also told Selchow to come to his apartment to discuss the theft of the badge. Selchow agreed to meet with Ritter.

Ritter explained to young Selchow the seriousness of taking a police officer's badge. He told him about possible jail time, a police record, and the public stigma attached. Selchow stated that Ritter then asked, "What do you think an appropriate punishment would be for taking my badge? Would you be too embarrassed to take off all your clothes and masturbate in front of me? Would that be fair?" Selchow said that Ritter ordered him to take off his clothes, and that he complied with the bigger, stronger officer because the sergeant was shouting at him and he did not feel safe. Ritter allegedly fondled the naked Selchow and told him that he would not be treated as kindly by a prison roommate.

Punishment

Following Selchow's report, Tambo and the chief questioned Ritter about the incident. Ritter admitted that Selchow had been at his apartment but denied that anything beyond discussion of the theft of his badge had taken place. He said he could not understand why Selchow would say such things about him. Ritter acknowledged that he should not have met with the boy at his residence but said he was "just trying to help the kid out."

Attorney Rowe briefed the council on the situation, pointing out that the deposition provided evidence that one of the city's police officers had used his authority to demand and receive sexual favors as a form of plea bargaining. While the officer denied the allegation, he did admit to violating departmental policy by interrogating in his home. The council wanted Ritter discharged, but the attorney advised that without Selchow's testimony, successful prosecution of Ritter would be impossible, and even a hearing before the police commission would not necessarily secure a dismissal.

One member of the council suggested that they ask for Ritter's resignation and threaten to expose his homosexuality if he refused, but such a course of action would risk a countersuit claiming sexual preference harassment. Ritter could be given undesirable work assignments and pushed to resign, but that might be a long, slow process that could be disruptive to the rest of the department and lead to scandal in the community.

After lengthy discussion, the council agreed to suspend Ritter for five days, the maximum suspension possible without a hearing, and to assign him to a newly created desk job. Finally, the council ordered a psychological evaluation to ascertain whether Ritter was competent to continue as a police officer.

The police psychologist indicated that Ritter did not have a "normal" heterosexual personality; furthermore, he was a strong-willed individual with a need to dominate others in certain authority situations. Nevertheless, Ritter was qualified to serve as a policeman. He could continue to be a good officer as long as he was closely monitored when dealing with youth. He should be kept from scout leadership or youth officer work but could serve the department in other capacities. The psychologist suggested that counseling might be helpful to Ritter, but it wasn't mandatory for continued employment.

The council did not feel that the village had the responsibility or the resources to pay for future counseling. If Ritter needed further psychological counseling, they reasoned, he should pay for it. The attorney was uncertain if, based on the psychologist's findings, Ritter could be required to attend any additional counseling sessions.

The decision problem

Four months after Ritter was assigned the desk job, the department lost three of its twelve patrol officers. Regular personnel were working twelve-hour shifts, increased to eighteen if an officer called in sick. Tempers were becoming short. Morale was low and falling lower. Anderson himself was spending time on patrol and thus was not available to perform all of his duties as chief. At that point, Anderson requested that Ritter be allowed to return to patrol duties.

Ritter had been resentful of his restricted assignment. He wanted badly to be back on the street and used every opportunity to criticize the mayor and the council for keeping him indoors. He spent his time reviewing officer reports, enforcing rules to the letter, and blasting the telecommunicators and clerical personnel for minor errors. His desk assignment had eliminated his official contact with area youth, but many of them had his home phone number and could continue to contact him outside of work. In addition, through police reports he was able to keep track of problems involving his particular friends.

The sergeant's only other questionable contacts had been with youths who were of legal age. Certainly the village did not have the authority to dictate its employees' sexual preferences, but did it have the right to limit the social contacts of a police officer? The psychologist had stated that Ritter was not a threat and could return to patrol duty. Contacts in which Ritter needed to supervise youths had been eliminated.

Craig Bankhead had been the village manager for two months when he received Chief Anderson's request to put Ritter back on the street. Bankhead had been hired as Porterville's first manager after the community, experiencing rapid growth, decided to professionalize its administrative staff and operations.

Bankhead was already too familiar with the village's poor financial condition. He was aware of the morale problem in the police department and knew that it would improve with Ritter out of the office and back on the street. He knew, too, that something had to be done to relieve the stress in the department. Police officers were no longer always willing to cover for each other's sick leave. Training and vacations had been on hold for a month. Unless Ritter returned to patrol, there would be no training or vacation time for at least another two months. Officers were reported to be testing for jobs in other departments where the pay was higher and overtime was optional. Union organizers had met recently with patrol officers.

Bankhead weighed the psychologist's report against the other reports to him about Ritter. The psychologist had opined that Ritter could return to patrol duty, but he had not exactly given Ritter a clean bill of health. If Ritter was returned to patrol and there were further complaints about his behavior, the results could be disastrous. The village's financial condition certainly could not sustain the costs of litigation or the payment of damage assessments. The village was financially and morally responsible for Ritter's conduct as a police officer and could not fully deny awareness of Ritter's potential to cause problems.

Bankhead had to make a recommendation to the council.

Discussion questions

1. How should the manager decide whether Ritter would be a threat to the health, safety, or welfare of the community if he returned to patrol duty? What kinds of information should he seek? How could he obtain the information?

2. Bankhead could recommend that Ritter be returned to patrol duty, or he could advise against it. What options does he have? What are the advantages and disadvantages of each option?

3. Should the mayor and council have required Ritter to undergo therapy, and should the village have paid for it? Did the council have an obligation to pay these costs? Explain.

4. What, if any, are the limitations on village options to make employment and work assignment decisions on the basis of employee sexual preference? What should village policy be regarding employee sexual preference?

5. What questions of principle are involved in this case, and how do they apply? How should Bankhead advise the council regarding these principles?

6. Should the Ritter question, as now posed, serve as a basis for a reexamination of policies regarding police recruitment and candidate screening policies? If so, how should the village proceed? If not, explain why not.

7. What should Bankhead recommend, and why?

The aftermath

Bankhead recommended that Ritter be returned to patrol duty, and the council approved the recommendation. Ritter served as a patrol officer for nearly a year without incident.

The incident, when it happened, involved a 19-year-old youth who had been arrested by Detective Tambo for the theft of goods from an auto parts store. Tambo had asked the youth, Paul Trimble, to return the goods to the police station, but Trimble instead returned them to Ritter at Ritter's home. Trimble told Tambo that Ritter was a friend of his and had offered to save him a trip to the station. Ritter had helped him previously, he said, when he had been mixed up with a wild crowd, and Ritter was a person Trimble trusted. Anderson and Tambo interrogated Trimble and Ritter about the incident. Both denied that Ritter had ever threatened Trimble or suggested exchanges of favors. Trimble became visibly resentful of the insinuations behind the questions.

In the council election following this incident, two new members were elected who immediately called for a complete investigation of the rumors circulating about Ritter. Anderson and Tambo were to conduct an investigation into charges that Ritter had used his authority with the Porterville Police Department to compromise young men and boys.

The six-week internal investigation included telephone taps, surveillance of Ritter's apartment, interviews with previous employers, and contacts with persons who had been arrested by Ritter. The investigation did not uncover any illegal activities. Ritter had friendships with several young men, had taken them on fishing or camping trips, and had roommates from time to time. If the boys were under age, Ritter had always been careful to get the prior approval of their parents.

Some time later, city attorney Rowe received a phone call from attorney Garry Walsh, representing Paul Trimble. Walsh charged that Ritter had coerced Trimble into performing sexual acts by threatening him with arrest for an offense that could lead to a jail term. Walsh stated that if action was not immediately started to dismiss Ritter, he would file a lawsuit against the village.

Because Trimble had been reluctant to talk to Porterville officers, Chief Anderson recommended that the village invite the state police to investigate Ritter's activities. The state police agreed to investigate the alleged professional misconduct of Ritter, working closely with the Porterville Police Department and attorney Walsh. In the middle of this investigation, Ritter resigned.

Final discussion questions

1. Once a government has hired a police officer, what steps can be taken to ensure that incidents like those alleged against Ritter do not occur? If they do occur, what can be done to prevent recurrence?

2. What steps can a manager or chief administrative officer take to "police" the police?

3. Under what circumstances can or should a government use its police powers to increase revenues through fines?

4. Are there reasons other than the need for increased revenues that might lead a government to urge its police officers to enforce the laws stringently? If so, what are they? When can they be justified?

5. When Ritter was returned to patrol, what instructions should Bankhead have given to Chief Anderson?

6. Did the village leadership do enough to support and protect Ritter from the rumors and allegations? What else could it have done, staying within the bounds of ethics and professionalism?

7. What changes in village personnel policy should be made as a result of Porterville's experiences in this case?

15

Cedar Valley slowdown
David N. Ammons and M. Lyle Lacy, III

Editor's introduction

When they engage in collective action against their employer, local government employees usually have a distinct advantage. First, they can exercise economic leverage through job actions or threatened job actions—strikes where they are allowed, work slowdowns where they are not. Second, they can exercise political leverage by organizing themselves, their families and friends, and local community groups to vote for candidates who support their goals and to apply pressure on elected officials on their behalf.

Local government administrators, on the other hand, must restrict their behavior to actions officially approved by labor relations laws. Even when sympathetic to the demands of their employees, administrators may be constrained by budgetary limitations, the need for equity across departments, or public resistance to higher taxes.

This case describes the plight of the city administration in Cedar Valley as it attempts to respond to ill-timed wage demands—first from its police officers and then from its firefighters. The case has all the elements of a typical local government labor relations controversy: substantial employee demands, tight budgets and taxpayer resistance to tax hikes, lack of experience on both sides of the negotiations, and reluctance on the part of the city to negotiate with employee organizations. The case develops like a chess game—move, countermove; reaction, counterreaction—and finally produces frustration, anger, and lack of trust on the part of all concerned.

In the end, both sides resort to extreme tactics. The firefighters undertake a job action; the city considers contracting with a private firm for fire protection services. This move by the city raises a whole new set of questions: the efficacy of private contracts for public services, the feasibility of public-private partnerships, and the inevitable politics of proposing such an alternative in a labor relations context.

The case also provides a useful insight into a very common reaction by the general public. The firefighters mobilize support for their wage demands from the same public that resists tax increases. Nothing in the American political philosophy or tradition requires consistency from citizens, but the public administration tradition does require consistency and rationality in recommendations and proposals from management. This imbalance gives rise to a classic dilemma for the practicing local government administrator.

From such dilemmas is born the demand for administrative leadership, even in political settings. A characteristic of effective leadership is the ability to produce innovative solutions to seemingly intractable problems. Digging into their storehouse of organizational theory and administrative skills, the local government managers in Cedar Valley must search for such a solution.

Case 15
Cedar Valley slowdown

Background

Hot summer temperatures were mild compared with another kind of heat that plagued city officials well into autumn across the nation, particularly in the mid-South. Walkouts and slowdowns by public safety employees were occurring in rapid succession in several parts of Dixie. Each act of defiance seemed to encourage the next. Even those officials in the South who were not confronted with job actions could see them on all sides.

In that atmosphere, city officials in Cedar Valley probably should not have been caught off guard when police officers staged a work slowdown, but they were. Cedar Valley, a southern city of 30,000 residents, is a major center of employment in a sizable metropolitan area. Its municipal government is supported by significant property tax and sales tax bases and an unusually large component of intergovernmental revenues. It happened that the attention of city officials had been diverted to a hearing on the possible reduction or discontinuation of the intergovernmental revenues when twenty-three officers—one-half of Cedar Valley's total force—declared a work slowdown to dramatize their demands for higher pay, enhanced benefits, and improved working conditions. Among the most important demands were the following:

An immediate 15 percent increase in pay

"Hazardous duty" status in the city's classification plan

Extra pay for evening and midnight shifts, as well as time-and-a-half for weekend work

Incentive pay for education, physical fitness, and marksmanship

Discontinuation of the merit system in favor of automatic step increases and longevity pay

Establishment of an exercise facility

Improved insurance coverage and elimination of employee contributions for insurance and retirement

Enhanced benefits for the purchase and maintenance of police uniforms.

The demands were presented in a petition to the city council and city manager signed by twenty-three police officers. The timing could hardly have been worse.

The day on which the police officers made their declaration, September 7, was slightly more than two months into the city's fiscal year—too late to adjust the tax rate and 10 long months before any major changes could be made through the normal budget process. Furthermore, city officials were preoccupied at the moment with the possible loss of a major intergovernmental revenue source, a budding crisis that jeopardized even the current budget and made unthinkable the additional financial pressure that would be imposed if the police officers' demands were met.

Compounding the problem of poor timing was the relative inexperience of two key members of the city's management team. Although both had served previously in other capacities in Cedar Valley, Bill Martin had been city manager only three months, and his new principal assistant, Larry Bristol, had been director of administration for only one week.

If there was anything fortuitous about the timing of the police slowdown notification, it was that a hearing on intergovernmental revenues had drawn virtually the entire city council together in one place, and Martin was thus able immediately to brief the council on the slowdown. Council members assured Martin that they would avoid making any statements that might undermine his efforts to deal with the problem. Martin appreciated those personal assurances; he was especially pleased that council members made them not in private conversations with him but in the presence of one another.

The case

Martin, Bristol, and Police Chief Carl Angelo met to develop a response to the work slowdown notification. The initial result of the meeting was a memorandum to participating officers that informed them of the difficulties involved in attempting to meet their demands at that point in the fiscal year, cautioned them about the harmful effects that a job action could have on public confidence and cooperation, and ordered them to resume full police activities. Furthermore, the memorandum advised the officers that continuation of the job action might lead the city to cancel the police department's participation in an upcoming in-service training session, thereby jeopardizing the officers' ability to meet the criteria for supplemental pay from the state. Police officers were irritated by the potential loss of supplemental pay but were not persuaded to abandon the slowdown.

In an effort to counteract the adverse effects of the work slowdown, Angelo began assigning officers to high-visibility locations that had been the sites of major accidents. Angelo's intent was to address traffic safety concerns and to compensate for the officers' refusal to take initiative in traffic patrol. Thus, even officers participating in the slowdown could not help but be perceived by the public as part of the police presence in the community.

On September 12, the city council and city management received another blow. Only four days after the police officers had announced their work slowdown, forty-two members of Cedar Valley's fifty-one-member fire department issued a statement that they were joining the police officers in the work slowdown. Unlike the police job action, in which the participants were virtually all nonsupervisory officers, the fire department job action included several ranking officers.

Dealing with employee associations

State law did not regulate labor-management relations in Cedar Valley or in other local governments in the state; the law did not even require that municipal employee unions be recognized. In that environment, Cedar Valley officials staunchly resisted the union-like tactics of the police and fire groups, groups that officials regarded merely as employee "associations," even though one was affiliated with the Fraternal Order of Police and the other with the International Association of Fire Fighters.

Martin offered to meet with groups of three aggrieved employees at a time but resisted any action that might give the appearance of bargaining with the two or three persons who had emerged as "union" spokespersons. Officer Bob Jacksboro, president of the police association, had assumed that mantle on the police side. The ranking officer in the firefighters' association, Captain Bowie Camp, was its nominal spokesman, but Captain Hal Rockwood was more outspoken and appeared to be that group's driving force. Martin adamantly refused to strengthen their roles as leaders by meeting separately with Jacksboro, Camp, or Rockwood.

On September 14 Jacksboro notified Martin and the city council that individual officers were rejecting Martin's offer to meet with them in small groups rather than with their representatives and that the police officers and firefighters participating in the job action had voted to merge and to pursue their interests as one group. Four days later, the combined group staged a three-block march to city hall and pressed its demands at a meeting of the city council.

In response to the demands, Martin summarized city management's position. First, the salaries of city employees would be given top priority during budget considerations for the next fiscal year; public safety employees, however, would be considered in the context of the entire city workforce. Second, none of the grievances would be addressed as long as the work slowdown continued. Third, the city would not proceed on a course that would, in effect, recognize employee labor unions. The city council formally endorsed Martin's position.

By September 26 police and fire employees had begun to picket the mayor's place of employment, as an intended prelude to the picketing of all city council members. However, informal talks between city staff and attorneys representing the two employee groups headed off the second-phase picketing. By September 29 city staff had calculated the projected costs of implementing the group's demands. Those calculations were distributed to aggrieved public safety employees along with an invitation to meet with Martin, not in groups of three—as had been previously offered and rejected—but in entire work shifts. Jacksboro, still hoping to represent the police officers in negotiations with Martin, announced that shiftwide meetings were no more acceptable than meetings with three officers at a time.

Crisis

Police and fire employees aggressively pressed their case in the community and in the local media. Statements of support increased for public servants who were willing to risk their lives for the community; commercial marquees began to urge support for local police officers and firefighters; radio and newspaper coverage and commentary on the subject seemed more and more prominent. Meanwhile, city management had begun to explore options for providing public safety services, including contracting out the fire protection function.

By the end of September, Martin and his staff had grown impatient with the stalemate and with the employees' continuing defiance of orders to resume full duties. On October 5, exactly four weeks after police officers had begun the slowdown, participating police officers and firefighters were confronted face to face and ordered to resume full duties. This order was stronger than the order Martin had given the police officers several weeks earlier. This time the participants were told that unless they declared their intention to comply, they would be suspended without pay pending termination for insubordination and neglect of duty, as specified by the city's personnel ordinance.

Martin selected October 5 for the confrontation not only because it marked the end of the fourth week of stalemate but also because both Officer Jacksboro and Captain Rockwood were on duty that day. Martin and his staff hoped that, caught off guard, Jacksboro and Rockwood would either discontinue their participation in the slowdown or make a mistake that would undermine the job action. Both, however, held firm.

None of the aggrieved police officers and only three of the aggrieved fire department employees on duty that day decided against continuing. The others were suspended.

Word of the afternoon's events spread rapidly, and city management made final preparations to deal with a very volatile situation. Police Chief Angelo immediately instituted twelve-hour shifts for the remaining police force, which consisted primarily of supervisory employees. Fire Chief Joe Caro consolidated forces at one of the city's three fire stations, relying on a handful of veteran fire officers and firefighters supplemented by employees from other departments who could be persuaded to help.

Picket lines composed of police and fire personnel and members of their families formed late that afternoon. As the evening wore on, emotions ran high. The understaffed fire company was inundated by a rash of false alarms. In the early morning hours of October 6, three fires broke out, all of them later attributed to arson: two homes under construction and a former elementary school serving as a day care center were destroyed. The city's contingency plans had proven sufficient for police services and probably would have been adequate for normal fire responses. However, the rash of false alarms and the triple arson overwhelmed the skeleton firefighting force. Although no arrests were ever made in connection with the arsons, public support for the job action seemed to diminish after the evening's events.

When the next morning dawned, Martin and his staff faced the aftermath of a night that had surpassed everyone's worst-case scenario. All were sickened by the thought that this might have been only the first night of several like it. Efforts to prepare for a recurrence were only partially successful. A local industry that operated its own firefighting force agreed to place a pumper and crew at the city's main fire station, and the city manager of a neighboring community assured Martin that he would send a pumper to Cedar Valley on a moment's notice. State officials, however, refused to make the National Guard available, stating simply that the Guard could not step in unless fire losses were greater than they had been the first night.

Informal discussions between management staff and attorneys for the employee groups continued throughout the day. By late afternoon a return-to-work agreement had been reached that reinstated all suspended employees, ended the work slowdown, and instituted a forty-day cooling-off period.

During the cooling-off period, city staff attempted to respond positively to some of the less costly components of the employees' demands. For example, police officers were given access to the weight room of the local high school and a discount on uniform cleaning. Most of management's attention, however, focused on ways to solve the much greater problems of disgruntled employees and limited resources to provide vital public services. From the employees' perspective, the forty-day period passed with little visible progress.

Seeking solutions

Almost from the moment the demands had first been received, city management had been exploring service-delivery alternatives. Those efforts continued during the cooling-off period. For two reasons, attention was focused mostly on fire service options. First, because the fire service was a labor-intensive function characterized by extensive idle time, major changes in service-delivery patterns would be more manageable and more likely to achieve substantial benefits there than in the police function, where officers presumably spent their time between calls patrolling the community. Second, and perhaps more important, both Director of Administration Bristol and Fire Chief Caro were familiar with the reputation of Smokeater Systems, Inc. (SSI), a private company renowned for providing efficient fire services in a widely publicized contract arrangement in a neighboring state. If the firefighters persisted with their work slowdown, perhaps SSI could provide fire protection to Cedar Valley at a cost equal to or less than the current cost of service provision.

SSI was contacted, and by mid-October the city had a rough proposal in hand that promised to save $135,000 during the first year of operation. By early November that proposal had been refined: it contained a variety of service-level options that provided first-year savings ranging from $135,000 to $280,000. When local officials checked references, SSI got high marks for service quality and cost effectiveness.

Knowledge of the city's contact with SSI became widespread by mid-November, despite city officials' efforts to remain low key. Local firefighters were soon writing letters to the city council and the local newspaper editor suggesting that contract service would be unreliable, questioning SSI's willingness and ability to provide fire inspection and allied services, and raising the specter of increasing fire insurance premiums should SSI be hired. One writer asked, "Is the proposal to contract for fire services only another tactic to intimidate city employees?"

By November 20 all doubts about the seriousness of city management's interest in contracting with SSI had vanished. A memorandum from Martin invited the mayor and city council members to view a videotape of a nationally aired television segment on SSI's operation. A resolution authorizing a contract with SSI had been prepared by the city staff, although it was not considered at the council meeting that evening.

By mid-December most city council members had informed Martin, either directly or indirectly, that they were impressed by SSI's operation but that they preferred to make changes in the current operation, if possible, rather than scrap it and turn the fire service over to a contractor. Martin therefore instructed Bristol to continue his analysis of alternative methods of fire service delivery but to direct his attention particularly to the possibility of adapting various characteristics of the SSI operation to local use.

Different perceptions

By January the volatile situation of autumn had settled into an atmosphere of general mistrust. Firefighters and police officers viewed departmental administrators and the city's management staff suspiciously, privately and publicly attributing sinister motives to various actions. For example, they regarded management's unwillingness to negotiate with labor spokespersons and its willingness to consider contracting out fire services not as legitimate management strategies but as affronts to dedicated public safety employees, threats to their employment security, gestures of "bad faith" in the efforts to resolve the crisis, and reflections of management's indifference to the perspective of front-line police officers and firefighters.

Management, on the other hand, saw little to be gained by recognizing a bargaining unit when not required to do so by state law. Martin, Bristol, and many key management officials had little regard for the notion that a major purpose of local government is to provide jobs. They believed instead that the purpose of local government is to provide services and that pay and working conditions are productivity issues rather than humanitarian or social concerns. Accordingly, they viewed the consideration of contractual fire services as an entirely legitimate and even prudent management strategy.

These managers also resented the insinuations by police officers and firefighters that Martin and his colleagues cared little for the security of the community. They were angered by efforts to encourage residents and businesspersons to apply pressure on the city council and city management and by the inflammatory pronouncements and public appearances that delighted the local media. Particularly irritating were letters to the editor of the local newspaper that purported to speak for "the public," but in fact were written by relatives of police officers and firefighters.

Moreover, city management resented deeply what it believed to be desertion of managerial ranks and responsibilities by fire department middle management. It was true that city management had done little to create a strong sense of "management team" camaraderie with fire captains before or after the job action; but management was nevertheless offended not by supervisors' sympathy for the firefighter position (some of the captains who had stayed on the job probably also felt that) but by the overt leadership that some captains exercised in the job action.

Although contradictory, the views of both labor and management had some justification.

The decision problem

Against this backdrop, city management attempted to address what it perceived to be four fundamental problems:

1. Although the desired salary increase had been presented as an ultimatum rather than as a request and had come at a point during the fiscal year when the budget and the tax rate had already been established, Martin agreed fundamentally that salaries of public safety employees should be increased. His primary motivation, however, was to maintain a competitive compensation structure for city employees. The problem, therefore, was not a disagreement over the need for salary adjustments but rather the difficulty of developing a credible strategy to placate, or at least neutralize, disgruntled employees until the next budget cycle.
2. Because city resources were tight, the city council and the citizenry appeared to have little patience with suggestions that property taxes be raised to fund higher salaries. Substantial revenues, therefore, would have to be secured through money-saving changes in current operations.
3. Although Martin never sought a vote from the full city council, conversations between management and individual council members revealed little support for privatization of the fire service, despite substantial projected savings. As long as viable in-house options existed, council members appeared to prefer that route—a preference that effectively restricted the alternatives available to management.
4. Labor-management relations within the police and fire departments were severely strained. Each side viewed the other's comments and proposals cynically.

At Martin's request, in late January Bristol presented a staff analysis that explored five options.

The first option, continuation of the current operating mode, offered no solution to any of the existing problems. However, if the city could manage the existing situation until the next budget, it might be able to offer some concessions to the aggrieved employees and perhaps begin the process of rebuilding relationships with them. Furthermore, this option would require no long-term changes and therefore could appeal to anyone who thought the current problems might actually be short-term in nature.

The second option, simply cutting the number of fire department employees, would produce cost savings that could be used to make salary and other concessions. It would, however, also result inevitably in reductions in service level and in operating effectiveness. Layoffs or even reductions through attrition would be bitterly opposed, so this option did not even promise improved relations with the police and fire employees.

The third option was establishment of a public safety officer (PSO) program, in which police officers and firefighters would be cross-trained and deployed on patrol when not otherwise engaged in police or fire activities. Cross-trained public safety officers had been used successfully in some other cities despite chronic opposition from firefighters' associations. Locally, a PSO plan might produce some cost savings, but it had little administrative appeal to the police chief, the fire chief, or the city management team. Those officials had just experienced the difficulty of dealing with coordinated actions by police officers and firefighters and thus had little inclination to unite the two groups structurally.

The fourth option, contracting out fire protection, was the preference of the management team, but the council would almost certainly reject it. At a minimum, the management team would have to exert substantial effort to sell the council on this option, despite the substantial projected cost savings.

The fifth option was departmental reorganization and the adoption of a "fire specialist" program. As outlined by Bristol, this option would reduce fire department employment by 20 percent, from fifty-one to forty-one full-time employees, and establish new deployment patterns. Under this program, station-based firefighters responding to a structural alarm would be supplemented at the scene by other city employees who had been trained as firefighters and equipped on assigned standby days with a fire department pickup, turnout gear, a two-way radio, and a pager. If the alarm occurred during working hours, the fire specialists from other city departments who were on standby that day would leave their jobs and respond immediately. If the alarm occurred after working hours or on the weekend, they would respond from wherever they happened to be within their assigned response zones. The net effect of the plan was an increase in response strength—from seven or eight firefighters per standard structural alarm under the old system to nine under the new system—despite a reduction in the number of station-based firefighters.

Unlike the rotational pattern used by SSI that required standby personnel to be on call several days in succession, the rotational pattern for standby assignments in Cedar Valley would be one day on and the next two days off. Thus, local firefighters would be able to serve as fire specialists on "off" days in their own 24-hours-on/48-hours-off work cycle. This arrangement served at least three strategic purposes. First and most important, it would tap the most highly trained pool for fire specialist expertise. Second, it would offer firefighters a source of supplemental income that would make use of their skills and impose minimal disruption on normal activities. Third, participation in the fire specialist program by full-time firefighters would do much to blunt criticism of the program, increase the program's chances for long-term survival, and reduce the tendency to view employees from other departments as "scabs" who were seizing jobs from fire department employees. If employees had to be recruited from other departments, it would be because off-duty firefighters had declined to serve as front-line fire specialists.

When fully implemented, the restructured fire service was expected to produce annual savings exceeding $135,000. For two reasons, however, initial savings were expected to be considerably lower. First, city management recommended using normal attrition rather than layoffs to effect employment reductions; in addition, management recommended against salary reductions, even in cases where cutbacks resulted in downward reclassifications of workers. Second, city management recommended that a substantial portion of the first three years' savings be devoted to a smoke detector rebate program to improve fire safety in existing dwellings.

In February, Martin recommended the fifth option—departmental reorganization and adoption of the fire specialist program—to the city council. Martin and his staff perceived the immediate reaction from the community to be either positive or, at worst, noncommittal, except among firefighters and their friends, their relatives, and others who had been their principal supporters during the autumn work slowdown.

Management staff held meetings with firefighters to describe the plan in detail, to discuss its ramifications, and to receive suggestions for improvement. The atmosphere of the sessions was tense; most questions from firefighters were designed less to elicit information than to express opinions and challenge the management plan. The response of the firefighters was decidedly negative. A press release in late February stated the firefighters' position:

The Cedar Valley Firefighters Association wants the public to know the truth about the city administration's so-called "reorganization plan" and some of the dangers this plan poses to our community.

The number of professional firefighters on duty during an average shift would be reduced by 20 percent and supplemented by an unspecified number of "civilian specialists" who are not professional firefighters. They have not been trained in the skills and sciences necessary for a successful firefighting operation, such as hydraulics, fire chemistry, rescue and first aid, ventilation, physics, building construction, arson investigation, and fire prevention and inspection.

Members of a fire company *must* train together as a team and work together as a team; they must stay abreast of new techniques and equipment to help them save lives and preserve property. Under our present system, the Cedar Valley Fire Department has an enviable record of success, proving that adequate manpower, responding together as a team, prevents loss. *The saving of lives and the preservation of property are difficult to evaluate in dollars and cents.*

The city administration claims that the proposed plan will cost the taxpayers less than our present, successful system. Actually, implementation of the new plan alone, including the purchase and maintenance of four radio-equipped pickup trucks and between twelve and eighteen pagers, along with the payment of civilian salaries, will negate most, if not all, of the savings.

The Cedar Valley Firefighters Association urges all citizens to read our newspaper ads carefully and to call city council and express concern over this hasty action.

The battle lines of the previous fall were still clearly in place as the focus of attention shifted to the deliberations of the city council. "If they're going to fight me every step of the way," thought Martin, "maybe I should have pushed harder for option 4, the contractual arrangement. Maybe I should revert to that option even now."

Discussion questions

1. Early in the crisis, Martin expressed strong disapproval but nevertheless tolerated a work slowdown for four weeks before forcing action to break the impasse. Was he too patient or too impatient? What action could he have taken earlier that might have produced more favorable results?

2. Was Martin wise in refusing to treat the police and fire employee associations as negotiating units? Why or why not?

3. Did Martin proceed properly? Should he have given in a little more and complied with additional demands? Should he have "battened down the hatches" and attempted to ride out the storm? Should he have focused less on substantive issues and more on smoothing out relationships? Or was he correct in risking further antagonism by considering major changes in the status quo that would be likely to face stiff opposition from firefighters or police officers? In essence, should he have retreated a bit, dug in, sought a truce, or mounted a charge? Explain your answer.

4. Sometimes the most effective political leadership is achieved by keeping a low profile and avoiding confrontation while waiting for a solution to make itself obvious. Is it possible that Martin, as a new city manager, felt that he had to prove his leadership ability by taking

direct action? What would you have advised him to do? If he had chosen to keep a low profile, what, if anything, should he have done to speed the emergence of a solution?

5. Are there other options that should have been added to Martin's list? If so, what are they? Evaluate them.

6. Martin's original preference was option 4, contractual fire protection. If no other option appears as promising, and the firefighters are opposed even to option 5, should Martin return to his first choice and attempt to sell it to the council? If so, how should he proceed? If not, why not?

7. Are there modifications that could be made in either option 4 or option 5 that might make it more acceptable to the firefighters? If so, what are they? What costs might they entail?

8. If you were Martin, how would you proceed? Why?

9. Realistically, what is the best outcome that Martin can hope to achieve?

The aftermath

Despite firefighter opposition, Martin continued to advocate option 5. In his presentation of the fire specialist proposal to the council, he stressed that this option would actually increase the fire department's response strength at fires and that it would produce significant savings, releasing funds that could be used to improve fire safety through the smoke detector program and to upgrade the city's compensation plan. He acknowledged the firefighters' opposition, but he urged the council not to allow its policy-making prerogatives to be blocked by the intransigent self-interest of employee groups.

Despite persistent opposition by many fire department employees, the city council approved the reorganization plan. By the end of February, Chief Caro had started to recruit personnel for the twelve fire specialist positions required for the program. The initial invitation to join the specialist ranks was extended to fire department employees. Preliminary reactions among fire department employees swung from one extreme to another. At one point it appeared that they might boycott the program, and at another it looked as if they would use their priority status to lock up all fire specialist positions, thereby blocking other city employees from significant involvement.

Eventually, nine fire department employees joined the fire specialist program, thereby risking almost certain ostracism by the most zealous of the work slowdown advocates. Even more galling to program opponents was the fact that four police officers, including Jacksboro, who had been a leader in the police work slowdown, became fire specialists. Six employees from other city departments also joined the initial class of trainees. (Some of the specialists would serve only in backup roles, temporarily filling in when regular specialists could not serve on standby.) By late May all participants had received at least thirty hours of training, and all necessary equipment had been obtained. On June 1 the fire specialist program began operating.

The fire specialist program proved overwhelmingly successful on virtually every measure. The first several months were characterized not by traffic accidents or by a devastating fire, as city management had secretly feared, but by incident after incident in which an early-arriving fire specialist was instrumental in controlling a small fire. City officials rarely missed an opportunity to report program successes, noting that having four fire specialists on standby more than doubled the points from which fire responses originated and thereby made possible quicker response to at least some emergencies. The effectiveness of fire specialists at larger fires was similarly documented and publicized.

However, implementation of the fire specialist program was not problem free. A few supervisors from other departments resented what they perceived as an intrusion on their authority over employees who served as fire specialists; these supervisors relented only when upper management made its commitment to program success absolutely clear. In addition, fire department officials discovered that their responsibilities were much broader and a bit more complex as they learned how to supervise standby personnel. For example, they were forced at an early stage to administer quick and decisive discipline when a fire specialist's decision while on standby reflected adversely on the program: A specialist was suspended for thirty days for exercising poor judgment in going to a local tavern while on standby, even though he insisted that he had consumed no alcoholic beverages. Program successes, however, far outweighed any problems, suggesting a long-term role for fire specialists in the Cedar Valley fire service.

Final discussion questions

1.   The city council in this case expected the city manager to maintain control of the situation and to keep the council informed of developments. With few exceptions, council members did not attempt to move to the forefront of the controversy or to go public with their opinions, choosing instead to allow the manager room to operate. How important is such a stance by the council to the outcome of a crisis? How could a different scenario have affected the outcome? What can a manager do to secure such support from the council?

2.   How important is a long-term commitment by city management to nurturing labor-management relations? Could management in this case have involved labor more effectively in resolving the crisis or in designing program improvements? Given state law and existing policy, should management have made more of an effort to do so before the crisis developed? What can, or should, be done along this line in communities that do not have collective bargaining or an organized program of labor-management relations?

3.   If more money could have been saved by contracting out fire services than by any other reasonable means, should Martin have pushed harder for that option? Why or why not?

4.   Some experts argue that productivity improvements are most likely to occur in a stable environment. How did organizational turmoil and resource constraints affect the outcome of this case?

5.   What can a newly appointed manager do to create a good relationship with workers and an environment favorable to worker productivity?

6.   How would you advise Martin to improve the labor-management environment in Cedar Valley in the aftermath of this crisis?

Part seven:
Finance and
budgeting

Introduction to part seven: Finance and budgeting

Nothing is more vital to the daily process of government than money, and no concern poses a wider range of policy and management issues. The cases in Part Seven demonstrate the breadth of these issues, starting with those that are, or should be, purely managerial in nature and progressing through those with political overtones and those that involve principles of enduring significance.

The first case, a dispute over the amount and use of funds for the payment of overtime in a county correctional facility, raises issues that are essentially managerial in nature. They concern the efforts of a budget office staff to ensure that operating departments cooperate in a cost containment program and the challenge of developing new administrative policies to reduce the level of public spending.

The second case is distinctly political; it poses policy problems that should ultimately be resolved by legislative action. Such resolution, however, is typically preceded by administrative recommendations, and this case suggests the kinds of questions that need to be resolved before such recommendations can be developed.

The third case poses an even more fundamental issue: the basic principles that should guide and direct government policy formation, in this instance in economic development. Unfortunately, considerations of basic principles seldom if ever occur in a vacuum; they arise in the context of specific problems requiring specific decisions. Even though the establishment of such principles is a major legislative responsibility, it inevitably occurs through the adoption of solutions to existing problems. Thus, the resolution of questions of principle still starts on the desks of the government's administrative staff.

It is perhaps appropriate that this book should present questions of finance and questions of principle in the same context. Principle and policy, whether of high or low order, most frequently are addressed within the context of budgetary and fiscal issues. Ideally, principles should be formulated independently of monetary considerations, especially where public principles and public funds are concerned. Regrettably, in government as in life, the ideal is rarely achieved. It is easy for government to applaud ideas and proposals; it is hard for government to finance programs. Thus, it is within the financial decision-making process that most public policy is ultimately made and implemented.

The following cases demonstrate the truth of this classic scholarly observation.

16

County prison overtime
Tom Mills

Editor's introduction

The politics of the budgetary process certainly do not end when the budget is adopted. Administrative problems continue: Line items have to be stretched over the year; costs must be contained; budgetary policies must be enforced; and the budget office must continue to seek economies in spending practices.

Thus is the stage set for continuing dialog, and sometimes confrontation, between the budget office and line departments. This case describes such a dialog and a resulting confrontation between department heads. It provides a classic example of the politics of budget administration and the line-staff conflict so commonly found in organizational theory and management.

The dispute itself follows a classic pattern. What starts as an exchange of memos between fellow department heads becomes acrimonious. The ensuing dialog involves questions of jurisdiction and expertise and even a suspicion of motives. The dispute soon involves the county administrator, but not before the matter has come to the attention of the county board chair.

As is almost always the case in such management problems, there is no clear right or wrong. And with two valuable and competent subordinates involved, the administrator finds himself searching for a win-win solution, or at least one that will not present an obvious defeat or embarrassment for either party. An overriding consideration is the need for a solution that falls within the constraints posed by local politics.

For the reader, this case provides a glimpse into a little-known and -understood public service function: the management of a county correctional facility. The dispute centers on overtime pay for correctional officers, and the solution must take account of the undeniable need for, and the working conditions of, such officers. As is so often the case with public safety personnel, any budgetary savings must be accomplished without reduction in service or increased danger to the public.

The solution thus requires good analysis of relevant data, faithfulness to operating budgetary policies, sensitivity to the personalities of those involved, and an eye on the politicians watching from the sidelines. In short, this case poses a typical challenge to the creativity of the public-sector decisionmaker.

Case 16
County prison overtime

Background

Franklin County is a suburban/rural county located in one of the Mid-Atlantic states; it adjoins a large eastern city. Franklin County has a land area of 650 square miles; a population of approximately 500,000; and 45 local governments that consist of boroughs, villages, and townships. The local governments have their own police forces but lack secure holding facilities for defendants arrested and bound over by local magistrates for trial in the county courts.

The county provides all criminal justice system services from the county courthouse located in Franklinville, the county seat. On a tract of county-owned land just outside of Franklinville, the county operates two detention facilities: a small medium-security facility for juveniles and a large, modern medium-security facility for both male and female adult detainees. The latter facility, called the county prison, has a capacity of approximately 340 inmates and is maintained and operated by a staff of 181 employees.

Franklin County's chief lawmaking and administrative authority is the elected county commission, which is vested with both executive and legislative powers. Voters also elect a number of administrative officers—including the sheriff, the controller, and the district attorney—and the judges of the county court, called the supreme court of common pleas.

The county commission consists of three members elected countywide for four-year terms. The county code requires that one of the three commissioners be a member of the opposing, or minority, party. The county is predominantly Republican, and members of that party regularly control the countywide elective offices. The county commission, perhaps owing to its higher visibility, has occasionally been controlled by a Democratic majority.

The county commissioners appoint a county administrator, all nonelected department heads, and the members of most county boards and commissions. The day-to-day operation of the county is the responsibility of the county administrator, who is a professional local government manager recruited and appointed on the basis of technical competence. The county boasts a commitment to professionalism. The county administrator recruits and hires his or her own staff and has been responsible for securing the appointments of the finance director, the personnel director, and the director of purchasing.

The county code constrains the county commissioners' powers of appointment in some instances. The power to appoint the director of the department of corrections, who oversees both the county prison and the juvenile rehabilitation center, is vested in a prison board. The prison board is composed of the president judge of the supreme court of common pleas or that judge's designee, the district attorney, the sheriff, the controller, and the three county commissioners. Five of the seven members of the board were Republicans at the time this case begins.

The case

In the previous election, the Democratic party had won the majority of seats on the county commission by taking what proved to be the more popular position on a critical environmental issue. In hopes of reelection, the Democratic commissioners instituted a cost containment program that, if successful, would enable them to complete their term without raising taxes. The commissioners issued a directive to all department heads instructing them to implement economies wherever possible. The county administrator, George Truly, was given the principal responsibility for implementing the cost containment program. He, in turn, had charged the finance director, Donald Dexter, with much of the operating responsibility for the program.

After monitoring the expenditures of the county prison, Dexter was convinced that overtime expenditures were out of control. He had met on several occasions with Charles Goodheart, the director of corrections, and had called him almost weekly in an effort to reduce overtime costs. In Dexter's view, those contacts had been of little value, since overtime expenditures continued at what he regarded as an excessive rate. Somewhat reluctantly, he decided to go "on record." He dictated what was to be the first in a series of memorandums.

March 12
TO:　　　Charles R. Goodheart, Director of Corrections
FROM:　　Donald D. Dexter, Finance Director
SUBJECT:　Excessive Prison Overtime

Pursuant to the county commissioners' directive of January 8 establishing the cost containment program, my staff and I have been closely monitoring the overtime expenditures incurred in the operation of the county prison. We have had several meetings and numerous telephone conversations regarding this matter with both you and your key staff members—all to no avail. Overtime expenditures have continued to rise and might well exceed the budget allocation. This I find to be particularly distressing, since we had every hope that this was one area of your operation in which we could effect significant savings.

I would greatly appreciate it if you would provide me, at your first opportunity, with a detailed justification for the current rate of overtime usage and your plans to keep such expenditures to an absolute minimum.

cc:　　George S. Truly, County Administrator
　　　　Frank Friendly, Personnel Director

Before sending this memorandum, Dexter had given the action considerable thought and had concluded that, even if the memorandum was a bit strong, it was warranted in this case.

In the weeks that followed, Dexter continued to scrutinize the prison payroll records but did not observe any reduction in the use of overtime. He was about to schedule yet another meeting with Goodheart when he received the following memorandum.

April 5
TO:　　　Donald D. Dexter, Finance Director
FROM:　　Charles R. Goodheart, Director of Corrections
SUBJECT:　Response to Your Request for Information Regarding Overtime
　　　　　Expenditures

You indicated in your memorandum of March 12 that you felt we were utilizing an excessive amount of overtime. I welcome the opportunity to explain what might appear to be excessive overtime usage, but which really is no more than prudent prison management.

You will recall that during the budget hearings last year, I shared with you information on overtime usage in the four surrounding counties. Each of these counties has a comparable prison system, and, as I noted then, each uses more overtime than we do.

You must remember that I requested $434,400 as an overtime allocation for the current fiscal year (including holiday overtime). The overtime figure that was allocated to this department was substantially less. When budget allocations were announced, there was no explanation for the reduced overtime figure other than a general statement—which certainly is appropriate for you as finance director to make—that times were difficult, money was tight, and every effort must be made to curtail unnecessary expenditures. Although I accept these comments in the spirit in which they were made, I still am held responsible and accountable to the prison board for operating a safe and secure correctional institution. Prisons are potentially very dangerous, and that danger can be averted only by keeping staffing levels at safe and realistic levels.

As we both know, there are many justifiable causes for overtime usage in a prison setting. In the following paragraphs I'll attempt to identify the major causes.

Turnover During last year and continuing into this year, we have experienced high levels of turnover among our correctional officers. When staff members leave we are required to fill their posts, which we do through the use of overtime. The problem continues during recruitment for replacements and during the three-week training course to which all recruits are sent. When you add the two-to-four-week delay in filling positions to the three-week training period, you can readily see that a considerable amount of overtime might be involved. Turnover is perhaps our most critical problem. Previously I sent you a detailed commentary on our turnover experience. Over the past several years, I have told everyone willing to listen that there is a strong relationship between turnover in a correctional institution and overtime expenditures.

First of all, entry-level correctional officers are poorly paid, and, as I've told the county commissioners at every budget hearing, that is certainly true in our case. Second, this is a very difficult profession, and prison personnel are continually required to work at very high stress levels. Finally, we enjoy very little public esteem, and the working conditions can on occasion be very unpleasant. Small wonder that there is high turnover not only in our prisons but in prisons all across this country. When a staff member leaves, the need to fill the post continues. Unless the prison board tells me that it does not want me to fill vacant posts, I will continue to do so, and I have no choice but to use overtime.

Hospital watches Whenever an inmate requires inpatient treatment in a local hospital, I must provide the necessary security. Recently, two inmates were hospitalized. For each day of hospitalization, we provided two correctional officers per shift, three shifts per day, for a total of forty-eight hours of coverage. As you can see, the time mounts up rapidly. We have no fat in our shift complements; therefore, when a need like this arises, it must be covered with overtime.

Emergency situations Whenever there is reason to believe that inmates might be planning an action that could endanger the security of the institution, I adopt an emergency plan that puts all supervisors on twelve-hour shifts. I do not place this institution on an emergency footing for any trivial or illusory cause. Those instances in which I have used emergency overtime have been fully justified, and I stand by my actions.

Sick leave Our sick leave usage compares favorably with that of other county departments that enjoy less trying working conditions. Still, when a correctional officer calls in sick, his or her position must be filled, and it is usually filled by the use of overtime. We can't call in a replacement on one hour's notice on the person's day off, upset his or her family life, and worsen a bad morale situation simply to cover an eight-hour shift. We feel that the use of overtime in these situations is the most sensible solution.

Workers' compensation I have frequently remarked on this problem in the past. Today we are filling two posts that are vacant as a result of workers' compensation claims against the county. When an employee is injured on the job and a doctor certifies that he or she may not work, I have no choice but to utilize overtime to fill the post. I simply don't have any slack resources that would permit me to do otherwise.

Reserve duty Under the laws of this state, all staff members who are members of bona fide military reserve units are authorized to take fifteen days of paid military leave annually. When they depart for their military training, their posts remain, and we are responsible for filling them. The problem is exacerbated by the tendency of both military leave and vacations to cluster in the summer months. Another aspect of military reserve duty also generates overtime. Our correctional officers are scheduled around the clock and frequently are scheduled to work on a weekend when they are expected to attend reserve drills. Under the policy adopted by the county commissioners, the reservists may take "no-pay" time and fulfill their reserve obligations. While the county saves their straight-time pay, I am forced to use overtime to fill their posts.

Vacations   We do make a concerted effort to schedule vacations so as not to result in overtime expenditures. Unfortunately, as a direct result of our lean staffing, on occasion we must resort to overtime to permit our correctional officers to enjoy the vacations they have earned.

Training programs   Compared to the standard advocated by national authorities, our training efforts are extremely modest. We provide equal employment opportunity training, particularly with respect to our female correctional officers, and some supervisory training. In addition, we provide training in interpersonal communication skills—training I regard as essential in an institution such as ours. Since our shift schedules contain no fat, personnel must be brought in for training on their days off, which, of course, results in overtime.

The major causes of our overtime expenditures are as noted above. I have brought these problems and their causes to the attention of the county commissioners at every budget hearing over the past nine years. Our staff utilization records and overtime documentation are available to anyone who wishes to review them. We have nothing to hide.

I don't mean to be flippant or discourteous, but frankly I'm no wizard. I cannot operate this institution without a reasonable overtime allocation any more than the Jews of antiquity could make bricks without straw. For you to insist that I do so strikes me as being every bit as unreasonable as was the order of the Pharaoh's overseer.

If you can provide specific suggestions regarding policies or methodologies that you feel will assist in overtime reduction without compromising safe and efficient operation of this institution, please be assured that we will be happy to work with you in implementing them. We are open to any thoughtful and constructive recommendations that you or your staff may have. In the meantime, you might consider funding a comprehensive study of our staffing needs, including the need for overtime, by a nationally recognized group specializing in the field of corrections.

cc: Members of the County Prison Board
       George S. Truly, County Administrator
       Frank Friendly, Personnel Director

Dexter read the memorandum twice, his feelings alternating between anger and frustration. He regarded Goodheart highly, knowing him to be a caring individual and a respected corrections professional. "But clearly," thought Dexter, "he's no administrator. I asked him for a detailed justification of his use of overtime and his plans to keep those expenditures to a minimum, and what did he do? He offered me a lesson in biblical history and tried to put the monkey on my back with that bit about 'any thoughtful and constructive recommendations' I might have—baloney!" Dexter noted that Goodheart had twice mentioned his accountability to the county prison board and had been ingracious enough to copy the prison board members on the memorandum. "That," thought Dexter sourly, "is just a brazen example of saber rattling. Maybe he thinks that if he can broaden the controversy by bringing in the prison board, he can get me off his case. Not likely!" Still angry, he spun in his chair, picked up the mike of his recording machine, and dictated his reply.

Meanwhile, Jim Kirby, chair of the county commission, was enjoying his new role. He was no stranger to county government; he had been the minority commissioner for eight years under Republican administrations; but that, he felt, was essentially a "nay-sayer" role. Now, as chairman in a Democratic administration, he was in a position to take the lead on policy decisions, and he was enjoying it. He had founded a very successful business in the county and had called the shots there for more than thirty years. Although Kirby had often mused that government and business were much more different than alike—at least on paper—he relished his leadership role in the county.

Kirby prided himself on his capacity for work and made every effort to keep on top of things. He regretted that he had not read Goodheart's memorandum of April 5 before attending the monthly prison board meeting. He hated to be blindsided! The president judge of common pleas court, Harvey Strickland, who was also president of the prison board, had shown Kirby his copy of the memorandum as well as a copy of Dexter's memorandum of March 12, which had prompted Goodheart's reply. Strickland had been his usual amiable self, but Kirby knew from long experience that with him, you worried not about what he said but about what he left unsaid. The fact that Strickland had brought the memorandums with him to the meeting and his oblique references to "those in this life who are penny-wise and pound-foolish" convinced Kirby that trouble was brewing.

As soon as Kirby got back to his office, he called George Truly, the county administrator, and asked him to stop by. Truly was the perfect balance to Kirby. Kirby was "born to lead"—an activist by nature, full of ideas and restless energy and impatient with detail. Truly, on the other hand, was a "doer." A professional administrator with substantial background in local government, he disliked the publicity and pressure of policy leadership, preferring instead the satisfaction that came from making policies work and seeing that services were delivered. The two men understood each other and had developed an effective working relationship. Neither one worried about the line between policy and administration; each one understood the overlap between the two activities and freely advised the other about county problems.

As Truly walked through the doorway, Kirby asked him, "Are you familiar with Don Dexter's memo of March 12 and Charlie Goodheart's reply?"

Truly said that he was and that he had already spoken to Dexter about them but that he had been too late.

"What do you mean, too late?" Kirby asked. "This thing looks to me like it can still be salvaged."

"Then," Truly replied, "I guess you haven't seen Don's memorandum of April 7."

April 7
TO: Charles R. Goodheart, Director of Corrections
FROM: Donald D. Dexter, Finance Director
SUBJECT: Your Evasive Memorandum of April 5

In a sincere effort to implement the county commissioners' directive establishing a countywide cost containment program, I wrote to you on March 12. In my memorandum I asked you to provide me with a detailed justification for the current rate of overtime usage and your plans to keep such expenditures to an absolute minimum.

In reply, you gave me three pages of generalities and gratuitous comments. You're the prison expert, not me. If I had any good ideas on how you could run your operation more efficiently or economically, you can be sure I'd offer them. But as I see it, that's your job, not mine. My job is to see to the financial well-being of this county, and I can't do my job if I don't get cooperation. That's all I'm asking for—your cooperation in achieving the goals set for all of us by the county commissioners. Your knowledge of the Old Testament is doubtless better than mine, but I do know that the Pharaoh didn't pay overtime. As far as I am concerned, you can have all the straw you want, but cut down on the overtime.

cc: George S. Truly, County Administrator
     Frank Friendly, Personnel Director

The decision problem

After Kirby had finished reading Dexter's memo of April 7, he sighed wearily, laid it aside, looked up at Truly, and said, "I see what you mean. Any suggestions?"

Truly was a career administrator who had spent twenty-two years in a series of increasingly demanding city management jobs before being recruited by Kirby to serve as Franklin County administrator. He had been given carte blanche in the recruitment of his administrative staff, and he had picked, among others, Don Dexter. Dexter was extremely bright; he had been the controller for a large manufacturing firm in the county—quite an accomplishment for a man who was not yet thirty. "But," Truly reflected, "he's never swum in political waters before, and there's no question that he's in over his head."

As the two men reviewed the situation, they tried to define the problem specifically, to identify possible courses of action, and to anticipate the probable outcomes of those alternatives.

It was evident that whatever they did, they had to do it quickly. Strickland could not yet have seen Dexter's memorandum of April 7. If he had, he would have had it with him at the meeting, and he would not have been so affable.

The cost containment program was important to Kirby and the other Democrat on the county commission. It was probably their best hope of reelection. If they exempted the county prison from the program for fear of what the prison board might do, the program could be weakened throughout the county. After all, why should the other departments conform if the prison wasn't expected to do its part?

Under the county code, the prison board, not the county commission, was responsible for approving all prison-related expenditures. The board, with its Republican majority, could give Goodheart a blank check if they wanted to, and the commissioners would be able to do nothing about it. "Well not exactly 'nothing,' " groused Kirby. "We could direct the county solicitor to sue the prison board, but since the president of the board is also the president judge, that's more of a theoretical than a practical remedy."

In fact, it was much more likely that the prison board would wind up suing the county commissioners. If the board alleged that an imminent threat to public safety was created by the refusal of the commissioners and their agents to fund the county prison adequately, it could bring an action *in mandamus*. In that event, the prison board would not be likely to limit the action to the question of prison overtime but would, in all likelihood, open a Pandora's box of problems. Goodheart had documented many of these problems in his memorandum of April 5, and that memo would probably be Exhibit A at a trial. Issues most likely to be litigated included the needs for adequate prison staffing levels, proactive strategies to combat the high rate of turnover, and higher salaries for correctional officers.

Kirby knew that if political warfare broke out, the Republicans would move quickly to seize the high ground. They would allege that the Democrats were jeopardizing the safety and tranquility of the community for the sake of a few paltry dollars. Kirby was too old a hand to suppose that arguments of efficiency and economy would carry any weight with the public in such a debate—especially if people were convinced that they were going to be murdered in their beds.

Since all the elected officials in the county were Republicans with the exception of Kirby and the other Democratic commissioner, they could really make things untenable. So far, the elected officials had been cooperating in the cost containment program. If, however, they chose to support the prison board in a confrontation with the commission, the cost containment program would be thoroughly scuttled.

"Don Dexter really put us in a box," remarked Kirby.

"Yes, but he's young and bright; he won't make the same mistake again," replied Truly.

"If the president judge gets him in his sights, he won't have the opportunity," observed Kirby solemnly.

"Funny thing," Kirby continued, "Don was right; that memorandum from Charlie was evasive, but Don should have known better than to say so. More than that, he shouldn't have written at all. In a situation like that, you go to see the guy. Writing is a very incomplete, very limited way to communicate. It's a lot easier to talk tough to your dictating machine than to an adversary. My rules have always been, never write a letter if you can avoid it, and never throw one away."

After almost an hour of discussion, the two men had identified five alternative approaches to the problem. Unfortunately, none of them were without risk.

1.   Exempt the prison from the cost containment program. Under this alternative, Kirby would contact Strickland informally and intimate that the commission would not be unduly concerned if the prison did not achieve its cost containment objectives. The justification offered would be that as a public safety and law enforcement agency, the prison ought not be held to the same standard of cost reduction as other agencies, lest public safety suffer. The main problem with this approach was that party loyalty was paramount in this county, and Strickland was certain to share this information with the other elected officials, especially the district attorney and the sheriff, who headed justice system agencies. Once the commissioners had yielded on the prison, it would be difficult for them to hold the line on other justice system agencies, and the cost containment program would be seriously jeopardized. The result could be that the majority commissioners would be branded as weak men of little resolve, and that could have serious spillover effects in other areas.

2.   Fund an in-depth study of the prison by a nationally recognized group specializing in corrections. Since this was a solution proposed by the director of corrections, it would most likely gain the acceptance of the prison board. Apart from the cost of such a study, which could be considerable, its recommendations were not likely to be favorable to the county administration. Through long experience, Kirby and Truly had come to believe that special interest groups of whatever ilk rarely supported anything antithetical to their special interest. Worse yet, a comprehensive study might only document and verify the types of complaints that the director of corrections had been making for years. It was one thing to ignore his complaints; it would be something quite different were the county administration to ignore the studied recommendations of nationally recognized experts.

3.   Conduct an in-house study of the need for prison overtime. This alternative appeared to have a good deal to recommend it. The county

had a small management analysis team that reported directly to the county administrator. The supervisor of the team was a thoroughly honest and objective career professional who had been a founding member of the Association of Management Analysts in State and Local Government (MASLIG) and was well respected both within the county and beyond its borders. The problem, of course, was one of credibility. Despite his excellent reputation, his objectivity might be questioned in the partisan political climate that prevailed in Franklin County. Moreover, the prison board might refuse to approve such a study. A study could be undertaken without the prison board's concurrence, as a prerogative of the majority commissioners, but in that event, the prison board might view the study as flawed.

4. Attempt to find an "honest broker" to conduct a study of prison overtime. "Honest" in this context meant someone who would be considered honest in the eyes of the prison board—someone they would perceive as having no ax to grind. Ideally, this person should already work for the county and be known by, and enjoy the confidence of, the prison board. But who? The downside of this alternative, assuming that such a person could be found, was that the "honest broker" might not be all that honest. Should such a person be selected with the prison board's concurrence, that person might very well take the prison board's side, to the considerable embarrassment of the county administration.

5. Invite Strickland to undertake the overtime study with members of his staff. The court's administrative staff included several career professionals in court administration who were graduates of the Institute for Court Management. They were undoubtedly capable of conducting the study, and Strickland and the prison board, which he clearly dominated, would certainly find them acceptable. The question, again, was one of objectivity. Truly favored this alternative, arguing that if, as he believed, they were really professionals, they would be objective. Kirby's response was insightful: "I don't recall book and verse, but somewhere in the scripture it is written, 'Whose bread I eat, his song I sing,' and those fellows eat court bread."

What really was needed was a dispassionate review of prison overtime usage, the development of sound recommendations that would reduce overtime expenses without endangering the public, and an appraisal of the adequacy of the current budgetary allocation for prison overtime. This last point was particularly important. Goodheart continually reminded the prison board that his overtime request had been cut arbitrarily by the finance department without consultation or even explanation. True, there were other important questions that the study could appropriately consider, such as the adequacy of entry-level salaries for correctional officers and the appropriateness of current staffing levels. But solutions to both of these problems would be likely to cost the county more money. Given a choice, Kirby would prefer to postpone consideration of all problems that might result in increased cost to the county until after the next election.

Fortunately, the collective bargaining agreement with the local union that represented the correctional officers was due to expire in September. The study would certainly be completed well before then, and any recommendations requiring work-rule changes could be negotiated as part of the contract settlement.

Kirby turned to Truly and said, "George, give this some thought—and quickly! See what you can come up with."

Truly knew he had to work fast to answer two questions: (1) Which of the alternatives should be recommended? and (2) If a study were to be undertaken, what kind of person should be given the assignment?

Discussion questions

1. Judging from the statements and actions of the principal actors in the case, in what ways did their value premises differ?

2. What purposes, if any, are served by "going on record," as Dexter did in his first memorandum?

3. Instead of dictating his reply to Goodheart's memorandum of April 5 while he was still angry, what should Dexter have done?

4. Was Kirby correct in his observation that "writing is a very incomplete, very limited way to communicate"?

5. Are Kirby's and Truly's reservations about the objectivity of a nationally recognized group of corrections experts well founded? Would the recommendations of such a group be more likely to support or oppose the director of corrections? Why?

6. Which of the five alternatives, or what combination of the alternatives, should Truly recommend?

7. If the county administrator's recommendation involves a study, what kind of person should be selected to head it? Should it be a member of the county staff or an outsider? Should partisan affiliation be a consideration? Should the prison board be consulted on the choice? How important is reputation in such an assignment?

8. If a study is to be commissioned, what instructions or "charge" should be given to the analysts?

The aftermath

Truly's recommendation was a combination of alternatives 3, 4, and 5. He saw no reason to exempt the prison from measures that applied to all other parts of the county government, and he believed that the only way to obtain data for an objective approach to the issue was to commission a study, preferably by an "honest broker." After considering and rejecting several possibilities, Truly recommended that a study be conducted by a team to be headed by Geraldine Eager, administrative assistant to the minority commissioner. Eager was the daughter of the county chair of the Republican party. All of the Republican majority members of the prison board had known her since she was an infant, and all were beholden to her father. Eager had just completed her work for an M.P.A. degree and was looking forward to a career as a professional local government manager. She had interned in Truly's office, and he had established a mentoring relationship with her. She was relatively inexperienced, but that problem could be overcome by having the county's management analysis staff assist her in the study.

Kirby suggested the arrangement to minority commissioner Joe Finley, Eager's boss. He felt reasonably certain that Finley would jump at the idea. Kirby knew that Finley had promised Eager's father to give Eager responsible work and that Finley had thus far been unable to deliver on that promise. Kirby also knew from his own experience that in the commission form of government, minority commissioners, themselves, have little challenging and responsible work to do.

Finley agreed to propose the arrangement to the prison board. The board concurred in the study plan, imposing the condition at Strickland's suggestion that a member of the court administrative staff be on the study team.

The study team reviewed finance department and prison budget files, central payroll records, prison overtime expenditure reports, staffing plans, and shift staffing schedules. By using several different methods of calculating overtime budget estimates, the team determined that a reasonable overtime budget request from the prison would have ranged between $294,200 and $348,600, well below the $434,400 requested by the prison but in line with the finance department's allocation of $319,000.

The study team also found that the prison's estimate of overtime needed for holidays had been overstated by nearly $100,000 and that overtime costs had been inflated because higher-paid employees were working appreciably more overtime than their lower-paid co-workers. Finally, the study team found that 12.5 percent of all nonholiday overtime was occasioned by turnover, thus supporting Goodheart's contention that turnover was a serious problem.

In discussing possible solutions, the team came up with the concept of a correctional officer pool. Under this plan, twenty more correctional officers than were authorized in the budget would be recruited and sent to the three-week training program. On completing their training, they would be placed in a pool from which permanent appointments would be made as vacancies occurred. In the meantime, they would be on call to cover overtime assignments, but at a straight-time rate. In effect, until they achieved their permanent appointments, they would be per diem employees. The start-up costs of the pool were estimated at $16,152, and approval by the collective bargaining agent for the correctional officers was required, since this was a fundamental change in work rules.

The politics of the study worked out as well as the analysis did. The prison board accepted the study and endorsed the the pool concept, which was subsequently implemented. Kirby gave the prison board credit for the $50,000 in annual overtime savings realized by the pool arrangement. Potentially embarrassing aspects of the study were downplayed from the outset. The $100,000 overstatement of holiday overtime requirements was shrugged off by Goodheart with the quip that since he was sure that Dexter was going to cut his overtime request, it was just good budgetary strategy to build in a safety margin. This time, Dexter did not dispute his explanation.

Final discussion questions

1. Was the "political" appointment of an inexperienced person to head the study a good choice, or was Truly just lucky in this instance?

2. Why did the study team take the trouble to use several different bases of computation to compute the estimated overtime budget request? Was this necessary?

3. Was the prison administration justified in giving the higher-paid employees a larger share of the overtime work? What might be the rationale for this practice?

4. Was Goodheart's deliberate overestimation of his holiday overtime requirements the act of an unscrupulous administrator or simply smart budgetary practice?

5. Were Kirby and Truly wise to give the prison board credit for the $50,000 in overtime savings achieved by the study team? Would there have been benefits to sharing the credit?

6. Did Truly allow politics to play too large a role in this decision?

7. If you were Truly, how would you have dealt with Dexter after discovering his memos? How would you have dealt with him after receiving the study team's report?

Dollars, development, and decisions

Irene S. Rubin

Editor's introduction

Planning, budgeting, choices, decisions. These are all part of one unending process, but a process of monumental proportions, as this case demonstrates. Arrington is a community that has been run in the good old down-home manner. Dedicated, hard-working elected officials and community volunteers have made the government work, managed the community's development, and kept taxes low.

Why, then, are there problems? The community has a TIF district with revenues, but it has no idea how to spend the money. The general fund has been having deficit problems; a past default on a bond issue complicates the ability to borrow money; and the water and sewer tap-on fees that have enabled the city to keep its water rates low are about to end as the last remaining undeveloped parcels of land disappear. Voters want the tax revenues from commercial development without the traffic that such development attracts.

Faced with this scenario, Arrington recognizes the need to undertake long-term financial planning. But such planning presents still more problems: Service levels have to be established; resource allocation decisions have to be made; and whatever is decided has to be managed in a way that will prevent the mistakes of the past.

Yet Arrington is also inhibited by an even more common scenario: local reluctance to abandon the ways of the past. The community has managed "just fine" without a budget. Why is one necessary now? The general fund is already tight, so how can the community afford an administrator? The community knows it needs to change, but it doesn't want to.

From this dilemma the case pulls a number of decisions and problems that need to be addressed. How should Arrington manage its TIF district and economic development efforts? How should it establish its long-term tax and revenue policies? How should it allocate scarce resources, particularly on needed public works projects? How should it manage change?

The decisionmaker in this case is an outside consultant—a "hired gun"—although she could just as easily have been a city or county manager faced with the same kinds of decisions in the same political environment. In this case, however, the absence of a professional manager adds a different dimension; it illustrates the consequences of piecemeal decision making without professional management involvement, and it poses substantive and political questions regarding the desirability of, and strategies for, employing such an official.

Fundamentally, however, this is a case about budgeting, about the kinds of decisions that are involved in developing long-range plans for financial management and resource allocation. It addresses both the problems of making such decisions and the process by which they should be made.

Case 17
Dollars, development, and decisions

Background

Arrington is a small suburban city in a very large and growing metropolitan area. Although council-manager government is common in the region, and Arrington has long exceeded the size at which many of its neighbors adopted the council-manager form, Arrington itself has never hired a professional administrator to work with the council, mayor, and staff to manage the city's affairs. The community has a strong culture of volunteerism, which has helped provide able leadership inexpensively, but at times the lack of professionally trained talent has led to financial oversights, deficits in particular funds, or, as occurred once, a bond default.

At the time this case begins, the city had been experiencing particularly rapid growth and had begun to anticipate the development of its last major undeveloped parcel of land. This large parcel, a mined-out quarry, would have significant impacts on the city if it were fully developed. Providing water to the site would require considerable planning and entail substantial expenditures; the early development phase would overburden the city's planning and legal staff; and public works and police services would have to expand to accommodate the growth. The quarry area had been designated a tax increment financing (TIF) district. Under state law, a TIF district is an area that has been designated for development or redevelopment; to finance new local services (such as water and sewer) that are essential for such development, the city may borrow money against the anticipated future increase in tax revenues from the area. It repays the debt from increases in property tax revenues occurring in the district. To make such revenue increases possible, property tax levels are "frozen" at pre-TIF levels for all governments or special districts serving the area in which the TIF district is located.

In the past, Arrington's policy had been to require developers to underwrite and construct all infrastructure improvements in areas being developed, so the council was uncertain about what might constitute an appropriate expenditure of public funds in the TIF district. Since development was likely to occur anyway, without the TIF district designation or public expenditures, council members were concerned that they had frozen property taxes to other districts, especially the school district, for hard-to-justify reasons.

With or without the development of the last major piece of open space, the city was reaching its "natural" size, barring more intensive use of the land. The citizens and the council had agreed that keeping the semirural character of the suburb was important and that high-rises should be kept out. As a result, the fiscal dividends of growth, such as the building permit fees and water and sewer tap-on fees, would soon come to an end. The water fund in particular had come to depend on these fees to keep water rates down.

The city had become dependent on the growth dividend in another way, as well. The rapid growth in the city's share of state-levied and -collected income tax and sales tax had exceeded predictions year after year, often bailing out a budget that might easily have been in deficit.

As growth questions assumed increasing importance, the city, in order to set goals, cooperated with the county planning office to conduct a citizen survey identifying the key issues facing the city and their relative importance. The report prepared by the county planning office on the basis of the survey highlighted a kind of suburban schizophrenia with respect to economic development. On the one hand, respondents wanted to protect the existing neighborhoods from encroaching strip development; but on the other hand, they wanted to encourage businesses to come to the city so that residents could shop there and stop the dollar leakage. Respondents wanted to control growth on the high-traffic corridors, but they also wanted to increase the city's assessed valuation to keep taxes low.

Arrington faced other financial issues as well. First, the city had recently refinanced a water bond, only to find out that the long-forgotten bond default of the 1970s was still relevant to the bond market and that the bond underwriters had specific requirements for good financial management. Second, a recent state evaluation of the city's fiscal health, requested by the council, highlighted some weaknesses as well as strengths in the city's finances. Third, deficits in the city's general fund, resolved only by resort to new tax options, underscored the absence of long-range planning by the city. Fourth, council sentiment was growing for a new city hall—a building that would be larger, more suited to municipal needs, and a better symbol of the city's civic pride—but no strategies for financing such a building were evident.

Spurred by these considerations, the council decided to develop a five-year financial plan for Arrington. The process was organized by the chairman of the council finance committee, Roger Carlson. The council appropriated $17,000 for him to hire consultants and cover the staff time needed to gather historical data on revenues and expenditures. To provide this backup data, the city hired a part-time temporary staffer. Two consultants were also hired. The first, John Erickson, was a former city manager with an engineering background, whose usual consulting work for the city was with the public works department. The second consultant, Verna Fox, was a professor who taught local government finance and budgeting at a nearby university.

Meetings of the council and selected staff were scheduled on various topics throughout the fall and winter. Early topics included the overall financial condition of the city, the city's revenues and fund balances, problems of space and the possibility of a new city hall, and the need for a professional manager or administrator. Later sessions discussed the progress of the TIF district, including when development was likely to begin, whether the city could hold firm in dealing with the developers, what policies should guide the spending of the TIF district revenues, and whether the TIF district should be abandoned or redrawn. There were separate meetings to discuss the future costs of public works and police services. Following these discussions, there was a session with invited members of the public. The purpose of this meeting was to get suggestions from active citizens—representatives from homeowners' associations, planning commissions, candidates for office, the chamber of commerce, volunteers, and former officials—about what crucial issues the city should include in the five-year plan.

Verna Fox's assignment was to synthesize the information gathered from these meetings and from the historical financial data and to act as general facilitator of the five-year plan initiated by the council. There was initially no requirement for a consultant's report, but such a requirement emerged about halfway through the process. In preparing the report, Fox would eventually find herself taking on the responsibility of deciding what action to recommend to the council.

Several meetings were scheduled later for the council to review Fox's report, wrap up the process, and provide whatever policy guidance it could at that stage. The council also assured the public that it would have time to review and comment on the five-year plan.

The case

After the council had decided to prepare the five-year plan, Mayor Michael Riggs and Carlson met with Fox and gave her an overview of the city's recent financial history. They also delivered a packet of documents she had requested, including downtown development plans, the report of the county goals-planning session, a set of audit reports, bond ordinances and prospectuses, and the financial condition report prepared by the state. Interestingly, there were no budgets, as the city had not been operating from one.

In her role as facilitator of the planning process, Fox found herself treated as staff; for example, she was present on the platform with the council during public meetings. Specific questions were posed to her from time to time, such as how cities generally handle the funding of sidewalks or what kind of funding is available for building city halls.

At times the council asked the same question of both Fox and Erickson. Sometimes the two consultants agreed, and sometimes they gave contradictory advice or advice based on different assumptions. Fox perceived that her answers were oriented to what could reasonably be done and that Erickson's answers were more oriented to what should be done or what was technically correct. For example, one difference occurred over how long to assume a road would last: Erickson suggested fifteen to twenty years; Fox said around ten years. Erickson was assuming a road with an adequate foundation; Fox was assuming roads built on less than perfect foundations by cost-conscious councils. When the advice differed, it focused attention on such differences of perspective.

The planning meetings were held in council chambers. Present along with Fox and Erickson were Mayor Riggs, Finance Chairman Carlson, whatever council members could attend, whatever staff were involved in the subject at hand, any other relevant consultants, and sometimes citizens, especially those on relevant advisory boards. Carlson posed a series of questions in advance to each of the city's department heads; each department then prepared a presentation for discussion by the group. The questions covered issues circulating around city hall that had financial implications.

For example, one staff member prepared a report that described the space needs at city hall and compared Arrington city hall with city halls in similar cities. She also provided estimates of construction costs and in general made a case for a new city hall. The council then discussed the potential timing of such a project, possible sites, and financing options. They asked Fox to describe some possible financing techniques for city halls. This question, like many others, came on the spur of the moment, allowing almost no time for her to research or prepare answers. The council, she realized, was relying on her general expertise and advice rather expecting her to undertake research.

A number of policy issues were raised during these meetings, some of which were resolved, others of which were sharpened and focused.

Development issues

When the council started to review the overall revenue situation of the city, Fox noted that they did not seem to think there was a particular problem, despite recent deficits in the general fund and the anticipated decline in the water fund as the city's growth—and tap-on fees—came to an end. They believed that revenues were sufficiently inelastic that the city would not be unduly threatened by revenue shortfalls caused by economic recession. The problem of funding the water department with one-time revenues from tap-on fees was raised and discussed, and this time the advice of Fox and Erickson coincided: raise water rates gradually but regularly to cover operating costs. Beyond giving the matter the status of a problem, no decision was made on this issue during the meetings, and it was not clear what action would be taken. Later in the process, Chairman Carlson did include water department funding as an issue that would have to be resolved in the five-year plan.

The council also discussed the issue of hiring professional staff. For this part of the discussion, there was no staff report, no structured questions or analysis. Mayor Riggs and some council members described some of the city's concerns in this area, but there was no discussion of the advantages and disadvantages of such an action. Although the consultants felt that the need for professional staff was apparent, Fox was unable to read from the discussion whether there was a consensus on this issue.

The city hall proposal was more structured, and the response to it suggested considerable council support for the idea—until specific funding options were discussed. Once the matter got down to finances and tax burdens, some of the support evaporated. The issue came down to two questions: what the level of public support was, and whether a utility tax should be levied to pay for such a project. The issues were linked, because if the proposal to build a new city hall went to referendum, the public might reject it. A utility tax would not require a referendum, but levying the tax without one might provoke considerable public unhappiness. The underlying issue was whether the council could impose on the citizens a cost that the council wanted and the staff needed even though the citizens did not want it. The argument seemed to depend on the level of need, but the need had not been established to the council's satisfaction, leaving the city hall matter undecided at the end of its session. Fox later advised that the city wait on a new city hall until the development of the quarry site had brought the city staff to its peak and the need for new quarters was more obvious and convincing.

Consideration of the city's TIF district included discussion of the obstacles to development and the likely timing of such development, as well as its impacts on city hall staffing and budget. No single staff member had responsibility for economic development or for this particular project. Public works staff was able to discuss roads and water, but the council itself discussed TIF revenues, planning goals, water sources and costs, and how the TIF money could reasonably be spent. Unlike many other cities, Arrington did not have a plan for how TIF money would be spent once the city received it. Because parts of the property had been reclassified as agricultural, the assessed value had actually gone down, but the city was receiving some money from the state sales tax on the working part of the quarry. The council asked Fox to report on developments in the state law and in other cities using TIF financing.

This TIF district discussion was inconclusive. No development had yet occurred on the site; the site was scheduled to be quarried out by the end of the next year, but quarrels among the owners threatened to delay the development, possibly for many years or even indefinitely. At the same time, the council accepted that the quarry would be developed, that the development would entail many expenses for the city, and that it would generate considerable revenue. However, much of that revenue would be earmarked for the TIF district and legally had to be spent in the TIF district (which was coterminous with the quarry site) for the purpose of increasing the assessed value of the site. What complicated the matter was that normal city policy required builders to be responsible for installing their own infrastructure. In other words, city funds would not ordinarily be used for such expenditures. The council noted that the city had insufficient water to deliver to any large development and discussed several possible options for the site, each of which had some problems. Because no consensus was reached, the city did not know what expenditures it was supposed to make. Furthermore, the city suspected that the land value would increase by itself without the expenditure of public money.

Later in the planning process the township reassessed the land as the prime location for development that it was, raising assessments dramatically and creating a windfall of TIF funds that the city had not yet decided how to spend, and that were not a result of any city action. These monies touched off a debate on whether the new revenue belonged in large part to the school districts, and thus should be voluntarily returned to the schools, or whether the city should create legitimate ways to spend the money, even if the TIF district boundaries had to be changed in order to do it.

In the bind of having urgent revenue needs elsewhere in its budget, especially for roads, the city faced the prospect that at some indefinite time in the future, it would have too much revenue locked up in TIF funding, where it might not be needed. In the interim, funding for the public schools and other special districts dependent on the property tax would be held up as development progressed in the TIF district. The possibility of dissolving the TIF district was raised. These issues were aired but not resolved. Carlson submitted a list of existing city policies that concerned TIF funding, including one that prohibited spending TIF money just because it was there. But the policy statement only clarified the city's dilemma; it gave no solution to it.

Police issues

The discussion of the police department was much more straightforward. The chief had presented a bound report predicting the impact of growth on the department and requesting increases in future staffing levels. He argued for continued participation in a countywide drug program, to which the city loaned staff, and presented a justification of staff levels based on the number of calls, the time spent on calls, and a certain amount of patrol time per hour. Fox contested this justification, asserting that not every call had to be answered, nor did every call warrant sending a uniformed officer. She argued that calls should be ranked by importance and by "solvability." Crimes where the trail was cold should not warrant an immediate response but should be answered when an officer was freed up. She also argued for nonuniformed police to respond to certain types of calls. These arguments sparked response on the council. Mayor Riggs argued that citizens expected a quick response to all calls; it was a service they wanted and one that the city could provide. One of the council members argued that people were reassured by the police uniform and that what appeared routine might turn out to be dangerous. No policy was formulated at this meeting.

Public works issues

The public works discussion ranged over a number of controversial and difficult issues, but Fox felt that the matters were presented and discussed cogently, in terms of concrete departmental proposals. Erickson was present at this meeting, and he argued forcefully for the adoption of specific policies. Some of the issues were resolved at the meeting; others would be raised again during the following few months for resolution in the five-year plan. The issue of sidewalks was raised and for the most part resolved. One key question was whether sidewalks should be extended throughout the city. But the discussion quickly expanded to include repairs on existing sidewalks and financing construction versus repair of sidewalks. With Erickson's help, the council agreed to a policy in which sidewalks that needed it would be repaired by the city at city expense when streets were being reconstructed or resurfaced. If residents wanted repairs at other times or if sidewalks had become dangerous, repairs would be made by the city on a cost-shared basis with the owners of the property. This policy left unanswered the issue of extending sidewalks to other parts of the city.

The absence of sidewalks in much of the city left bicyclists on the increasingly busy main streets, creating a need for bicycle routes and possibly bicycle paths. A number of recent bicycle fatalities made this a pressing concern. High estimates of the cost for bicycle paths of appropriate quality and safety forestalled a decision to go ahead and build the paths. At the end of the discussion, it seemed likely that the city would build one segment of a bicycle path and probably designate a bicycle route through parts of the city. At the session for public input, this issue came up again when citizens made an impassioned plea for safer bicycle routes.

The bicycle route issue initially arose in the context of public works, but it was part of the larger issue of recreation, which came up only tangentially during the council discussions. During the police department discussion, the chief's prediction of an increase in teenage crime led the group to consider increased recreation facilities as a reasonable response. In the public works discussion, the issue of recreation surfaced with respect to bicycle paths and drainage and detention ponds, since detention ponds can be used as recreation areas during the drier months of the year. Then, at the meeting for public input, volunteers who ran the existing recreation programs urged that the city purchase land for playgrounds, since such purchases were beyond the capacity of volunteers, no matter how dedicated. The issue of recreation also made its way onto Carlson's list of issues to be resolved in the five-year plan, despite the fact that it had never been presented as a formal proposal and costed out.

Sewer and water issues were also presented by the director of public works. There were two key issues here. The city contracted for sewage treatment with a neighboring city, having sold its old treatment plant a number of years earlier. The council questioned whether the city should consider building its own treatment plant again. The public works director spoke against such a plan, arguing that the city lacked personnel with the requisite technical skills to deal with particular disposal problems. Lack of technical expertise made it likely that the city would violate EPA regulations and be fined for it. The second issue was the extension of sewer and water service to all households and lots in the city. It was city policy to force hookups and tap-ons in areas where utility services were available, but the policy was meeting with considerable resistance from affected citizens. Not discussed in this context, but perhaps part of the reason for the policy, was the fact that keeping tap-on revenues high was keeping the water rates down. Fox asked if the policy of forced tap-ons could be justified on the basis of public health. The mayor confirmed that health and odor were concerns. The group agreed to maintain and enforce the city policy of extending city water and sewer services to all residents.

The question that remained was how to cover the cost of extending such services to new areas—by special assessment or by general revenues—and whether such costs should be split between the residents and the city and, if so, in what proportions. The consensus seemed to be that residents should bear the costs of extending the system. The unsettled question was whether the city should subsidize extension of utilities to undeveloped parcels likely to be developed as commercial properties, given that these properties would later increase in assessed valuation and bring in additional tax revenues. The argument was made that some parcels had not been developed because the owners could not afford both the costs of construction and the costs of bringing in utilities. Carlson argued that development was likely to occur without city assistance. No clear policy statement was made on this issue.

The key issue for public works was the condition of the roads, many of which were chip and seal and had been blacktopped so many times that the level of the roads was higher than the surrounding property, creating runoff problems. Ditches at the sides of the roads provided drainage for many of the city's roads. The public works department prepared a list of costs involved in routine maintenance and also a list of roads that needed to be rebuilt with proper foundations. The technical arguments were clear, but the costs to the city were well beyond its budget. Fox recommended slowing down the rate of conversion from chip and seal to roads with foundations and edging down the quality of roads with less traffic. This was another issue that made its way to the list of policy decisions that would require resolution in the five-year plan. One of the key issues here, as elsewhere in the discussions, was how to pay for road reconstruction and what the city's share of the expenditures should be.

One of the council members asked how the public works department had chosen the roads that were proposed for reconstruction. The answer was that the department head and Erickson had driven around the city, taken a census of road conditions, and drawn up the list accordingly. The list thus had no political sensitivity—no balance among parts of the city or among election districts.

The public was invited to comment at a regular council meeting on the ideas discussed during the special planning sessions. About ten persons and groups asked for permission to submit testimony. They included representatives of the chamber of commerce, the homeowners' associations in the new parts of the city, the volunteers running the recreation programs, members of the planning commission, and a former member of the park board. They made pleas for bicycle paths, city acquisition of ball fields, preservation of the city's historic homes, and protection of the neighborhoods from encroaching development. The chamber of commerce presented a pointed list for consideration, including more funding for the economic development commission to enable it to go after the specific businesses the council said it wanted to have in the city. The chamber also urged the council to pick a style or image for the city and to appoint an architectural board to review plans for conformity with the city's desired image. The chamber spokesman made a general plea for the council to take control and not simply let things happen.

The decision problem

With the discussion process completed, the next step was the preparation of a consultant's report presenting recommendations for consideration by the city. Fox's task was to set forth specific proposals, with accompanying rationales, that would establish goals for the city, would be reasonably certain either of gaining acceptance or at least of avoiding prolonged controversy, would provide the impetus for action to achieve those goals, would establish a long-term basis for improved and sustained city fiscal health, and would sustain her credibility with the council, the staff, and the public.

The first phase of the planning process had raised issues that underlie routine budgets but that seldom get discussed in the budget process. These issues included almost all the major policy decisions that cities make. The process had brought to light unfunded liabilities of the city—in particular, the roads that had been constructed without foundations or drainage, which were increasingly difficult to maintain and repair and that were not cost effective over time. The process had also revealed unmet needs in the community, such as the need for recreation. One of the most important effects of the planning process had been to focus attention on how major capital needs were to be met and on whom the burden of payment would fall. The focus of much of the discussion had been the choice between general taxation and user fees.

The chamber of commerce presentation had raised the crucial issue of what the city wanted to become—whether it wanted to take action to shape the future or be passive and allow change to occur in an undirected manner. The chamber spokesman had also raised the crucial issue of mechanism, creating the link between goals and outcomes. He had argued for more funding of the economic development commission, but the same outcome could be achieved by hiring more staff at city hall.

Fox developed a list of approximately twenty issues that had emerged from the planning process and that needed to be addressed in any five-year plan, but she considered three issues to be central. The first of these was the employment of professional management staff to provide central direction and coordination not only for the development of a five-year plan, but also for its implementation. The council was wavering on the commitment of funds for such a staff. It was caught between its preference for the city's tradition of volunteerism and its own penchant for managing the affairs of the city directly, on the one hand, and, on the other hand, its awareness of past problems—such as the bond default and general fund deficits—that had arisen because of the council's own managerial limitations. Fox believed that the employment of a manager was essential, but the council remained unconvinced.

The second issue was the development of a budget: Fox believed that the city had to develop a budget process to achieve and sustain fiscal health over the long term; but, again, the council remained unconvinced. Council members had varying and sometimes contradictory attitudes about shifting from an annual appropriations ordinance (which required only a list of possible expenditures and depended on continuous cash balances for financial control) to a real budget. Sometimes the council argued that it used a budget informally, anyway, so that such a process would not represent a change. At other times, members of the council would contend that a real budget, setting forth estimated revenues, expenditures, and expenditure limitations, would hamper their administrative flexibility and discretion.

The third major issue was the development of the quarry land and the problems pertaining to the TIF district. Fox considered three different recommendations that she might make. One recommendation would be that in each year that development does not occur, the money earmarked for the TIF be released for normal uses: the educational portion be given back to the school district, and the city portion be released for general expenditures.

A second possible recommendation would be to dissolve the TIF district. The purpose of such a district is to encourage development that would not otherwise occur, and it was clear that the site would be developed without public assistance. While this position might be the moral high ground, it would be certain to provoke opposition from council members. Some felt that participation in the project would give the city more control over the nature of the development; others felt that it would entitle the city to take credit for the development; still others felt that the project would improve the city's capacity to carry out other needed projects, despite the legal constraints on how the money would be spent.

Third, Fox could recommend that the city alter its policy requiring developers to pay all infrastructure costs. The city could assume the unusual costs of preparing the site for construction, including relocating major city drainage ponds. The costs of engineering and planning could be taken immediately from TIF funds. However, there were disadvantages to such a recommendation. City funds spent for these purposes would not be available for other uses; if the city assumed these responsibilities, either more staff or more consultants would have to be hired; and neither the status of the land nor the nature of the development had yet been determined, nor was it known when such issues would be resolved.

Clearly, the matter of the TIF district was an issue that divided the council, and hence it was an issue with which Fox would have to deal circumspectly.

Although Fox considered the resolution of these three major issue areas— professional staff, a budget process, and the TIF issues—as prerequisites to the development of a five-year plan, it was not clear that the council agreed with her assessment regarding their centrality. Yet her job was to prepare a report that would provide the basis for the development of that five-year plan and that would address all of the issues raised during the planning process. Professor Fox, now Consultant Fox, had to devise a strategy and formulate recommendations.

Discussion questions

1. What additional information does Fox need before proceeding?

2. In addition to the issues discussed at the sessions, what other policy issues will have to be addressed as proposals are formulated and discussed? In particular, what specific issues regarding alternative revenue sources, size and allocation of tax burdens, and determination of service levels will have to be resolved?

3. What service areas and issues were overlooked by the council? If Fox assumes that the council's failure to address them means that these issues have low saliency to the council, should she take the initiative to raise them, or should she limit herself to the problems and issues perceived by the council?

4. What criteria should be used to decide whether projects such as sidewalk or road improvements should be funded by general revenues or by special assessments?

5. If you were Fox, what would you recommend regarding the employment of professional staff, and what strategy would you employ to sell your recommendation to the council?

6. What should Fox recommend to the council about the use of budgeting methods? What strategy should she use to sell this recommendation?

7. What should Fox recommend regarding the TIF district? Why?

8. Prepare a list of the other issues that Fox should address. What disposition should she make of these issues?

The aftermath

Fox decided not to tackle all the issues simultaneously but to address the matter of professional staff first. There were two arguments for this decision. First, she reasoned, it is easier to get council agreement on a single issue than it is to resolve several complex issues, especially several interrelated issues. She feared that council members, as well as others in city hall and in the community, might use her recommendations on other issues as justification for opposing her recommendation that the city hire a professional chief administrator, or city manager.

Second, she felt that the presence of a city manager would facilitate resolution of the other issues. A manager would bring another perspective to the city. Further, the manager would be responsible for implementing the fiscal decisions made as a result of the long-term plan, and such implementation was more apt to be politically and administratively successful if the manager had played a role in developing the plan itself. In particular, a recommendation regarding the development and use of a budget would be more concrete, and perhaps more salable, if the recommendation contained the details of the budget system that the city's first manager preferred to implement and administer.

Fox thus recommended to the council that it start the second stage of the planning process by resolving the question of professional staff. She urged that a city manager be hired to assist the council not only with the planning process but primarily with the administration of daily affairs and the implementation of the fiscal plan that would be adopted. The council agreed to hire a manager and began the process of searching for such a person, hoping that the newly employed manager would come on board just at the end of the long-term planning process.

Final discussion questions

1. How could this planning process have been improved? How would you design such a process if you were charged with preparing a long-term financial plan? What can you learn from Arrington's experiences—the parts that worked well and the parts that did not work so well?

2. Would you employ consultants to assist with such planning even if the local government had staff time available? Why or why not? What do consultants bring to such a project? What did they bring to the Arrington long-term financial plan? Did they act primarily in place of staff?

3. If you had been Fox, and had just secured council agreement to hire a manager for Arrington, what would have been your next steps in helping the council develop its five-year plan? What would you have recommended? Why?

4. In developing recommendations on substantive issues to further the development of the five-year financial plan, what policies would you recommend regarding the long-term revision of Arrington's tax and revenue structure? What would you recommend on the use of general revenues or special assessments to fund infrastructure developments? On city development of its own sewage treatment system? On a new city hall? On roads? On bicycle paths? On other recreational needs? On sidewalks? On police services? What further information would you need? How would you develop a rationale for balancing competing needs against the government's anticipated revenue?

5. The new manager will have to convince a wavering council that it should adopt a real budget and then find a way to implement the budget process that will cement the council's loyalty to it. As the new manager, how would you solve these problems?

6. The new manager will also have to resolve the uncertainty surrounding the development of the quarry site and the TIF funding plan. Which of Fox's three optional recommendations would you, as the new manager, support, or would you develop still other options? Explain.

7. Assume that Fox had been Arrington's city manager throughout this planning process, rather than a hired consultant. How might this have affected the role she played? What could or should she have done differently? Apart from the professional staffing question, how should she have handled the decision problem? Explain.

Goodbye, Sampson, Inc.?

Jeffrey A. Raffel and Kevin C. McGonegal

Editor's introduction

Economic development and financial administration are intrinsically related. The pace and kind of economic development affects local government revenues and, in turn, imposes demands for additional government expenditures to pay for new and expanded local services. The relationship is even more serious, however, in communities where the local economy is declining or stagnating. Such communities frequently find it necessary to offer financial incentives—tax breaks or financial support—to attract or, as in this case, retain business firms.

This case examines the linkage between economic development and local government finance, demonstrating the kinds of policy and management decisions that must be made as a result of this linkage. Such decisions cover a broad range of concerns—setting policy precedents, managing intergovernmental and public-private relations, and synthesizing opposing points of view within the management staff itself.

The case also portrays the critical linkage between economic development policies and local neighborhoods. In this case, the proposed development would help revitalize the city's central business district, but at the same time it would have an impact on adjacent residential neighborhoods with their aging housing stock and diverse racial and socioeconomic makeup. Along with economic development, then, are classic problems of city social and land use planning.

Redevelopment, whether of downtown business districts or of aging residential neighborhoods, has been a vital issue for local governments for more than a half century. The threatened departure of Sampson, Inc., in this case threatens a severe loss of jobs; its retention could be the foundation for downtown redevelopment. But at what cost should the city intervene? Should the costs to affected neighborhoods and displaced residents be considered along with costs to the city treasury?

Economic development rarely proceeds without complex intergovernmental interaction, and this case is no exception. It demonstrates not only the role of different governments, but also the different objectives being pursued by each. Distinct, but also related, is the necessary effort to involve the private business sector in the total development effort.

Most important, however, the case poses the central policy issue of economic development: What is the role of government, and what, if any, incentives should the public sector provide to the private sector in order to promote the overall welfare of the community?

Case 18
Goodbye, Sampson, Inc.?

Background

The city of Metropolis faced a major economic development crisis. Its second-largest employer, Sampson, Inc., was considering a move to the suburbs, and city officials had to decide what actions they could and should take to persuade Sampson to stay.

Metropolis, a city of approximately 80,000 people, is the state's largest city and is Tower County's urban core. Metropolis' 15.77 square miles of land is bounded on the east by a river and on the remaining boundaries by suburban areas. The city's location on the Eastern Seaboard makes it an important link in the Boston-to-Washington megalopolis; approximately 30 percent of the U.S. population is within a 350-mile radius of the city.

Metropolis is particularly significant to the state's economy, as it is an important center for banking, health and social services, communication, cultural and historical facilities, and education. The city has a thirteen-member elected city council and a mayor elected at large every four years at the same time as the national presidential election.

At the time this case unfolds, Metropolis had been experiencing problems similar to those of other cities in the Northeast in the 1960s and 1970s—a declining population and tax base, a loss of business and industry, obsolescence of its manufacturing facilities, housing stock, and public facilities, and a concentration of elderly, poor, and disadvantaged populations within the city. The number of manufacturing jobs was declining, while managerial, professional, and clerical jobs held by suburban commuters increased as a proportion of total city jobs. No new nonmanufacturing firms had been established since 1950, and the twelve major nonmanufacturing firms in the city had shown negligible growth in that period. Unemployment in Metropolis was significantly higher than in the surrounding county and in the rest of the state.

Metropolis' central business district (CBD), in particular, was aging and economically threatened. The CBD was located between two rivers, the picturesque Lamar River on the north and the Lomax River on the south. Residential neighborhoods bordered the district on its east and west sides. The district sorely needed to retain the level of business activity in the city, not only to retain and increase its own employment levels but also to provide jobs for the residents of surrounding neighborhoods and to encourage redevelopment efforts in the area.

Sampson, Inc., which began life as a divested part of the well-known and huge Clemson Chemical Company, had spent its entire existence in the shadow of the larger company. A successful Fortune 500 firm in its own right, Sampson was a diversified chemical company that developed and manufactured plastics, synthetic fibers, textiles, agricultural chemicals, detergents, and protective coatings. Originally named the Sampson Firepowder Company, it had expanded greatly from its beginnings as a manufacturer of explosives, but it still maintained a significant presence in that field with products for mining, quarrying, and even ballistic missiles.

When Harold Hammer, an experienced and dynamic executive, took the reins at Sampson as president and chief executive officer, he was determined to establish a stronger, separate corporate identity for the company.

Sampson, which was leasing 360,000 square feet of office space in Metropolis, needed 600,000 square feet for a new corporate headquarters. Its 1,350 employees at the downtown location made it the second-largest employer in the city, after Clemson. It was considering various relocation options, including a suburban location that was already home to its research center and its country club.

Hammer was particularly upset with the state's personal income tax structure, which taxed top income levels at 20 percent. His feeling, and that of other business leaders, was that this high rate of taxation kept other corporations out of the state, thus hurting the state's image as a business center. He went so far as to threaten to move the corporate headquarters out of state, and in fact was talking to a city in California about relocating there. Excerpts from a newspaper article written the day after President Hammer's speech to the Metropolis Rotary Club describe Hammer's position (see Exhibit 1).

Whether or not he would have followed through on his threats, Hammer certainly got the attention of the governor and the general assembly. Work was begun on a state income tax cut, which subsequently passed, dropping the top rate from 20 percent to 14 percent. The governor also realized that the economic

---

Exhibit 1   Excerpts from newspaper article   Sampson, Inc., an important element in the state's economy since its founding in 1913, could well sever the historic relationship to find a better business climate elsewhere, its chief executive made clear in a carefully worded speech yesterday.

Though avoiding any explicit threat, President and Chief Executive Harold H. Hammer left no doubt that the financially struggling chemical company was giving real thought to uprooting its highly paid 1,350 employees currently headquartered in downtown Metropolis.

The state's business leaders have for some time been grumbling that the state's policies, especially the personal income tax, hurt economic development, but this week could go down as the time they went public.

In a speech to the Rotary Club, Hammer centered his attack on the top rate of 20 percent in the state's personal income tax structure.

Sprinkling the talk with general references to business moves, Hammer rammed home his point by saying Sampson would be watching the state legislature's tax action and noting that the headquarters occupies leased space.

"There is a greater tendency on the part of business today to maintain flexibility.

Many companies rent or lease office space instead of building on their own. This, of course, gives greater flexibility. Sampson, for example, leases its space in the Sampson Tower. . . ."

The lease expires a year from December for the offices occupied by 1,350 employees in the Sampson Tower building. "No new lease has been signed," a spokesman said, adding, "It's not even time to sign one."

After the speech, a reporter asked Hammer whether he was threatening to leave. "We have no plan to pull out of the state at this time," he replied. "I will not voice threats. We will do what business prudence tells us to do."

Describing the state as a perfect geographic location that was being shunned by business, Hammer said state government was making little effort to solve basic revenue problems.

Apparently agreeing were the more than two hundred corporate executives, lawyers, surgeons, insurance representatives, and others who jammed the Rotary meeting. Hearty applause continued for twenty-five seconds at the end, and several came to their feet clapping.

Sampson will study the revenue committee's recommendations for tax legislation, Hammer said.

health of the state's major city was crucial to the overall economic health of the state. Metropolis was the "core of the apple," and it was in the state's best interest for Metropolis to retain its second-largest employer and stay as self-sufficient as possible.

Following the tax cut, Hammer announced that Sampson intended to remain in the state. But this decision by no means meant that Sampson would remain in the city.

Another article in the *Metropolis News* reported Hammer's decision to move the company from the Sampson Tower building into a new leased complex, but Hammer said no decision had been made as to whether it would be in Metropolis.

"I think one of the reasons we're not talking about building ourselves a building, but rather about leasing, is because we're a little skeptical about the long range," said Hammer. In the same press conference he went on to point out that the corporate office of Sampson, Inc., represented an annual contribution to Metropolis of about $100 million. He also dropped broad hints that Sampson was being courted by industrial development officials from other states but denied that he was seriously considering an out-of-state move.

The press report went on to say that city and state officials, in an effort to retain Sampson, had hired two consultants to help them make proposals for a Sampson headquarters. They talked to Sampson about several "concepts" in the $70 million price range with government-subsidized financing. Photographs of the proposed building at three different sites had one thing in common: a forty-two-story cyclinder that towered over the Clemson Chemical Company's complex.

The case

In its search for a new headquarters site, Sampson soon limited its options to two. One was the suburban land already owned by the corporation. The other was a city site made up of two parcels on the northern edge of the downtown area along the Lamar River; one parcel was a vacant lot owned by the Clemson Chemical Company, and the other was occupied by an old vocational/technical school building. The company offered to remain in Metropolis if the costs of the city site were made comparable to those of the suburban location.

Immediately adjacent to the city site, and to the west, was a residential neighborhood called Midtown Lamar, which had been undergoing a transition with fairly extensive housing renovations and rehabilitation. It was now populated with young black and white professionals and lower-income black renters and homeowners (Table 1). Only 3.9 percent of the families in this neighborhood were below poverty level, and the median income equaled the mean for the entire city. A strong neighborhood organization attempted to maintain the racial and economic mix.

To the east of the site was Eastside, a predominantly black, lower-income neighborhood composed of a large number of long-term homeowners and some elderly renters. According to the U.S. census, the median income of Eastside families was one-third less than that of the whole city, and about 30 percent of the families had an income below the poverty level. The area had experienced a 41 percent decline in population in the decade between the last two Census counts; urban renewal was the cause of about half of this figure.

The residents of these two areas expressed a number of concerns to city officials regarding the possibility of a major office structure in their midst. Construction problems for the neighborhoods, such as dirt and construction debris, were short-term issues; of more significance were the longer-term issues such as traffic congestion, design considerations, and displacement. Related concerns included the high unemployment rate among Eastside residents and the deterioration of certain parts of the neighborhoods.

Table 1   Demographic data.

	Census tract		
	City	Eastside	Mid-Town Lamar
Population (total)	80,386	2,945	787
White	44,901	94	266
Black	35,072	3,844	511
Percent black	43.6	96.6	64.9
% 16–21 years, not high school graduates, not enrolled in school	20.7	21.0	11.8
Persons 25 years & over	46,204	1,816	444
Median school yrs. completed	10.9	8.8	11.2
% high school graduates	39.7	20.9	43.2
Male, 16 years & over	25,317	1,046	265
In labor force	18,462	626	224
Female, 16 years & over	32,123	1,176	296
In labor force	14,549	688	187
Income below poverty level			
Families (% of all families)	3,084 (16.0)	201 (29.7)	6 (3.9)
Persons (% of all persons)	16,991 (21.4)	1,111 (37.9)	59 (8.1)
Households (% of all households)	5,245 (21.0)	270 (36.5)	43 (15.0)

Source: U.S. Census of Population and Housing.

The cost differential between the urban and suburban sites was substantial. First, the cost of the city parcel owned by Clemson was $3.9 million. Since Sampson owned the land outside the city, there would be no out-of-pocket expense for purchasing land for a suburban headquarters. Of course, choosing the suburban site would mean a lost opportunity for other development on that site. Second, since the downtown location would be a high-rise structure rather than a low-rise office park structure, the construction costs would be $9.7 million more in the city. Third, a parking garage would be needed in the city, adding $12.7 million to the project cost. Fourth, costs that were proportional to the total project costs, such as contingencies, architects' and engineers' fees, transfer taxes, and financing expenses, all increased roughly in proportion to the overall budget. All in all, the cost of the city location was higher by $32.3 million, or 42 percent, than the cost of the suburban location (Table 2).

Table 2   Proposed Sampson headquarters building: Cost differential between urban and suburban sites.

Cost component	Urban	Suburban	Differential
Building	$ 45,967,000	$36,256,000	$ 9,711,000
Fixed equipment	1,552,000	1,552,000	—
Site development	1,694,000	2,971,000	−1,277,000
Parking landscaping	1,200,000	—	1,200,000
Parking garage	12,700,000	—	12,700,000
Arch. & eng. fees	3,443,000	2,447,000	996,000
Construction/contractor	3,000,000	3,000,000	—
Owners' admin. expenses	976,000	930,000	46,000
Land	3,878,000	—	3,878,000
Furnishing	10,750,000	10,750,000	—
Interior designer fee	850,000	850,000	—
Contingency	6,352,000	4,700,000	1,652,000
Legal fees	72,500	65,800	6,700
Closing costs	10,000	10,000	—
Title insurance	63,000	47,500	15,500
Transfer tax	2,100,000	1,054,000	1,046,000
Construction financing	14,201,000	12,045,000	2,156,000
Application fee	160,000	—	160,000
Total	$108,968,500	$76,678,300	$32,290,200

Metropolis had several models to draw on. A few economic development projects had been undertaken in the city, though not really as part of an overall development plan. Most notable among these were a pedestrian shopping mall on Main Street and a hotel constructed over a downtown parking garage, a project that had been financed in part by a federal grant. This grant was part of a federal program to encourage urban development projects by making low-interest loans available to businesses locating in economically depressed areas. The process was competitive among cities, and the cities receiving the grants could, in turn, loan the funds to the project businesses. The businesses would repay the loans to the city over a period of time. Other federal grants had been used by the city to aid development in recent years, including grants for community development, public works, urban parks, and job-training programs.

City administrators estimated that approximately $10 to $20 million could be available through various federal programs to help close the gap between the costs of a city site and the costs of a suburban site for Sampson. A primary goal of the federal government was to create long-term economic growth opportunities for distressed cities like Metropolis; therefore, the government would evaluate any proposal on the extent to which it involved a partnership with the private sector that would increase investment in the city and lead to new long-term employment opportunities, especially for the city's unemployed minorities. To secure the investment from Sampson, and to reduce the city-suburban gap, the city realized that it would need to provide incentives or concessions. These might be in the form of a property tax abatement (a new Sampson headquarters was expected to increase Sampson's property taxes by $360,000 per year), a waiver of the property transfer tax, or other actions that might lower the cost of the city site.

Modest state funds, perhaps as much as $5 million, also could be available for this project. The state's interest, however, had been limited ever since Hammer announced that Sampson was staying in the state.

Thus, outside funds could be available to the city, but city officials would have to determine what they would be willing to "pay" for them and under what conditions. Furthermore, officials would have to decide how to make the development package as attractive as possible to these funding sources.

The loss of the Sampson corporation would be a severe blow to Metropolis—first, because the company was the second-largest employer in the city. The company's 1,350 employees represented over $92,000 in "head-tax" payments (levied on employers according to number of employees over a minimum of five) and $300,000 in wage tax payments (levied on all employees living or working in the city at 1 percent of annual wages). The city depended a great deal on this wage or "municipal user tax," receiving about 30 percent of its $30 million budget from it. Second, a ripple effect on the city economy would be felt by the numerous services employed by the company, such as copying firms, travel agencies, and janitorial services. Third, Sampson employees had a significant impact on retail sales in the central business district. The city planning department estimated that each Sampson employee spent an average of $830 per year downtown, totaling about $1.1 million annually.

The decision problem

David Dunworthy, chief administrative officer of Metropolis and the top aide to Mayor William Williams, was charged with recommending a strategy to meet the Sampson threat. The members of the mayor's administrative cabinet who were involved in this decision had different views and concerns regarding the situation.

The budget director was concerned with the price that the city might have to pay to keep Sampson in town. Trying to reduce the cost of the city site might set a precedent for which the city would pay dearly in later years when other corporations tried to gain similar advantages. He did not feel that the city was in a financial position to make tax concessions to Sampson to make up for the added cost to Sampson of remaining in the city. Yet, the budget director reasoned, the city must also be concerned about the loss of taxes and revenue that the flight of Sampson would inflict on the city tax base. He thought that Hammer might well be bluffing, and at times he advocated calling his bluff.

The commerce director believed that it was imperative to keep Sampson in the city. If Metropolis' number two employer left town, who knew what firm might be next? And word would get around that Metropolis couldn't hold its own corporations. He therefore advocated doing whatever was necessary to keep Sampson in the city.

The planning director viewed the situation as an opportunity to develop the downtown area more rationally. However, he was concerned about the objections of the neighborhoods adjacent to the site; he did not want an antidevelopment mood to dominate the city's political life for the next five years. He estimated that ten families and businesses would need to be relocated if the headquarters were built on the vocational school site.

The mayor was adamantly against "losing Sampson," but he was also concerned about losing the goodwill of the adjacent neighborhoods.

The city of Metropolis, therefore, had a classic dilemma: it could not afford to lose Sampson, and it could not afford to keep Sampson.

City officials determined that if Sampson left for the suburbs, the city would incur the following costs:

Loss of city wage taxes estimated at $300,000 and head taxes of $92,000

Loss of retail sales in the CBD totaling about $1.1 million annually

Loss, not easily measured, of the secondary economic benefits of services employed by the company and the associated wage and head taxes

Loss of economic development "goodwill" and reputation.

Given a total city budget of $30 million and a declining tax and economic base, the loss of more than $400,000 in taxes loomed large.

Yet the city of Metropolis could not afford, by itself, to reduce the city-suburban gap of $32 million to induce Sampson, Inc., to stay. Even if the city's revenue losses were estimated at $1 million per year, the current value of this loss would represent only about $9.1 million at a 10 percent discount rate over twenty-five years. The city could not justify spending much more to keep Sampson. Nor was it clear that Metropolis could raise the money to do this, in any case.

In formulating his recommendation, Dunworthy had several decisions to make. First, should the city take direct action to further influence Sampson to stay in Metropolis?

Second, if the city took direct action, what strategy should be used, and what conditions should be negotiated?

Third, what actions could the city take to close the cost differential between the city site and the suburban site? What amount would be enough to convince Sampson to stay? And what cost elements (listed in Table 2) were the most appropriate to alter?

Fourth, what effect would the new Sampson building have on the surrounding neighborhood, and what steps could be taken to mitigate any negative impacts?

Discussion questions

1. Realistically, does Dunworthy have any choice but to recommend that the city work to keep Sampson? If not, why not? If so, how could

failure to act be justified to the city's business community? How important are matters of public perception, business attitudes about the city, and precedents when economic development policies are being made?

2. How should Dunworthy handle the department heads in this situation, given the difference in opinion among them?

3. Assuming that a strategy will be developed to attempt to keep Sampson in the city, what principles should guide the city's choice regarding (a) the development costs that the public sector should be asked to assume and (b) the tax concessions that the city should consider offering to keep Sampson? What alternatives might be considered in each case? What would you recommend?

4. What role could the state be asked to play in an effort to keep Sampson, and what arguments can be advanced to justify the state's cooperation?

5. What role could the private business section in Metropolis be asked to assume in this development effort? How should the business community be approached, and what inducements should be offered?

6. What assistance should be sought from the federal government, and how?

7. How would you organize an effort to keep Sampson? Given the players involved (the city, private organizations such as the chamber of commerce, and other interested parties), where should responsibility for the development of the campaign's policy be located? Who should participate in that policy-making effort? Where should administrative responsibility for the effort be located? What would be the advantages and disadvantages of creating a special economic development organization?

8. What can and should be done to prevent or minimize neighborhood opposition? What should be done to involve the neighborhoods in the process? Are there specific benefits that should be offered to each neighborhood to allay its concerns?

The aftermath

Dunworthy decided that, for political reasons, he could not suggest that the city make no effort to retain Sampson. Such a recommendation would generate too much adverse reaction. No matter what the various policy preferences or the economics of the situation might be, he reasoned, he had to suggest a course of action that might enable Metropolis to keep Sampson. Otherwise, no matter what the outcome, the city administration would take the sole blame for the loss of Sampson. Dunworthy's recommendations provided the structure upon which subsequent developments were built.

Given the the potential political repercussions of Sampson's departure, the city's elected officials agreed that they had to make an effort to keep Sampson. Furthermore, they realized that to be successful, the city must leverage federal and state money. This would require not only good economic reasoning but excellent politics as well. The interested parties included the city of Metropolis, the state, the federal government, Sampson, the business community, and the neighborhoods surrounding the proposed site. A package had to be developed to meet the objectives of all of these parties.

Economically, the city wanted to maximize federal and state funds and minimize city funds. The state had no direct financial interest in Sampson's location—since the city and the county were both subject to state taxes, the state would lose no revenue if Sampson moved to the suburbs. But city financial problems resulting from a Sampson move, and the possibility of subsequent business departures, could increase demands on state coffers to help the city. Furthermore, keeping Sampson in the city would also make it unnecessary for the state to help fund improvements in the supporting infrastructure at the suburban location. These considerations, argued effectively by local public- and private-sector leaders and state legislators, led to a modest willingness on the part of the state to help the city keep Sampson in town.

To acquire federal funds, the city had to convince the federal government that its national policy objectives would be advanced by keeping Sampson in the metropolitan region's central business district. This meant that the federal government had to be convinced that there was a need to encourage private investment in Metropolis' CBD and that such investment would increase job opportunities for the city's unemployed minorities and promote still more investment and employment through economic multiplier effects. The city thus linked a more comprehensive planning/economic development strategy to its economic and political strategies.

Finally, Sampson had to be convinced that it would be part of a revitalized downtown, not an island of affluence in a sea of economic and social decay.

The strategy recommended by Dunworthy and the city administration thus was built on a comprehensive development scheme for the city's CBD. That scheme, labeled the Lamar and Lomax Gateways plan, envisioned a "river-to-river" development concept that would capitalize on the city's two waterfronts on either end of the downtown area and direct economic development efforts to those two locations. The city's leadership embraced the concept in a formal announcement.

The anchor of the Lamar Gateway was to be a new headquarters for Sampson. Financing was to be handled through the Lamar Gateway Corporation (LGC), a newly established economic development agency composed of city and state officials. An application was submitted to the federal government for a $16 million Urban Development Action Grant (UDAG), to be used for financing assistance to the Sampson project. The city would use $3.9 million to purchase the land from Clemson and then sell it to Sampson for $1.00. Then, through the LGC, the city would loan $12.1 million to Integrated Resources, the owner-developer of the proposed building, at 5 percent interest, repayable over twenty-five years.

The city received a second grant, of $1.5 million, from the federal Economic Development Agency (EDA), to help finance an adjoining parking garage to be built by the Metropolis Parking Authority (MPA). The MPA would receive a portion of the UDAG payback from LGC to offset the debt service costs on the new garage.

To secure these grants, Sampson had to commit to a long-term (twenty-five-year) lease at the new location, justifying the $80 million expenditure on the building by Integrated Resources, and make commitments to use good-faith efforts to hire economically disadvantaged city residents. To aid in these efforts, the city of Metropolis pledged a portion of its job-training funds to train and refer candidates. The state agreed to demolish the vocational/technical building and construct a park between the new building and the river, along with significant road and access improvements in the immediate area. Finally, Metropolis agreed to provide a graduated property tax abatement to Sampson of 100 percent for the first seven years, 75 percent in the eighth year, 50 percent in the ninth, and 25 percent in the abatement's final year.

The city (and state) had carefully considered which cost elements of the city-suburban differential to address. Reducing the transfer tax (which required legislation), for example, would result in a loss to the city that would never be recovered. Property tax abatements, however, could be phased out over time. Subsidizing interior planning or building costs might be hard to justify to the city's residents, who would never see the results of the spending. Subsidizing parking, landscaping, and site development were more in line with traditional city service and infrastructure development, and revenues from the parking garage would be forthcoming to the city in the years ahead.

In order to secure citizen support for this project, the city took a novel approach to offset neighborhood concerns about traffic congestion, design issues, and possible displacement. After numerous meetings, a city-neighborhood development agreement was signed to handle these types of problems contractually. Central to this agreement was the creation of the InterNeighborhood Foundation (INF), whose board was composed of neighborhood residents. The INF was promised $6.9 million in paybacks from the UDAG loan, which it was to use on neighborhood projects.

While all of these efforts together did not make up the entire $32 million differential, the combination of free land, a parking garage built by the Metropolis Parking Authority, a low-interest loan covering a critical part of the project cost, and the prospect of an impressive new building in a high-profile location were enough to convince Sampson to stay in the city. The federal government was persuaded to award the UDAG because of the 5-to-1 loan ratio, the job retention figures, the hiring commitments, and the unique benefits accruing to the community through the INF agreement. The state decided that it should act to promote the economic health and self-sufficiency of its major city, thereby improving its own economic climate and setting a precedent for future city-state economic development efforts. The city of Metropolis not only saved the direct tax payments of over $400,000 a year that it was receiving from Sampson but also gained a $90 million building that would ultimately be added to the property tax base. Moreover, this building would be a major anchor for future development in the CBD.

As a result of the cooperative effort to keep Sampson, leaders from the city, the state, and the private sector developed a working relationship that resulted in state legislation to attract banks and insurance companies to the state and the city. Several new office buildings were constructed and filled. The Lomax Gateway, at the other end of the downtown, became the focus of plans for a new office building, a revitalized train station, and several new projects (including three more office towers and a marketplace). Metropolis' CBD came to be considered a rapidly developing waterfront area. In fact, when city officials failed to come up with a package to stop the local newspaper from relocating its offices and plant outside the city limits, few people were concerned that Metropolis' economic future would be threatened, because Metropolis had become known as "the place" for certain types of businesses.

Final discussion questions

1.   Could Metropolis have done anything to avoid the Sampson crisis? Could the state have? What role did the crisis mentality play in this case? Is a crisis necessary for change?

2.   How should city officials balance economic objectives with neighborhood concerns in decisions like the one Metropolis faced?

3. In negotiating to set up the INF, what role, if any, should the city have retained for itself to influence, or perhaps veto, future uses of the money the foundation was to receive from the paybacks? Is there a broader public interest in the use of such funds? If so, does the city have an obligation to protect that interest? Should the city have negotiated away such a role in bargaining for neighborhood support for the Sampson project?

4. In creating an economic development support package for a particular private organization, any city is concerned about setting precedents. Which of the benefits and concessions given to Sampson should the city be prepared to offer routinely to future developers? Which benefits and concessions can the city not afford to offer to other developers? How can the city legitimately deny future developers' demands for those benefits and concessions?

5. In negotiating these benefits and concessions, what role should be played by the mayor? By the professional chief administrative officer? Is the role of the latter any different if he or she is a city or county manager rather than a CAO serving a strong elected executive? If so, how? If not, why?

Part eight:
Ethics

Introduction to part eight: Ethics

Despite its placement at the end of this book, ethics is neither an afterthought nor a secondary consideration in the professional activities of the local government manager. Quite to the contrary, ethics should be a central, all-encompassing, ever-present characteristic of professional local government management. At some level, ethical considerations are, or should be, a part of every managerial decision or action.

Because of the centrality of ethics in professional management, ethical questions have emerged in many earlier cases in this book. There are, in fact, at least six cases in which ethical questions are explicitly posed for the reader's consideration: Cases 1, 7, 11, and 14, as well as Cases 19 and 20, which follow. Other cases have ethical components as well. Case 18 deals with the use of public funds to aid a private business. Case 3 questions the appropriateness of public intervention in the private housing market. And a number of ethical principles underscore the efforts to establish a pricing policy for the delivery of public services to a private group in Case 6.

Taken together, these cases give a sense of the range of local government matters that have an ethical dimension. For example, Case 1 describes conflict between principle and political expediency; Case 7 presents a circumstance in which a manager is tempted to act beyond his legal authority to resolve a crisis; Case 11 portrays the ethical dilemma of an analyst who perceives herself under pressure to develop numbers supportive of a policy option that she feels is not in the public interest; and Case 14 tackles questions involving sexual preference, job performance, and the personal right to privacy.

The next two cases pose still more ethical questions. The first examines the ethics of the relationship between elected officials and the professional administrator; the second poses questions of ethics in a personnel decision. The first demonstrates the pressures that come to bear when an ethical stance may cost a manager his job. The second demonstrates the difficulty of applying ethical principles when a complicated set of individual circumstances obscures questions of right and wrong.

The special virtue of the cases that follow is the message they convey about ethics in government. They underscore the difficulty that even highly ethical people can have in trying to determine right and wrong and in trying to decide how best to respond to particular situations. They clearly communicate that ethical behavior requires, first and foremost, conscious awareness of the ethical dimensions of the problem at hand and thoughtful deliberation in selecting a policy option or an appropriate course of action. Perhaps most of all, these cases suggest that ethical judgments should not be made hastily, either when determining one's own course of action or when judging the decisions, actions, or behavior of others.

19 Principles under pressure

Harry G. Gerken

Editor's introduction

The central characteristic of council-manager government, and professional administration in local government, is its nonpolitical nature. True to the description first set forth by Woodrow Wilson, professional local government administrators eschew involvement in local politics. Indeed, the Code of Ethics set forth by the International City Management Association specifically rejects such involvement.

What, then, should the local administrator do when external circumstances seem to make it impossible to avoid politics? How does the code apply when normal patterns of relationships between elected officials and the appointed administrator break down? That is the issue posed by this case.

While the instant reaction of most professional administrators would be to condemn political involvement regardless of the circumstances, real-life situations rarely lack mitigating circumstances, and this case is no different. The manager's failure to get involved could undermine the integrity of the council-manager form of government as practiced in the community and probably cost the manager his job as well.

Adding to the complexity of the manager's decision is the potential for codes of ethics, in this case the ICMA Code, to send apparently conflicting signals to the embattled manager. The case thus affords an opportunity not only to apply ethical principles in practice, but also to reconcile different sections of the code with the help of their accompanying guidelines. The ICMA Code of Ethics, together with the guidelines, appears in the appendix to this book.

Case 19
Principles under pressure

Background

In the mid-1970s the ripples of Watergate reached down to many local governments. Perhaps prompted by the almost daily revelations of wrongdoing at the federal level, some citizens of Centerville formed a group known as Taxpayers Against Corruption (TAC).

Centerville, a sprawling community of 35,000, contained large tracts of undeveloped land. Intensive development pressure created immediate growth-related problems, such as insufficient sewer capacity, roads, and schools. With growth came residents demanding services, which inevitably caused property taxes to increase each year.

With a government chartered under the council-manager form, Centerville's citizens alternately elected four at-large and five ward council members in nonpartisan elections every other May. The mayor, chosen by and from members of the council, was elected to serve a one-year term at the annual reorganization meeting held each July 1.

Taxes, development, and the legacy of Watergate provided fuel for a bitter and highly politicized at-large election in May 1975. Taxpayers Against Corruption (TAC) raised questions about virtually all activity in the municipal building. Legitimate bills for consulting engineering services and legal advice were suggested by TAC as reasons that property taxes were skyrocketing. TAC-supported candidates made allegations of conflict of interest involving both elected and appointed officials of the community. Republicans, holding a slim 5-to-4 majority on the council, jumped on the TAC bandwagon by endorsing both the actions and the candidates of the Taxpayers Against Corruption.

When the votes were counted, TAC candidates swept the four at-large seats, giving the Republicans an 8-to-1 majority on the annual reorganization day. Following the swearing in of the new council members, the city manager asked to be recognized. The next day's headlines read "City Manager Resigns: TAC Takes Control."

Despite Centerville's reputation as a politically explosive community, over eighty applicants sought the city manager's position. In a move questioned by the press, the public, and city employees, the council hired a local resident with no prior governmental experience.

John Newman, the council's choice for city manager, had impressive credentials in private-sector management. His weakness, voiced by an unidentified city employee in the next day's paper, was his appointment by the TAC-dominated council. Terms such as "hatchet man" and "political hack" appeared in early press reports, always attributed to sources who wished to remain anonymous. In fact, Newman was a two-year resident of Centerville who had no political affiliation. His only contact with local officials was as a volunteer with Centerville's conservation commission.

Newman spent much of his time during his first few months meeting and talking with city employees, community leaders, and appointed officials of Centerville. The bitter election campaign had polarized the community and caused tremendous tension among staff members. Some employees actively supported the TAC candidates, while others worked against them. One of Newman's tactics included meeting with small groups of employees to assure them that no one's job was in jeopardy for past political involvement. The caveat was that any future activity would result in appropriate disciplinary action.

During his first eighteen months in office, Newman succeeded in returning some sense of stability to the local government. TAC lost much of its punch once the "reformers" became the policymakers. Concerns over property taxes, corruption, and other perceived evils of government abated as the election approached for the five ward seats on the council.

The case

A few weeks before the candidate filing date for the next ward election, Sue Farwell, a long-time employee in Centerville's accounting department, requested an unpaid leave of absence to campaign for the ward seat on the council in the area in which she lived. Farwell had been an active supporter of the TAC candidates in the previous election, but she had abided by Newman's directive to avoid continued involvement in political activity. After consulting with the city attorney, Newman granted Farwell's request, which expired, at her request, the day after the election.

On the second Tuesday in May, voters returned most of the Republicans to office; one ward council seat went Democratic, creating a 7-to-2 split. Included among the winners was Sue Farwell.

The morning after the election, Newman received a letter from Farwell.

Instead of offering the expected resignation, Farwell informed her soon-to-be subordinate that she was under a doctor's care for physical and mental exhaustion. The letter requested that she be placed on paid sick leave and was accompanied by a letter from her doctor attesting to her condition. The doctor suggested that she could be expected to return in four to six weeks. Farwell's role as a council member was to begin on July 1.

Newman again asked the city attorney for a written opinion on whether the city was required to grant this sick leave. The attorney advised that under the circumstances, Farwell's request could not be denied.

Five weeks later, two days before Farwell was sworn into office, Newman received a letter of resignation from Farwell as an employee so that she could assume her duties as a council member. Along with the letter was a doctor's certification that she was in good health.

With a check for six weeks of sick pay and a letter of best wishes from her former boss, Farwell began a four-year term as an elected member of the Centerville City Council. During the first few months of her term, relations between the city manager and his former employee were cordial. In the winter, however, Newman began to detect possible violations of state law governing council-manager relations. A number of residents of Farwell's ward called city offices indicating that they had been promised services that Centerville could not legally provide. In the spring Newman found himself rejecting employment applicants who had been promised positions by Farwell. The manager also learned that certain employees had been promised promotions or raises by Farwell.

In an effort to stop these activities and to avoid public embarrassment of a council member, Newman asked the mayor and other members of the majority party to discuss the city manager's concerns privately with Farwell. When Farwell's husband approached Newman and other members of Centerville's staff for campaign contributions, Newman realized that his efforts to solve the problem through informal means had been unsuccessful. With the next ward election still eighteen months away, Newman believed he had to take some action.

Newman wrote a personal and confidential letter to Farwell detailing his concerns over the incidents of the previous thirty months. He advised Farwell that any future violation of the state laws governing council members' relations with local government employees and interference in personnel matters would be reported immediately to appropriate state officials.

The final year of Farwell's four-year term was marked by cool and sometimes hostile relations between Farwell and the city manager. Newman's Republican supporters tried to distance themselves from Farwell. As relations deteriorated among members of the governing body, Newman became the frequent target of Farwell's comments to the press. To counter Farwell's attacks, the Republican majority strongly backed the manager's performance.

When the Republicans met in January to pick candidates for the ward election in May, Farwell did not receive her party's endorsement. Undaunted by the rejection, she decided to run an independent campaign for her ward seat against a weak Republican and an unknown Democrat.

The election campaign was anything but nonpartisan, although nonpartisan elections were required by law. The Democrats, who had gained another seat in the at-large election two years earlier, recognized the lack of unity in their Republican opponents. A Democratic victory in four of the five seats would mean control of the council for the first time in decades. The Republicans needed just two seats to continue control. Clearly, both sides desperately needed to win the ward seat occupied by Farwell.

In the May election, Farwell, running as an Independent, received 48 percent of the vote, the Democratic candidate received 28 percent, and the Republican candidate received 24 percent. State election law dictated that the successful candidate must have 50 percent plus one vote; therefore, a runoff election between Farwell and the Democratic challenger was scheduled for the second Tuesday in June.

In typical Centerville fashion, the May election created chaos for the political parties. Excluding Farwell's seat, each side had won four seats. The Democrats, out of power for years, needed only to pull an upset in the runoff election to become the majority party. The Republicans suddenly found themselves with four seats and no candidate for the runoff election. To retain majority control, the Republicans' only alternative was to support Farwell's candidacy in the June election, just four weeks away.

Given the 4-to-4 split between the parties, Farwell was in a strong negotiating position. Her terms for continued Republican control of the council were very simple. First, she was to be named mayor. Second, Newman, now in his sixth year as city manager, must be replaced. Should the Republicans not agree to her terms, Farwell would approach the four Democratic members with the same offer. The incumbent Republicans reluctantly agreed to Farwell's terms. The Democratic party put all of its support behind its own candidate.

As the four-week campaign for the remaining seat began, Newman was besieged by the press and the public for comment on the situation. Members of both parties were aware that Newman and Farwell had clashed on a number of issues, and in the first week of the campaign, leaders of the Democratic party demanded that Newman disclose all written memoranda, legal opinions, and personnel records that related to his problems with Farwell.

Newman realized that he was in a bind. To release any information or to comment publicly could easily be construed as partisan political activity because it would be damaging to Farwell. It would also be construed as self-interested, of course, since Newman's only hope of continued employment as city manager rested with a Democratic victory, given the deal struck by the Republicans and Farwell. Failure to release the information or to comment, however, could also be regarded as partisan activity—specifically as an endorsement of Farwell's past actions, if not of her candidacy.

Looking for guidance, and hoping to avoid professional suicide, Newman turned to the ICMA Code of Ethics, which hung prominently on his office wall, and at the guidelines for interpreting the Code (see Appendix). Tenet 7 of the Code clearly stated, "Refrain from participation in the election of the members of the employing legislative body, and from all partisan political activities which would impair performance as a professional administrator."

Yet tenet 3 required that Newman "be dedicated to the highest ideals of honor and integrity in all public and personal relationships in order that the member may merit the respect and confidence of the elected officials, of other officials and employees, and of the public." Respect, honor, and integrity seemed hollow words in such circumstances.

Article 4 affirmed that ICMA members must "recognize that the chief function of local government at all times is to serve the best interests of all of the people."

Tenet 10 added another twist, particularly its guideline requiring the manager to "openly share information with the governing body." But what worried Newman the most was tenet 12, with its guideline on confidential information: It stated clearly that members "should not disclose to others, or use to further their personal interest, confidential information acquired by them in the course of their official duties."

The decision problem

Newman faced both a personal and a professional ethical crisis. Releasing the information on Farwell's past activities clearly would give the Democratic party a potent and perhaps valid campaign issue for the runoff election. The Republican members had agreed that should Farwell win, they would make her mayor and discharge Newman from his position.

In considering the Code of Ethics, Newman decided that from his perspective, the best interests of all of Centerville's residents—as well as his own interests—would probably best be served if Farwell were defeated. He believed that Farwell's conduct throughout her tenure as an elected official was consistently unethical, if not illegal.

The tenet on "honor and integrity" also seemed to support Newman's initial inclination. Did not honor and integrity demand that the city manager release facts about Farwell's unethical conduct? Would silence on the subject be construed as condoning unethical activity on the part of an elected official?

Still, Newman could not reconcile this position with the prohibition against participation in partisan politics. To release the information would be construed by the Republicans as partisan activity. However, not to release the information would be construed by the Democrats as partisan activity, since they would be deprived of a major campaign issue.

To complicate his dilemma further, Newman had an uneasy feeling that the material in question might fall into the category of "confidential information" that he had acquired in the course of his duties and that to divulge it would certainly further his personal interests.

Weighing all of these considerations, what should Newman do?

Discussion questions

1. In most states, the city manager is required by law to enforce all municipal and state laws in the community. Did Newman violate his oath of office by not contacting law enforcement officers at the first hint of Farwell's unethical and perhaps illegal conduct?

2. Was Newman's response to the request for campaign contributions the most appropriate one? What else might he have done?

3. Newman's initial approach to solve the problem involved a private meeting with the mayor and Farwell's Republican colleagues. Should the two members of the minority party have been included? Why?

4. Were there other steps that Newman could have taken to deal with the Farwell situation prior to the election campaign?

5. Do you agree with Newman that failure to release the information would be construed by the Democrats as partisan?

6. Could Newman have solved his dilemma by seeing that the information was "leaked" to the press anonymously? Is this strategy practical? Is it ethical?

7. What is the best course of action for the manager in this case? Are there other ethically acceptable courses of action? If so, what are they?

The aftermath

Studying a professional code of ethics did not give Newman a clear-cut solution to his dilemma. The guidelines contained in the ICMA Code are precisely that—suggested standards of behavior grounded in principles of the profession.

While initially tempted to justify the release of information under the guise of acting for the public good, Newman came to the conclusion that such action would be construed as partisan political activity; that much of the information was of a confidential nature, and that unethical behavior by an elected official would not and could not justify unethical behavior on his part.

Immediately after reaching his decision, Newman requested a meeting of leaders of both parties. He informed representatives that he would not release what he considered to be confidential, partisan information and that he would offer his resignation the day after the election, some three weeks away.

Ten days before the runoff election, state officials revealed that Farwell and her husband were under investigation for absentee ballot fraud and voter intimidation.

Centerville voters rejected Farwell's candidacy by a slim margin. On July 1 the Democratic majority took office and rejected Newman's letter of resignation. Three months later Newman took a position in another community.

Six weeks after the election, Farwell and her husband were indicted by a grand jury.

Final discussion questions

1. What role, if any, does a professional city manager have as a "whistleblower"? Would such a role appear to be a violation of the Code of Ethics?

2. If Farwell had been elected in the runoff election, would Newman have been justified in releasing damaging information in his letter of resignation?

3. If the grand jury had returned its indictments earlier, would Newman have been justified in releasing the information before the election?

4. Should Newman have resigned so soon after the council rejected his postelection resignation? Did he show a lack of appreciation for the support the council had given him?

20 Personnel or people?

John Doe

Editor's introduction

Whenever the subject of governmental ethics arises, people inevitably anticipate some form of corruption. Specters of bribes or kickbacks, conflict of interest, compromising circumstances, sexual improprieties, vote trading, or influence peddling immediately come to mind.

The most common ethical problems, however, involve none of these. Rather, they involve the way people behave toward each other in the course of daily activities. Most ethical issues arise in the treatment of people by other people.

Sometimes this treatment is part of routine transactions, such as promptness in keeping appointments or cordiality in dealings with others. At other times, this treatment arises in the context of special or unusual circumstances: How much time off with pay can a public employee be given to attend to a sick child, for example? Regardless of the circumstances or the answers, the behavior and decisions involved are rooted in the application of ethical principles.

Such is the situation in this case, which calls for a decision about the treatment of a fire chief who is discovered to be appropriating city property for personal use. What appears to call for a simple, straightforward application of principle, however, becomes complicated by idiosyncratic circumstances: by alcoholic illness and an opportunity for rehabilitation, by impending retirement, and by special family considerations and needs. Ultimately, the question becomes a classic nightmare for the administrator: Should the case be handled "by the book," or should established rules be sacrificed in favor of more sensitive and humane treatment? Posed in this fashion, there is no simple, universally applicable answer. Each case must be decided on its own merits.

It is just such a case that now faces the city manager of Annsburg.

Case 20
Personnel or people?

Background

As a result of the national transition from a manufacturing economy to a service economy, many communities faced a sudden and severe loss of their industrial tax base. Annsburg, a one-industry town, was one of those communities; its one industry had closed its doors.

The production process used by the industry had left the facilities unfit for alternative uses, so they had to be completely dismantled, and the site had to be cleared. This loss not only deprived Annsburg of an opportunity for economic recovery based on a reuse of the facility, but it also devastated the city's property tax base. Five years after the company closed its doors, the city was operating on less than one-half of its prior tax base.

Annsburg's political leadership consists of a city council elected on a nonpartisan basis for four-year, overlapping terms. The council annually selects a chairperson, or mayor, from among its ranks. The traditional practice is to rotate the position of chairperson through the council to equalize influence among the council members. The city attorney also serves as the prosecuting attorney, a nonpartisan elected position.

Among appointed officials in any community, the police chief and the fire chief exert significant political force. This was particularly true in Annsburg at the time of this case because of the general political environment and because each man had worked his way up through the ranks during more than twenty years of service.

The loss of the dominant industry in a one-industry town creates a political as well as an economic vacuum. Instability and divisiveness are natural results of the struggle to reestablish political order. In Annsburg a charter election to abandon the council-manager form of government in favor of the strong-mayor form was defeated at the polls, but the referendum was symptomatic of the political instability associated with the changes taking place. Annsburg was a community in transition when Paul Daniels became city manager.

When the previous city manager had left Annsburg, the vacancy sparked an extended public debate on whether the new manager should be a local candidate with knowledge of the community or a professional with education and experience in the field. Finally the city council retained Daniels, a professional city manager who came to Annsburg from a community in another state.

Because of the severely distressed local economy, Daniels' mandate was clear. The decline in the tax base meant that the government must get smaller. Each department must be reduced, and some services and programs must be eliminated.

As he set out, department by department, to address long-term expenditures, Daniels discovered that a major challenge would be the fire chief.

The case

Daniels became familiar with Fire Chief Roger Eleson when he revived a plan first developed by his predecessor to supplement the full-time fire department with volunteer personnel. Although the unionized firefighters had grudgingly agreed to terms that would permit the supplemental use of volunteer firefighters, the environment in the fire hall was such that each time a volunteer was recruited, he was ostracized and eventually quit. These problems made it obvious that change was needed, and the fire chief had to be made a change agent.

Under the charter, the fire chief was a council appointee. The council had appointed Eleson without the previous city manager's support. Prior to Daniels' appointment, Eleson had faced charges three times as a result of performance problems. He had always managed to retain his job, however, because of his political connections, the council's fear of adverse economic consequences (earlier discharges had cost the city tens of thousands of dollars in civil damages), and his retention of an effective attorney to represent him.

Eleson went through periods of good performance and intermittent periods of poor performance. He and Daniels developed a system to add volunteer firefighters to the department that was acceptable to the full-time firefighters. It would permit the number of full-time firefighters to be reduced by attrition, without reducing service levels. Including fringe benefits, each position eliminated could save $40,000 per year. This success temporarily enhanced the fire chief's standing in the city.

Then the police chief, Harold Bales, told Daniels that he suspected the fire chief of stealing city property, including gasoline from the city pumps. Too many five-gallon cans of gasoline were being filled and placed in the fire chief's car for transport. The small power tools at the fire hall could not be using that much gas. Bales and Daniels decided to say nothing about their suspicions but to have Eleson followed the next time he picked up gas.

Several months passed before Bales noticed Eleson at the gas pumps. True to form, Eleson filled two five-gallon cans and placed them in the trunk of the vehicle. Bales directed a patrolman in the police station to follow Eleson and report back by telephone (Eleson had a police radio in his vehicle). As the patrolman followed, Eleson went home, took the gas cans out of the trunk of the city car, and placed them in front of his private vehicle parked off the alley. Eleson then proceeded to the fire hall. The patrolman telephoned Police Chief Bales with his report.

Bales and Daniels discussed the situation and telephoned the city attorney to see whether they could obtain a search warrant, which would be necessary to gather evidence if Eleson were to be prosecuted. The city attorney expressed reluctance on the basis that it would be difficult to prosecute a fire chief for the petty theft of ten gallons of gasoline. Bales directed the patrolman to continue visual surveillance pending a decision.

The theft of ten gallons of gasoline, while only petty theft, did constitute a breach of the public trust by a high-ranking, visible public official. By itself, however, it would not be sufficient to uphold a discharge under state statute. Daniels presumed that the theft was a result of the fire chief's problem with alcohol, which had contributed to the charges brought on the three previous occasions.

The problem of alcohol

Daniels suspected, but could not confirm, that Eleson drank on duty. If this were true, it could create enormous liability for the city, in light of the chief's public safety responsibilities. Fire department morale, improving since the smooth implementation of the volunteer system, was at stake. If the city manager suspected that the fire chief was an alcoholic, members of the fire department, who worked more closely with the chief, must certainly be aware of related problems. Daniels also considered the fiscal implications. If the chief resigned or were discharged, his position would be filled from within the department, the net result being the elimination of one position. An opportunity for action existed, but it carried risks.

Daniels drafted two letters. The first was a letter of immediate resignation, which would be offered to Eleson. The second was a letter from the city manager to the fire chief announcing Eleson's immediate suspension with intent to prosecute and discharge him.

Daniels summoned the unsuspecting Eleson to his office, explained the facts, and indicated that the fire chief had a choice: Either he could sign the letter of resignation, or Daniels would sign the letter of suspension with intent to prosecute and discharge. Eleson said he would take no action until he had telephoned his attorney. He had faced charges before. Unable to contact his attorney, he continued to delay, searching for alternatives. Daniels telephoned the city attorney in the fire chief's presence and directed that a search warrant be issued to impound the evidence. He signed the letter of suspension with intent to prosecute and discharge and handed it to Eleson. Eleson hesitated, then signed the letter of resignation and left, appearing somewhat shaken.

The next day Daniels heard that Eleson had started drinking after this confrontation and had set out to find and get even with the patrolman who had caused him this difficulty. Unable to locate the patrolman, he had gone home to tell his family of the injustice to which he was being subjected. After years of living with an alcoholic, his family had given him no sympathy. Finally confronted at home and at work with the effects of his alcoholism, Eleson had broken down: He had admitted his alcoholism and asked for help.

Daniels met with the three shift commanders of the fire department. Uncertain whether he could make the previous day's resignation stand up and unclear about exactly what had occurred the previous evening, Daniels advised the shift commanders to treat the situation as if the fire chief were on vacation. No permanent assignments would be made, but the senior fire captain would be acting chief, as would be the case during a vacation leave. Daniels gave a status report to each council member by telephone and discussed the situation with the fire chief's attorney. Rumors began to circulate throughout the community.

Legal and political complications

Eleson entered the hospital for inpatient treatment. After several days Eleson's attorney asked Daniels to meet with him and the doctor to discuss the chief's condition. The doctor indicated that the chief was in the advanced stages of alcoholism but that a more critical problem was the interaction between alcohol and the chief's diabetic condition. The doctor stated that the chief's physical condition was such that he almost certainly lacked the mental capacity to make rational decisions; furthermore, that condition had certainly existed on the day that he had signed his resignation. The attorney then said that since Eleson lacked mental capacity, his resignation was invalid.

Daniels indicated that the attorney was free to argue diminished mental capacity at Eleson's trial for theft, but he pointed out that such a trial would undoubtedly be a very public one, with personal repercussions for the fire chief and his family. Positions were thus established.

At their next meeting, the city council went into executive session to hear an update on the situation. Rumors had reached the local media. One reporter accepted the confidential nature of the incident, but another insisted on full disclosure. When not permitted to attend the executive session, he outlined the various rumors in his next day's article.

The stands taken by the actors in this scenario were related to their positions in the community. The city council generally took a neutral stand on the fire chief's resignation. Eleson had been charged too many times, and his political support had eroded. He had signed a letter of resignation, but it was not clear that the resignation would stand up in light of his "diminished capacity." The council feared that the city might again have to pay thousands of dollars in settlement of a wrongful-discharge suit.

To Police Chief Bales the case was black and white: He had caught a thief. The prosecuting attorney hoped for a negotiated settlement to avoid having to prosecute Eleson. The city manager was adamant; if Eleson managed to return to active-duty status, Daniels would lose credibility. Eleson's attorney was obligated to represent his client. The public watched expectantly, fed regularly by articles and rumors.

The decision problem

Negotiations began in earnest between Daniels and the fire chief's attorney when the chief was about halfway through his twenty-eight-day inpatient therapy. All parties agreed that it was in their mutual interest to have the matter resolved before the chief was released from the hospital. Daniels needed a definitive answer to satisfy the council and the public. Eleson needed a definitive answer so his recovery from alcoholism could proceed. The chief's attorney offered extended sick leave as a solution.

Although a medical disability was available, it would provide Eleson less income than full retirement, for which he would become eligible in just eight months. He had available to him twelve months of sick leave, which would normally be paid out at 25 cents on the dollar at retirement. The attorney proposed that the resignation be redated with the chief's full retirement date and that he be placed on sick leave until that time. That would address the city manager's major concern that the fire chief never again have active-duty status. Keeping the chief on sick leave would cost about $10,000 more than paying off his sick leave on the basis of his original resignation date.

Daniels agreed to put Eleson on sick leave while he was in the hospital but would not accept a $10,000 price for what he perceived as the discharge of an alcoholic thief. Negotiations broke down.

The city manager met again with the council in executive session to report on the status of negotiations. The following morning's headlines would proclaim a "secret meeting" to discuss the still-unconfirmed status of the fire chief. The meeting itself was inconclusive. Daniels believed that he had enough rope either to tie up the problem or to hang himself.

Following additional discussions with Daniels, the fire chief's attorney agreed that it was not in his client's best interest to return to active-duty status. However, Eleson had a family to support, with children in college and in high school. In order to recover from the disease of alcoholism, he would need the self-esteem associated with supporting that family. He would need full retirement. The attorney asked Daniels to meet with Eleson's family so he could understand the situation better.

Reluctantly, Daniels agreed to do so and asked that the council chairperson also attend. Meeting with the wife and children of an employee he was trying to force out was bound to be uncomfortable.

Daniels was taken by surprise when the chief's wife started by thanking him for what he had done. For the first time in their married life, her husband had admitted that he was an alcoholic, and she had hope for a recovery. Because of what Daniels had done, the family now had a chance at a new beginning, a chance to have a real father and husband. The children expressed the same hope.

But in order to recover, the children told Daniels, their father would need help in retraining and in finding a new job. And this would require money. The difference between full retirement and medical disability was over $250 per month for the rest of Eleson's life. That meant college, tuition, books, a future for them and for their father. Daniels had helped by making their father admit his alcoholism. Couldn't he help a little bit more now and let their father get to a full retirement?

What should Daniels do now?

Discussion questions

1. Should Daniels recommend that the chief be permitted to remain on paid sick leave for eight months, in order to prevent him from returning to active duty? Why or why not?

2. How should Daniels weigh the threat of a lawsuit and a possibly expensive damage settlement against his personal determination to uphold matters of principle? What consideration should he give to the city's constituents and taxpayers and to the pleas of the fire chief's family? What consideration should he give to the incident of theft?

3. Does an employer have an obligation to an employee who has been permitted to perform poorly over a long period of time before

definitive action is taken? If so, what is that obligation? If not, why not?

4. Of how much concern should the public image of the local government, particularly of the city manager, be in such circumstances? Should public image be a factor in the decision? Why or why not?

5. Evaluate the fiscal impacts of the situation: the up-front cost of $10,000 versus the potential costs of litigation (e.g., the legal fees plus the damages that might have to be paid). Is such a cost-benefit analysis appropriate when matters of principle are under consideration? Why or why not? Explain.

6. How should Daniels estimate the possible nonmonetary costs involved in the situation, including publicity, employee morale, public attitudes regarding the city government, and political repercussions for council members? Are these costs different if Daniels accepts a negotiated settlement in order to avoid possible litigation? What role should these considerations play in Daniels' decision?

Aftermath

Daniels agreed to allow Eleson to remain on sick leave until his full-retirement date and to help him find alternative employment. In exchange, the fire chief executed a new letter of resignation effective on the date he would be eligible for full retirement. In addition, he signed a waiver, a hold-harmless agreement, a release of liability, and a pledge of no litigation, all cosigned by his attorney. All parties quickly and quietly approved the settlement.

Final discussion questions

1. The settlement having been reached and accepted by the council, how should the matter be explained to the press and the public?

2. How should Daniels help Eleson with his efforts to find new employment? Should Daniels agree to provide Eleson with a letter of recommendation, and if so, what should he say in it?

3. What information should Daniels release to other members of the fire department regarding Eleson's behavior and resignation? What should he say to other city employees? Should the case be explained to deter similar behavior by other employees, or does Eleson's right to privacy preclude such disclosure?

4. How much consideration should be given to personal circumstances—in particular, to the welfare of an employee's dependents? Would such consideration be discriminatory, since it is not extended to persons without dependents? Does failure to consider such circumstances constitute insensitive treatment of the employee? How should the city reconcile these conflicting values?

5. What can and should Daniels do to establish policies and practices that will lead to better identification and treatment of drug and alcohol abuse problems among city employees?

Appendix

**ICMA Code of Ethics
with guidelines**

1. **Be dedicated to the concepts of effective and democratic local government by responsible elected officials and believe that professional general management is essential to the achievement of this objective.**

2. **Affirm the dignity and worth of the services rendered by government and maintain a constructive, creative, and practical attitude toward urban affairs and a deep sense of social responsibility as a trusted public servant.**

Guideline
Advice to Official of Other Municipalities. When members advise and respond to inquiries from elected or appointed officials of other municipalities, they should inform the administrators of those communities.

3. **Be dedicated to the highest ideals of honor and integrity in all public and personal relationships in order that the member may merit the respect and confidence of the elected officials, of other officials and employees, and of the public.**

Guidelines
Public Confidence. Members should conduct themselves so as to maintain public confidence in their profession, their local government, and in their performance of the public trust.

Impression of Influence. Members should conduct their official and personal affairs in such a manner so as to give the clear impression that they cannot be improperly influenced in the performance of their official duties.

Appointment Commitment. Members who accept an appointment to a position should not fail to report for that position. This does not preclude the possibility of a member considering several offers or seeking several positions at the same time, but once a bona fide offer of a position has been

accepted, that commitment should be honored. Oral acceptance of an employment offer is considered binding unless the employer makes fundamental changes in the terms of employment.

Credentials. An application for employment should be complete and accurate as to all pertinent details of education, experience, and personal history. Members should recognize that both omissions and inaccuracies must be avoided.

Professional Respect. Members seeking a management position should show professional respect for persons formerly holding the position or for others who might be applying for the same position. Professional respect does not preclude honest differences of opinion; it does preclude attacking a person's motives or integrity in order to be appointed to a position.

Confidentiality. Members should not discuss or divulge information with anyone about pending or completed ethics cases, except as specifically authorized by the Rules of Procedure for Enforcement of the Code of Ethics.

Seeking Employment. Members should not seek employment in a community having an incumbent administrator who has not resigned or been officially informed that his or her services are to be terminated.

4. **Recognize that the chief function of local government at all times is to serve the best interests of all of the people.**

Guideline
Length of Service. A minimum of two years generally is considered necessary in order to render a professional service to the municipality. A short tenure should be the exception rather than a recurring experience. However, under special circumstances it may be in the best interests of the municipality and the member to separate in a shorter time. Examples of such circum-

The Code of Ethics and guidelines as reproduced here were adopted by the ICMA Executive Board in May 1987.

stances would include refusal of the appointing authority to honor commitments concerning conditions of employment, a vote of no confidence in the member, or severe personal problems. It is the responsibility of an applicant for a position to ascertain conditions of employment. Inadequately determining terms of employment prior to arrival does not justify premature termination.

5. Submit policy proposals to elected officials; provide them with facts and advice on matters of policy as a basis for making decisions and setting community goals, and uphold and implement municipal policies adopted by elected officials.

Guideline
Conflicting Roles. Members who serve multiple roles—working as both city attorney and city manager for the same community, for example—should avoid participating in matters that create the appearance of a conflict of interest. They should disclose the potential conflict to the governing body so that other opinions may be solicited.

6. Recognize that elected representatives of the people are entitled to the credit for the establishment of municipal policies; responsibility for policy execution rests with the members.

7. Refrain from participation in the election of the members of the employing legislative body, and from all partisan political activities which would impair performance as a professional administrator.

Guidelines
Elections of the Governing Body. Members should maintain a reputation for serving equally and impartially all members of the governing body of the municipality they serve, regardless of party. To this end, they should not engage in active participation in the election campaign on behalf of or in opposition to candidates for the governing body.

Other Elections. Members share with their fellow citizens the right and responsibility to exercise their franchise and voice their opinion on public issues. However, in order not to impair their effectiveness on behalf of the municipalities they serve, they should not participate in election campaigns for representatives from their area to county, school, state, and federal offices.

Elections on the Council-Manager Plan. Members may assist in preparing and presenting materials that explain the council-manager form of government to the public

prior to an election on the use of the plan. If assistance is required by another community, members may respond. All activities regarding ballot issues should be conducted within local regulations and in a professional manner.

Presentation of Issues. Members may assist the governing body in presenting issues involved in referenda such as bond issues, annexations, and similar matters.

8. Make it a duty continually to improve the member's professional ability and to develop the competence of associates in the use of management techniques.

9. Keep the community informed on municipal affairs; encourage communication between the citizens and all municipal officers; emphasize friendly and courteous service to the public; and seek to improve the quality and image of public service.

10. Resist any encroachment on professional responsibilities, believing the member should be free to carry out official policies without interference, and handle each problem without discrimination on the basis of principle and justice.

Guideline
Information Sharing. The member should openly share information with the governing body while diligently carrying out the member's responsibilities as set forth in the charter or enabling legislation.

11. Handle all matters of personnel on the basis of merit so that fairness and impartiality govern a member's decisions, pertaining to appointments, pay adjustments, promotions, and discipline.

Guideline
Equal Opportunity. Members should develop a positive program that will ensure meaningful employment opportunities for all segments of the community. All programs, practices, and operations should: (1) provide equality of opportunity in employment for all persons; (2) prohibit discrimination because of race, color, religion, sex, national origin, political affiliation, physical handicaps, age, or marital status; and (3) promote continuing programs of affirmative action at every level within the organization.

It should be the member's personal and professional responsibility to actively recruit and hire minorities and women to serve on professional staffs throughout their organization.

12.   Seek no favor; believe that personal aggrandizement or profit secured by confidential information or by misuse of public time is dishonest.

Guidelines
Gifts. Members should not directly or indirectly solicit any gift or accept or receive any gift—whether it be money, services, loan, travel, entertainment, hospitality, promise, or any other form—under the following circumstances: (1) it could reasonably be inferred or expected that the gift was intended to influence them in the performance of their official duties; or (2) the gift was intended to serve as a reward for any official action on their part.

It is important that the prohibition of unsolicited gifts be limited to circumstances related to improper influence. In de minimus situations such as tobacco and meal checks for example, some modest maximum dollar value should be determined by the member as a guideline. The guideline is not intended to isolate members from normal social practices where gifts among friends, associates, and relatives are appropriate for certain occasions.

Investments in Conflict with Official Duties. Members should not invest or hold any investment, directly or indirectly, in any financial business, commercial, or other private transaction that creates a conflict with their official duties.

In the case of real estate, the potential use of confidential information and knowledge to further a member's personal interest requires special consideration. This guideline recognizes that members' official actions and decisions can be influenced if there is a conflict with personal investments. Purchases and sales which might be interpreted as speculation for quick profit ought to be avoided (see the section below on "Confidential Information").

Because personal investments may prejudice or may appear to influence official actions and decisions, members may, in concert with their governing body, provide for disclosure of such investments prior to accepting their position as municipal administrator or prior to any official action by the governing body that may affect such investments.

Personal Relationships. Members should disclose any personal relationship to the governing body in any instance where there could be the appearance of a conflict of interest. For example, if the manager's spouse works for a developer doing business with the local government, that fact should be disclosed.

Confidential Information. Members should not disclose to others, or use to further their personal interest, confidential information acquired by them in the course of their official duties.

Private Employment. Members should not engage in, solicit, negotiate for, or promise to accept private employment nor should they render services for private interests or conduct a private business when such employment, service, or business creates a conflict with or impairs the proper discharge of their official duties.

Teaching, lecturing, writing, or consulting are typical activities that may not involve conflict of interest or impair the proper discharge of their official duties. Prior notification of the governing body is appropriate in all cases of outside employment.

Representation. Members should not represent any outside interest before any agency, whether public or private, except with the authorization of or at the direction of the legislative body of the governmental unit they serve.

Endorsements. Members should not endorse commercial products by agreeing to use their photograph, endorsement, or quotation in paid advertisements, unless the endorsement is for a public purpose, is directed by the governing body, and the member receives no compensation. Examples of public purposes include economic development for the local government and the sale of local government products.

Members' observations, opinions, and analyses of commercial products used or tested by their municipalities are appropriate and useful to the profession when included as part of professional articles and reports.

List of contributors

James M. Banovetz (Editor) is professor of political science and public administration and director of the Division of Public Administration at Northern Illinois University. He is also president-elect of Pi Alpha Alpha, the national honorary society for public administration. An honorary member of ICMA since 1978, he is founder of the secretariat of the Illinois City Management Association and the Council of Governments of Cook County. He is a former staff member of the League of Minnesota Municipalities. He holds M.A.P.A. and Ph.D. degrees from the University of Minnesota.

Bill R. Adams (Case 7) has been public information officer for the city of Santee in San Diego County since early 1986. For ten years prior to taking this position, he worked in the news and information business in the private sector, primarily as a journalist. He covered local political scenes in Washington, D.C., and in the San Diego region. Adams holds a bachelor of arts degree from the University of Maryland, College Park, where he studied political science and journalism.

David N. Ammons (Case 15) is a research associate at the Carl Vinson Institute of Government and adjunct associate professor of political science at the University of Georgia. He earned a Ph.D. in political science at the University of Oklahoma. His experience in municipal government includes service in various administrative capacities in the cities of Fort Worth and Hurst, Texas; Phoenix, Arizona; and Oak Ridge, Tennessee.

Mary Timney Bailey (Case 12) is assistant professor in the Department of Political Science at the University of Cincinnati, where she has major responsibilities in the Master of Public Administration program. Prior to completing her Ph.D. in 1984, she worked in the private sector, was executive director of a nonprofit environmental organization, and was research analyst on energy management for a large city. Her current research interest is public-sector decision making, particularly for environmental policies.

Ronald L. Ballard (Case 7) is city manager for the city of Santee, a growing San Diego County municipality with a population of 52,000. He has worked in the public sector for twenty years, accepting his current position in 1983. Previously, Ballard held positions with several California cities, including that of assistant city manager for National City in San Diego County. Ballard holds a master's degree in public administration from San Diego State University and a bachelor of arts degree from Bethany College, Santa Cruz.

William R. Bridgeo (Case 1) is city manager of Canandaigua, New York. He served from 1979 to 1985 as city manager of Calais, Maine, and from 1976 to 1979 as assistant town manager of Killingly, Connecticut. He holds a bachelor's degree in political science from St. Michael's College, Vermont, and an M.P.A. from the University of Hartford, Connecticut.

Jacqueline Byrd (Case 8) is director of policy analysis and planning for a major metropolitan county. She is on the faculty of St. Mary's College and teaches in the graduate program in human and health services administration. Dr. Byrd has worked for many state and local agencies in public administration and policy analysis. She holds Ph.D. and master's degrees in educational policy and administration from the University of Minnesota. Her bachelor's degree, also from the University of Minnesota, is in English.

Jay Brent Covington (Case 9) is currently assistant to the city manager in Vancouver, Washington. He has worked for Vancouver since 1982 and directs the city's financial planning and council agenda functions, as well as providing executive direction to department directors. In addition, he is responsible for the development and administration of the city's data processing system and automation plans. Covington has an M.P.A. degree from Brigham Young University, Provo, Utah.

John Doe is a pseudonym for authors who wish to remain anonymous.

Mark Etling (Case 3) has been administrative assistant for housing development in Ferguson, Missouri, a suburb of St. Louis, since 1987. In that capacity he serves as director of the Ferguson Neighborhood Improvement Program, a not-for-profit housing corporation operating under city auspices. He has worked with various housing, neighborhood development, and social service organizations, including four years as president of the Village Hills Neighborhood Housing Services board of directors. Etling is also a doctoral candidate at St. Louis University.

John J. Gargan ("The Case Approach") is Professor of Political Science at Kent State University, Kent, Ohio. He holds a Ph.D. degree in political science from Syracuse University, and his major research interests are management capacity building in city government and strategic management.

Harry G. Gerken (Case 19) is executive director of the Southeast Morris County Municipal Utilities Authority. He has also served as city manager in two communities. Educated at Rutgers University, he received a National Endowment for the Humanities Fellowship in 1980 to attend the University of Kansas. Gerken has written a number of articles for local newspapers on local government issues and ethical problems confronting public officials. He has also taught courses on contemporary ethical problems.

Richard K. Ghere (Case 4) is assistant professor of political science at the University of Dayton, where he teaches extensively in a master's in public administration program. His teaching interests are organization theory, public-sector decision making, and fiscal administration. He has also directed an undergraduate public administration program at Winthrop College and taught in master's programs at three other universities.

Frederick R. Inscho (Case 4) is assistant professor of political science at the University of Dayton. He received his Ph.D. in political science in 1976 from the State University of New York at Buffalo. His major areas of interest in teaching and research are public finance and budgeting,

quantitative methods, strategic planning, and environmental policy. Inscho previously served on the faculty at the University of Tennessee and as editor of the newsletter of the American Society for Public Administration's Section on Natural Resources and Environmental Administration.

Ralph Jacob (Case 14) was village administrator for Algonquin, Illinois, from 1984 to 1988. He served as the first city manager of Paris, Illinois, in 1983 and 1984. Jacob was assistant administrator for Libertyville, Illinois, from 1979 to 1984 and superintendent of office services and information for West Chicago from 1975 to 1979. Jacob received a Master of Public Affairs degree from Northern Illinois University in 1979. He is currently employed by Rodeway Express in Elk Grove, Illinois.

Mary Theresa Karcz (Case 8) is a senior policy analyst in a major metropolitan county. She has a master's degree in economics from Syracuse University, with concentrations in public economy and urban and regional economics. Her bachelor's degree in economics is from Sangamon State University. Karcz has taught at the University of Wisconsin–Eau Claire, the University of Wisconsin–Stout, and Onondaga Community College. She has also been a consultant on several training and education-related projects.

M. Lyle Lacy, III (Case 15), is city manager of Alliance, Nebraska. He began his career in public management after receiving a bachelor of science degree from Hampden-Sydney College, Virginia, in 1969. Following assignments with the state of Virginia in personnel administration, Lacy received an M.P.A. from Texas Christian University in 1973. While attending TCU, he worked as a budget analyst in the Research and Budget Department of the city of Ft. Worth, Texas. He then joined the staff of the city of Oak Ridge, Tennessee, where he served in various administrative capacities, including city manager, for eight years. In 1986, he was appointed city manager of Marietta, Georgia, and served there two years.

Scott D. Lazenby (Cases 9 and 10) is director of management and budget for the city of Glendale, Arizona. He received his bachelor's degree in physics from Reed College and his master's degree in public management and policy from Carnegie-Mellon University. He has ten years' experience in general public management and was previously assistant to the city manager of Vancouver, Washington. He also has taught graduate-level public administration courses.

Jack Manahan (Case 11) is the village manager of Park Forest, Illinois. From 1985 to 1989 he was the director of management and budget for Johnson County, Kansas, where he directed annual, capital, and strategic planning and managed the operating budget. Prior to that he was the county's assistant director of finance. He has held adjunct faculty appointments at Johnson County Community College; Kansas City, Kansas, Community College; and at the University of Kansas, where he has taught graduate public administration classes. Manahan holds a bachelor of science degree in education and a master's degree in public administration from the University of Kansas.

Kevin C. McGonegal (Case 18) is a commercial realtor for Hunter Lott Realty Company in Wilmington, Delaware. From 1974 to 1987 he was employed by the city of Wilmington in the Personnel Department and the Office of the Mayor. Positions held included director of employment and training, deputy budget director, chief labor negotiator, director of the Office of Management and Budget, and chief administrative officer. A graduate of Fairfield University, McGonegal is an instructor for the College of Urban Affairs and Public Policy of the University of Delaware and for the business administration program of the Delaware Technical and Community College.

Tom Mills (Case 16) is a retired city official who, during a twenty-two-year career, served as deputy managing director, chief deputy court administrator, and first deputy finance director for the city of Philadelphia. Since 1983 Mills has been professor of public administration at Fairleigh Dickinson University (Rutherford campus). He also serves as director of executive education at the Fels Center of Government, University of Pennsylvania, and as a member of the Philadelphia Board of Education. Mills holds a B.S. degree in economics from the Wharton School, an M.B.A. in industrial management from Drexel University, and an M.A. and Ph.D. in political science from the University of Pennsylvania.

Nina Naffziger Nissen (Case 13) is the assistant personnel director for the City of Peoria, Illinois, and the former personnel director for Peoria County. She has a master's degree in public administration from Sangamon State University.

Joe P. Pisciotte (Case 5) is professor of government and director of the Hugo Wall Center for Urban Studies at Wichita State University. Previously he served as executive director of the Sixth Illinois Constitutional Convention and as director of the Illinois Department of Business and Economic Development. He holds a bachelor's degree in government from the University of Hawaii and a Ph.D. in government from the University of Colorado. His professional career has included extensive involvement in teaching, research, training, and consulting with state and local governments, and he has held numerous appointments on public boards and commissions.

Paul M. Plaisted (Case 1) has ten years of experience with Maine's criminal justice system. Currently assigned as assistant director of the state's Bureau of Inter-governmental Drug Enforcement, he has served as patrol officer, criminal investigator, chief deputy sheriff, and chief of police. Plaisted holds a bachelor's degree in public administration and a master's degree from the Yale School of Organization and Management.

Jeffrey A. Raffel (Case 18) is a professor in the College of Urban Affairs and Public Policy at the University of Delaware and director of the school's urban affairs programs. He is former director of the master's in public administration program. Raffel received his Ph.D. in political science from M.I.T. in 1972 and his bachelor of arts degree in political science from the University of Rochester in 1966.

Irene S. Rubin (Case 17) is associate professor of public administration at Northern Illinois University, DeKalb, Illinois. She writes on public budgeting, with particular focus on local budgeting. She holds a Ph.D. degree from the University of Chicago.

Terry Schutten (Case 8) has been executive director of a major metropolitan county for three years. Previous positions include eight years as county administrator for Lehigh County, Pennsylvania; four years as project manager for the National Association of Counties in Washington, D.C.; and two years as executive director of the Central Arizona Association of Governments. Schutten graduated from California State University at San Jose with a bachelor's degree in social sciences. He completed his master's degree in public administration at the University of Arizona–Tucson.

Steven A. Sherlock (Case 8) is a senior policy analyst for a major metropolitan county. He has worked in local government since 1980. Sherlock holds a Ph.D. from the University of Minnesota, with an emphasis in program evaluation and anthropology, a master's degree in anthropology from the University of Minnesota, and a bachelor's degree in political science from Purdue University.

Glen W. Sparrow (Case 7) is a professor at the School of Public Administration and Urban Studies, San Diego State University. His areas of specialization include state and local management and intergovernmental relations. He has been executive director of the Sacramento and San Francisco Charter Commissions and director of a Comprehensive Employment and Training Act (CETA) prime sponsor. In addition to teaching, he has provided consulting assistance to cities and counties in California, especially in the areas of incorporation, fiscal impact, and public-private partnerships. In 1986–87, while a Fulbright Professor at the Chinese University of Hong Kong, he lectured and consulted extensively in the People's Republic of China on municipal management and public administration curriculum.

Stephen A. Staub (Case 2) is director of graduate studies in the Department of Political Science at the University of Alabama at Tuscaloosa. He teaches courses on urban policy and public management.

Susan Von Mosch (Case 8) is a senior policy analyst for a major metropolitan county. She holds a bachelor's degree in history and political science from the University of Minnesota–Morris and a master's degree in public policy from the Humphrey Institute. She has worked for the U.S. Department of Housing and Urban Development in Washington, D.C., the City of St. Paul, and the Metropolitan Council.

Jon A. Walsh (Case 8) is a policy analyst for a major metropolitan county. He holds a master of arts degree in public administration from Hamline University.

Municipal Management Series

Managing Local Government: Cases in Decision Making

Text type
Times Roman, Helvetica

Composition
EPS Group, Inc.
Baltimore, Maryland

Printing and binding
Arcata Graphics/Kingsport Press
Kingsport, Tennessee